The
Price
of
Freedom

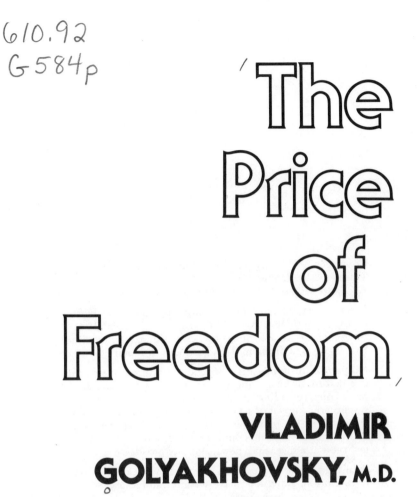

The Price of Freedom

VLADIMIR GOLYAKHOVSKY, M.D.

*Translated from the Russian
by Eugene Ostrovsky*

E. P. DUTTON | NEW YORK

Published in the United States by
E. P. Dutton, a division of New American Library,
2 Park Avenue, New York, N.Y. 10016.

Library of Congress Cataloging-in-Publication Data
Golyakhovsky, Vladimir.
The price of freedom.
1. Golyakhovsky, Vladimir.   2. Jews, Russian—United
States—Biography.   3. Jews—United States—Biography.
4. United States—Emigration and immigration—Biography.
5. Soviet Union—Emigration and immigration—Biography.
E184.J5G64   1986   617.3'0092'7 [B]   86-4257
ISBN 0-525-24449-2

Published simultaneously in Canada by
Fitzhenry & Whiteside, Ltd., Toronto

W

DESIGNED BY MARK O'CONNOR

10 9 8 7 6 5 4 3 2 1

First Edition

TO MY IRINA,
FOR RICHER OR POORER,
FOR BETTER OR WORSE

Preface

A Soviet Russian immigrating to the United States is like a denizen of the ocean deep abruptly hauled out of the water and lifted to a mountaintop. To survive under a radically different set of conditions, he has to adapt to the new environment and change himself to such an extent as to actually embark upon a new existence, a second life.

I was one of the quarter million sons and daughters of the Jewish people who joined the exodus from Russia over the past decade. In my autobiography, *Russian Doctor,* I described "the Communist paradise" as it really is, hell on earth, and told the story of our escape.

But I felt that surely there must be a paradise on this planet. And so my family, along with a hundred thousand other Russian immigrants, came to seek it in America. The very first brush with the new reality brought on psychological stress, tragedies of misunderstanding, and comedies of errors. The drama of two conflicting societies unfolded in our minds and souls: The deep of the past refused to relax its grip, while the rarefied atmosphere of the new was already at work producing its dizzying effect. The drama was particularly stark in New York City, a place where even immigrants from Alabama or Missouri are likely to feel depressed and uncomfortable.

This book tells the story of our Americanization and the cost we paid in the process. Hardly any other group of immigrants are less prepared for America than the Russians—but then so much more tragic, funny, and intriguing the story of their adaptation.

All events, facts, and human portraits in this book are real. All I did was to change certain circumstances and names.

And have we found what we sought in America—an earthly paradise? All I can say at this juncture is that first we had to go through purgatory. The rest of the story is in the book.

VLADIMIR GOLYAKHOVSKY, M.D.
New York City, 1986

The
Price
of
Freedom

1

$\mathcal{D}$arkness was gathering beyond the ports of our Boeing, at 7:00 P.M. on April 18, 1978, when the shores of the United States came into view. All we could see was a multitude of lights, scattered dots alternating with large constellations, and then all of a sudden they merged into a continuous sea of light far below the plane wings. "We are approaching New York City," the captain announced over the PA system. My heart beat in unison with the throbbing of the jet engines. The lights rushed toward us; the aircraft was descending. There was the characteristic rumble of the landing gear being extended, and in a few more seconds, the jet touched down at John F. Kennedy Airport and rolled down the runway, on American soil. The passengers burst into applause. I joined in. Then I grabbed my wife Irina's hand, and we looked at each other through tears of joy. At last we were in America!

History preserves bare facts and disregards emotions felt by the protagonists of historical events. But it is easy to imagine the emotional state of people under this or that set of circumstances hundreds or even thousands of years ago, for like human nature, human emotions are immutable. I am certain that our feelings at the instant of touchdown were not much different from what Christopher Columbus and his sailors felt when the bow of their boat hit the sandy beach of the New World. It is an emotion shared by all people upon attainment of a long-cherished goal.

We were faced with the last bureaucratic formality of our long journey: obtaining an alien registration number authorizing temporary residence in the United States under the Russian refugee quota. We were separated from the stream of Americans and foreigners who had been our companions during the flight. The procedure did not take long because everything had been taken care of in advance. It did not matter in what sequence my family would cross the invisible threshold of American territory, but all the same, I pushed Vladimir, Jr., ahead: He was the youngest; in this country he would live a longer life than the rest of the family, so let him be the first to set foot in our future.

We had arrived in New York two days before the Jewish holiday of Passover. At Customs a social worker from a private Jewish charity, the New York Association for New Americans (NYANA), handed us parcels with Passover gifts. Each parcel contained fifteen dollars in cash, Jewish cookies, and a brochure in Russian. The customs officials did not bother to check our luggage. Carrying our suitcases and parcels we emerged from the terminal building and had our first breath of New York air. A fierce wind was blowing, its gusts so strong that it was difficult to keep our balance. Bending forward into the wind, we followed the social worker Indian file toward the bus stop. I supported my father; Vladimir, Jr., helped my mother. Irina, choking on the wind blowing in her face, brought up the rear. I did not remember winds of such ferocity in Russia. Our first encounter with America's elements indicated that they were far less tame than their Russian counterparts.

Another first impression was the enormous size of the cars. While we were waiting for the bus, huge automobiles rolled past us in a continual stream. There was no question that America was indeed a world apart.

The magnificent expressway linking Kennedy Airport with the city also struck us speechless. Perched on the front seat of the bus, swiftly racing through the night, I stared ahead intently. A brightly lit building was discernible in the distance floating at a great height. I thought it stood atop a tall mountain. The NYANA official told me we were heading for Manhattan. I knew that Manhattan was part of New York City, but which part I had little idea. Maybe something like SoHo, I thought irresolutely, not very sure what SoHo was.

"What's that illuminated thing up there, on top of the mountain?" I asked our guide.

"What mountain?" she asked in surprise. "Oh, I see. It's not a mountain, it's just the illuminated upper portion of the Empire State Building."

I decided to refrain from further questions so as not to make a fool of myself. Then the guide said that we were on Broadway. Now I felt sure of my competence. Everybody knew that Broadway was New York's most fashionable street. I pressed my face to the window to see all I could. I was astonished at the sight of stupendously tall buildings and bright lights. The bus pulled to a stop, and we were told that we had arrived at our destination, the Greystone Hotel on West Ninety-first Street. We entered the hotel lobby and the first person we saw there was none other than my wonderful aunt, Lyuba.

Shriveled and frail at eighty-eight, she had sat in the lobby for over four hours, awaiting our arrival. It transpired that it was Lyuba who had prevailed upon NYANA to book us in the Greystone because she herself lived nearby, on West Ninety-sixth Street. Lyuba had cooked a festive dinner and insisted that we proceed to her place immediately. Because of the flight and emotional tension, we had been sleepless for twenty-four hours, but the joyous occasion clearly warranted a celebration.

A tall young man, the first black we encountered in America, took us up in the elevator to our room. He chewed gum, sang, jerked his legs to the beat of his own music, and nonchalantly pressed the elevator buttons, paying no attention whatsoever to his passengers. Having brought us to the required floor, he mumbled some indistinguishable words and hurled a plastic parcel after us. We understood neither his speech nor the purpose of the parcel. The room was small and uncomfortable, containing only two beds for the three of us. It was very cramped, particularly after we hauled our suitcases inside. Okay, there would be plenty of time to tackle the accommodations problem later on; we were in a hurry to get to Lyuba's place. The plastic bag was left untouched outside our door.

We traversed five Broadway blocks, from West Ninety-first Street to West Ninety-sixth Street, with a good deal of caution. It was almost 11:00 P.M., the streets were nearly empty, whether because of the late hour or the gusty, biting wind, and we encountered only a few eerie figures. We had no idea who they were or what their intentions could be, but to be on the safe side we tried to give them a lot of berth. We knew one thing: New York was a dangerous city.

By contrast, it was warm and cozy at Lyuba's. She lived with her friend of many years, Mrs. Augusta Rosen, also a widow, sharing a small apartment in a cooperative building. Since her friend was ill and away at the time, Lyuba lent her bedroom to my parents for the time being. They were incomparably better off in Lyuba's apartment than in our very modest hotel.

For many years I had corresponded with Lyuba at her address, and here I was, sitting for the first time at her table and discussing the first order of business for tomorrow. I boasted to Lyuba that permission for us to enter the United States had come through faster than for all other refugees, to which she responded, quietly and softly, as was her custom:

"It is because Senator Charles Percy interceded on your behalf and asked the U.S. ambassador in Rome to expedite your departure."

I was startled: "But how did the senator find out about our existence?"

4

"I asked a good friend of mine, who works on the senator's staff, to drop in a word for you."

So that's what it was!

"You'd better realize that here in America personal recommendations and patronage are enormously important," Aunt Lyuba said. "But then private enterprise is the king here. Unlike Russians, Americans are a very open sort, used to talking frankly on all subjects. If you get an opportunity to meet influential people, don't miss the chance. Your career will largely depend on the right connections."

"Aha!" I exclaimed. "Sounds familiar. In Russia, I had to do a lot of string pulling. The difference is that in Russia strings are pulled in contravention of the state system, which frowns upon private initiative, so patronage operates on the sly, as often as not illegally. Be that as it may, though, I'm grateful for your advice. But given my poor English, how am I supposed to talk to people and hope to be understood?"

Indeed, lack of linguistic proficiency was my single biggest handicap during our first days in New York. My English was roughly comparable to that of a three- or four-year-old toddler: helpless babble instead of talk. But what is cute in a child hardly becomes a grown man of forty-eight.

I was to start in my new life out of the language blocks. Or, as the Bible says, "In the beginning was the Word."

2

"And the Word was God."

How true in my case!

The next early morning I came out of the hotel to find a

synagogue, Congregation Young Israel, next to it. It was remarkable to see a synagogue, just like that, surrounded by residential buildings, an organic part of everyday life. All my life it had been a taboo. I could count on the fingers of one hand the number of times I had seen one, each time experiencing acute emotional turmoil—curiosity had pulled me inside while fear had held me back. And now everything was so clear and simple: Come in and pray, if you wish. I did not know how to pray, but I decided to visit during Passover.

It had been raining hard since late in the morning, so I went quickly back inside without really looking around. We had never witnessed a downpour that intense in Russia either. Still, Vladimir, Jr., twenty years old and consumed with a youthful urge to get to know America without delay, decided to brave the foul weather and take a heroic stroll down Broadway. In the meantime, I busied myself procuring another room for my family. Irina and I got down to the lobby. It was full of elderly men and women, clearly hotel guests. They stood and sat in twos and threes, conversing in a mixture of English, Yiddish, Polish, and Russian. Our appearance caused a general hush, and we became objects of intense scrutiny. This mute scene lasted several minutes. Finally, one of them approached us and opened a conversation in heavily accented Russian.

"By the looks of you, have just arrived," he said.

"That's right, late yesterday night."

"Welcome to America."

"Thank you."

"Maybe you need help? I'd be glad to . . . Just ask."

He spoke gently, obviously trying to be unobtrusive. The others stayed at a distance listening jealously, their faces animated. Several of them stepped closer and bombarded us with questions:

"Where are you from?" "Do you have a large family?" "What did you do in Russia?" "Do you speak English?"

Irina and I valiantly tried to cope with the avalanche until the first man came to our rescue and offered to talk to the manager on duty about a new room for us.

"There is a plastic bag at our door. What is it?" I asked him.

"What? Oh, the parcel . . . Didn't you guess? It's a Passover present—wine and cookies."

"I see."

"Well, you know, it's a tradition we have here."

The way the gift parcel was "presented" was an eye-opener. All Europeans, including the Russians, attach considerable importance to the formal side of intercourse. That parcel taught us the first lesson about America—protocol is almost totally disregarded here; hurling a parcel at your back in the corridor might turn out to be a courteous act of gift giving.

The manager was swayed by our arguments and gave us new accommodations: a nice, two-room suite on the fourth floor. We owed much of our success to our new friend, who negotiated with the hotel management on our behalf. It was still raining heavily, but we were to go to NYANA for the introductory briefing. I decided to call NYANA to find out if the appointment was on, but as it happened, I did not know how to use the pay phone. Our benefactor dropped in his own dime and got me through to NYANA. In spite of the rain, we were expected to come. But how were we supposed to get there? Again our benefactor came to the rescue; he handed us bus tokens and walked us to the Columbus Avenue stop of the M7 bus. He gave us detailed and very clear directions and volunteered to stay with us until the bus came, although he was drenched to the bone.

His name was Boris. He had left Russia immediately after World War II, having fought in all four years of the war. He was a lieutenant in the Soviet army but was unwilling to stay in his country on account of rampant anti-Semitism. Since then he had lived in New York for over three decades, running a newsstand for a living, but recently he had fallen ill and had retired. He was single and had lived in the Greystone for many years. The rest of the hotel residents, whom we met that first morning in the lobby, had roughly similar stories to tell. They all tried to help the new arrivals from Russia, who at that time were coming in droves. If not for their generous help, our first steps on American soil would have been far more difficult. We are deeply grateful to them all. But our "personal guardian," Boris, was particularly helpful. I consulted him on virtually all practical matters in the initial phases of immigration, and he, a simple and nice man, was always available when sound advice or help was needed.

The hotel guests were in a kind of race: who would beat the others in the speed and generosity of assistance to new immigrants. Occasionally I could not hold back a chuckle watching the jealous reaction of the losers to the triumph of the winner. They would get angry, denigrate his counsel, stop talking to one another, and bitterly watch, sardonic smiles playing on their lips, the lucky devil fussing proudly over his ward. The losers in the game looked like jilted roosters eyeing askance their triumphant rival and making a great show of bewilderment as to why the dumb hen made such a glaring mistake in choosing the clearly inferior specimen of manhood.

NYANA staged a celebration for us, with wine, cookies, and coffee. The fifty or so new immigrants present were addressed in Russian by one of NYANA's vice presidents. He gave us many important pointers essential at the early stage of adaptation, but one in particular stuck in my memory.

"America is the kind of country where one moves upward all the time," he declared sententiously and made a sweeping gesture suggesting an ascent of a steep mountain. "All of you are making a fresh start in life and many difficulties are going to confront you. But believe me, in a few short years all of you will be okay—rich and happy. This is America."

I listened with rapt attention. His oration contained no earthshaking revelations, but what he was saying tallied exactly with my own preconceived notion of America and gave me a boost. I can accurately point to that moment when I felt, for the first time, completely confident that my family really would be okay. That's the kind of country America is, you know . . . !

That day, our first in New York, Vladimir, Jr., returned home soaking wet and absolutely happy. He had walked the entire length of Broadway in the downpour—from West Ninety-first Street to the Battery and back; he had seen the Statue of

Liberty, the Columbus monument, and, in a word, everything there was to see. Needless to say, the window displays of electronic goods had made an indelible impression on him, what with their overflowing abundance of stereos, tape recorders, and turntables, the latest and most popular albums. Small wonder, nothing of the sort was available in Moscow, and for today's youth, modern music is god. Junior was boyishly excited, though shivering with cold. His mother and I managed somehow to overcome his resistance and talk him into a hot bath.

We were in a state of permanent astonishment at everything around us. Even the speed at which water gushed out of the faucet in our bathroom was a marvel. When I flushed the toilet for the first time, I had to restrain myself not to jump aside, so startled I was by the unheard-of power and noise of the flushing torrent. American technology was remarkable!

We were not able to take our first walk in the city until the next day. By morning, the rain clouds had scattered and beautiful weather set in; the speed with which the weather pattern changed was yet another novelty. And so, here it came— our first real day on the town. At least we had some vague notion of what awaited us in the streets of New York—huge buildings, even the vaunted skyscrapers we had only heard about but never seen; lavish window displays; endless streams of gigantic automobiles. . . . But it was far more interesting to have a maiden look at Americans—not lone Americans amid foreign crowds, but Americans en masse, American crowds. What were they like in a throng?

We decided to dress up, lest we spoil the harmony of the glittering crowd; after all, we, too, were Americans now, weren't we? I took my time selecting a tie that would not clash with my suit and shining my shoes; Irina donned a dark blue French suit, which became her wonderfully, and high-heeled shoes. Thus spruced up, we plunged into the Broadway crowd.

3
_____

I am not a connoisseur of Hollywood movies, but the few I had seen gave me the impression that New York was a city of stately skyscrapers and crowds of beautiful people. I pictured most male New Yorkers as replicas of John Wayne, and most women as look-alikes of Rita Hayworth. And all of them, in my imagination, strolled down magnificent Broadway.

We had a rude awakening. The first sight to meet our eyes was litter, litter everywhere: pieces of paper, plastic bags, rags, broken umbrellas, shreds of newspapers, even battered hulks of cars stripped of wheels, doors, and windows. All this refuse littered the street, attracting no attention whatsoever. Such an abundance of garbage was also something we had never seen anywhere before. But to hell with litter, let's look at the people. It was the morning of a business day, presumably a rush hour, but the street was packed with people moving at a leisurely pace, without undue haste or fuss. But wait, where were our "typical" Americans? I looked frantically around but could not see the John Waynes or the Rita Hayworths. An entirely different sort of person dominated the sidewalks: straight-haired swarthy or black men and women; most of them squat and some real shorties; most of them thickset and some outright obese; all of them shabbily dressed and some wearing rags. I looked at Irina in confusion, she returned a like look, and we both burst out laughing at the incongruity of reality and our expectations. I guess passersby had a lot of fun watching us: a well-dressed couple, newly arrived and obviously unaccustomed to Broadway, maybe tourists, roaring with laughter amid a throng of fat, squat, and drab New Yorkers.

Still, we could not figure out the natives. We walked hand in hand, looking closely at the people around and catching scraps of their conversation. The language they spoke was not English, of that we were sure. But what was it? We were able to recognize German, French, and Italian phonetically. But those people spoke some other tongue, in a rapid-fire fashion, rolling the hard *r,* and sounding quite disharmonious, I would say.

"Maybe it's Spanish," Irina ventured a guess.

"Are you kidding!" I exclaimed indignantly. "Spanish is so melodious, smooth, and beautiful, while their speech grates on the ears."

No, we positively could not place those people by the sound of their speech.

We approached a huge supermarket, Key Food, and decided to look inside.

The supermarket struck us by its opulence, size—and squalor. We decided to conduct a psychological experiment and watch who bought what, selecting as a subject a typical shopper: a shabbily dressed, fat black woman of about forty, pushing a shopping cart piled high with groceries down the aisle. When she approached the checkout counter, we followed suit, taking a pocket-size package from a shelf as a cover. We wanted to see what there was in her shopping cart and how much she would pay for the groceries.

The cashier proceeded to record the purchases, working her cash register nimbly, while a mound of packages, boxes, jars, fruit, vegetables, meat, and bread rose on her counter. Finally, she was done. I looked at the sum in the display window of the cash register and was stunned—eighty-five dollars, exactly the amount each of us received from NYANA as a monthly food allowance. To our surprise, the fat customer handed the cashier a stack of some sort of coupons instead of cash. The shopper squeezed her body through the narrow space between two counters and waited majestically while the pale, skinny cashier stacked up the bags with the groceries in her cart. Then, still impassive and important looking, she approached a huge old Cadillac, heaved her bulk behind the steering wheel, and whizzed away. My God, what a car!

We were totally confused. What kind of coupons had she used for money? Why was the obviously rich fat woman so shabbily dressed?

In the streets adjoining Broadway, on Amsterdam and Columbus avenues, we were shocked to see numerous dilapidated and half-destroyed houses, a general state of ruin, and dozens of people who looked like criminals, prostitutes, or beggars. Frightened, Irina huddled next to me. By now, though, we had left the slums behind us and were walking along clean, attractive streets full of tall, well-dressed Americans.

Our stroll took us to Central Park. Oh, how wonderful it was there! Cherry trees in blossom, a sea of white and pink blooms, fields of tulips and daffodils—even orchids, tender and majestic. We fell in love with Central Park at first sight; never before had we seen such a magnificent natural oasis in the middle of a huge metropolis. And what an oasis!

We returned to our hotel exhausted by the stroll and the flood of new impressions to find Boris, our personal protector, and the other residents manning their usual positions in the lobby.

"Well, did you have a good walk?" Boris asked.

"Marvelous," we replied. "But there were a lot of things we couldn't understand."

"You will, in due time," he observed, waving his arm. "All in good time, little by little."

"What language do most of those people speak?"

"Those people? Why, they speak Spanish."

"But it does not sound like Spanish."

"Oh, I see what you mean . . . they speak distorted Spanish."

"Who are they?"

"Most of them are Puerto Ricans, some hail from Haiti, others from Jamaica—in general from Caribbean islands."

"Aha, so that's what they are! But why are there so many of them in this place?"

"Here's where they live. This is the border of the so-called Spanish Harlem."

"What kind of coupons do they use instead of money at the supermarket?"

"You must be referring to food stamps."

"What are food stamps?"

"They are issued to the poor to supplement welfare payments so as to enable them to buy more food and avoid starvation. They are jobless and have no other source of income."

"Poor? Who is poor—those fat people? Why don't they work?"

"I see what you mean. . . . They are classified as poor because they have lots of kids—ten or even more per family. They get money allowances and also food stamps. And, yes, cheap housing subsidized by the city."

"But we saw a woman driving a luxury Cadillac the like of which we have never seen in our most extravagant dreams."

"Is that what bugs you? An old Cadillac? Maybe it cost a mere hundred bucks, or maybe nothing at all—just throwaway junk. Like I said, this is America. But don't worry, you'll get used to the way things are here, little by little."

All my life I had pictured poverty differently: A poor man should be hungry, skinny, and emaciated, ready to take any job, devouring a stale bread crust if it comes his way, and looking miserable because not a ray of hope lights up his life. The fat female, she of the Cadillac, who had bought a cartload of marvelous food with free food stamps, in no way corresponded to my notion of poverty, any argument to the contrary notwithstanding.

Well, apparently, that was America!

4

$\mathcal{S}$aturday morning, I went to a synagogue for the first time in my life to pray and thank God for our deliverance from the Communists. The synagogue was nearly empty. I lingered in the doorway, unsure of what I was supposed to do. I did wear a yarmulke, though; it had been included in the gift package sent flying after me in the hotel corridor. But the knowledge that one's head had to be covered in the temple just about summed up all I knew of such matters.

One of the few worshipers who was praying inside, a tall and thin man with a long beard who looked about seventy, came up and addressed me in Russian:

"You are fresh out of Russia, aren't you?"

"That's right."

"Welcome to our synagogue."

"Thank you."

"Well, put on a tallith, take a prayer book, and sit down with us; we'll tell you what to do."

"Thank you."

I draped my shoulders with a prayer shawl and felt very awkward. I could not read in Hebrew. All that I knew was that it read from right to left, so I opened the book at the end. Now what? All the men around me were swaying, mumbling softly, and staring at the floor. I tried to rock back and forth, back and forth, but immediately had symptoms of seasickness, and my head started to spin. No, it was definitely more prudent to sit still. But it was equally unseemly just to observe the others. So I decided to pray after my own fashion: recalling our journey all the way from Moscow to New York, piecing together the links in the chain of events, and looking for a common logical thread. After all, what was the Bible if not a history of the Jewish people, a record of their trials and tribulations, an account of their miraculous escapes from danger? Some 3,500 years ago, the Jews had escaped from Egyptian captivity, and today we were celebrating their deliverance as a high holy day. As for us, our exodus from Russia took place only two and a half months ago. I recalled what my family had lived through and drew parallels to the biblical Exodus.

The mass exodus of Jews from Russia in the 1970s was a significant historical event of the twentieth century and a major milestone in the history of the Jewish people. For the first time in over two centuries, since Catherine the Great had permitted Jews to settle in specified remote localities and engage in commerce and crafts, Jewish emigration was officially sanctioned. For the first time since our planet had been divided into the Communist and Free Worlds, a quarter of a million men, women, and children managed to break free. The process was set in motion in the late 1960s when Leonid Brezhnev's government approached the United States for economic assistance, including the sale of millions of tons of grain. Early in the 1970s the U.S. Congress passed the Jackson-Vanik Amendment that made trade concessions to Russia (most-favored-nation status) conditional on free Jewish emigration for family unification. Apparently, Brezhnev needed grain more than he did Jews. Hence the impossible: The Iron Curtain screechingly lifted a bit, and people started to get out.

Exit visas were granted on the strength of invitations sent through the mail from real or mythical relatives in Israel. But the KGB took control over the mails, and quite a few invitations failed to reach their destinations. The papers of would-be emigrés were checked for a long time, an average of twelve months, so that the KGB could make sure that the applicants were not privy to state secrets (although just about anything is regarded as a state secret in Russia). Those who were allowed to leave were stripped of their citizenship. Emigrés were permitted to take only a fraction of their possessions—household things, utensils, furniture, books—but all valuables, such as cash, antiques, art objects, or family jewels, were barred. Nor were they allowed to take any kind of official documents, even education certificates.

Of all emigrés only a handful really came out to be united with their kin, and barely half went to Israel. Most of the rest set their sights on the United States, which issued them entry permits under a quota for political refugees; though few, if any had been dissidents or victims of persecution. Most refugees had no political biases, but left out of dissatisfaction with their meager living standards and disgust with officially sanctioned anti-Semitism. The Jewish young, caught in the upwelling of national pride born of the creation of Israel, were almost without exception glad to have a chance to leave Russia. Even some of the older generation were prepared to cut loose and start life anew. And I was among them.

I was fed up with Russia, sick and tired of suffering the indignities of anti-Semitism and my dependent status all through the forty-eight years of my life. I was an orthopedic surgeon of some renown, but not a Communist. For this reason, I had to work extra hard for everything I sought: successful career, financial security, and peace of mind. The unequal fight had sapped me of strength so thoroughly that I decided to leave the country of my birth.

It took enormous willpower and a large dose of innate optimism to withstand the early immigration trials with equanimity. Irina lacked these qualities; she had never lived in such strained circumstances, never had to contend with such a lowly class of people. It is not surprising therefore that she was forever on edge.

"I agreed to leave Russia in order to live better, not to sink to the bottom," she repeated testily. "If it's always going to be like this, I don't see why we bothered to emigrate."

I tried to reassure her as best I could, but the trouble was I myself had a rather vague idea of what awaited us. I hoped and believed that sooner or later things would improve, but there was no telling when or how.

When we were finally called into the U.S. consul's sanctum in Rome, one at a time, I was the first to be ushered in. I was nervous—a tribute to the novelty of the situation. Besides, I desperately wanted to converse in English but feared that anxiety would interfere with my ability to understand and speak, pitifully limited as I was. My premonition was accurate enough.

At that point I noticed a sheaf of my documents translated into English and several reprints of my articles on the consul's desk. The consul said something to the aide who translated for my benefit:

"Our country is honored that a man of your stature has chosen it for resettlement."

I was deeply moved for I had not expected such a compliment. I somehow managed to stammer out my thanks in English. The very first official of the United States to talk to me about a matter of crucial importance to me praised me so highly! I had worked in Russia for a quarter of a century but never heard such kind words from anyone.

I left the consul's office, confident that not only would I be allowed to enter the United States, but that I had made the right choice—America was the country for me.

And here I was, praying with Congregation Young Israel in New York City. . . . Thank you, Almighty, for having delivered us.

The tall, elderly worshiper who spoke Russian (he had lived in Russia in his youth) sat down next to me and launched into a discourse on his own immigration story and the many hardships he had successfully endured.

"Anything you need, just let me know. I'll do whatever I can, and I can do a lot. I have excellent connections, particularly in commerce. I can buy or sell anything, you name it," he told me.

"Thank you ever so much, but I need connections in the world of medicine."

"That, too, I can do!" he exclaimed eagerly. "I can do anything!"

5

A crowd of immigrants always milled around in the lobby of the hotel or on the pavement outside, talking interminably. Everything struck them as disagreeably strange in the new country. Unable to grasp that they were in a different society, in a stratified world of private enterprise, they failed to understand the problems with which their new country was grappling. Frustration bred anger, and many of them never ceased to criticize America.

The ever-reasonable Boris tried to comfort them:

"Don't get excited. Little by little, you'll come to understand the American ways and like them, trust me."

"What's there to like?!" a former watchmaker from Kharkov, a bloated, sickly man past sixty, was beside himself with indignation, "Am I supposed to get to like their pigsty of a subway?! And to think I have to shell out half a dollar for the dubious privilege of riding in it! I wish they could see our Kharkov subway—clean as a whistle, and just five cents a ride!"

He put particular emphasis on the pronoun *they* in all its forms. All immigrants took pains to disassociate themselves from the Americans who in their parlance were *they, them, their*.

"All right," Boris replied, "but tell me, did you own a car in Kharkov?"

"A car?! How could I own a car? I wouldn't have been able to buy a car with the earnings of half a lifetime."

"You see? And here a man like you typically owns two or even three cars and thus has no need to use the subway."

"Come on, what kind of silly talk is that? 'Two or even three cars' in possession of a common watchmaker?" The immigrant was plainly incredulous.

"What's so unbelievable about it?" Boris asked. "Once you start working you'll become a car owner. Initially you will buy just one car, an old one most likely, then a second car, this time new. Little by little, you'll get everything you dream of. Why get nervous? Remember, this is America."

Public transportation in Russia is indeed cheaper and far more efficient than that in New York City. But in the whole of Russia, public transportation is the only way for urban dwellers to get around. Everybody depends on public transit, except for a handful of officials whisked around in state-owned, chauffeured limousines and a few private citizens with enough money to buy very expensive Soviet-made cars of inferior quality—altogether, not more than five percent of the country's population.

Irina and I went by subway to the Washington Heights area in Upper Manhattan to have a look at several vacant apartments, a list of which we had procured. The Ninety-sixth Street station where we boarded the train was dirty and half dark. The train did not come for thirty minutes. The cars were an ultimate in squalor, but mercifully half the lights were out and the appalling interior drowned in darkness. The train jerked and swayed so violently that keeping one's balance was nearly impossible.

But the passengers on station platforms and inside the cars struck us even more forcibly than the dirt and the discomfort. Almost half of them looked like criminals; they smoked, made a lot of noise, staggered in a drunken fashion, and even harassed other, normal passengers, who eyed the boisterous individuals with fear.

Irina was terrified. She clung to me, looking fearfully around. I tried to comfort her in a soft whisper.

Finally we made it to West 186th Street and started making the rounds of the available apartments, talking to residents and building managers. Irina kept asking the same question:

"How safe is this neighborhood?"

"You won't find an absolutely safe area in New York City" was the invariable answer. "That's the kind of town it is."

"But can one walk out at night?"

"No, when it's dark you'd better stay indoors."

"I don't want to live here," Irina told me. "I simply won't be able to exist in constant fear for our son, yourself, or myself."

We went to the Bronx: Maybe it was better there? The car of Number 2 train was half empty. Several young blacks, who looked between eighteen and twenty, were loudly arguing among themselves, the rest of the passengers casting furtive, fearful glances in their direction. All of a sudden a fight erupted. Two of the young men rolled on the floor in combat, knives flashed, and their companions jumped into the fray. It all happened without warning, right next to us. The passengers got up from their seats and rushed toward the passageway leading to the next car. As if on cue, Irina was off and running, dragging me by the sleeve. Then the train stopped in the tunnel between two stations, the conductor ran through the car to the fighters, and the engineer called the police. Irina was literally shaking, looking at the melee.

We did not make it to the Bronx; at the very next station, we took the train in the opposite direction.

Many of the immigrants chose to settle in Brooklyn, in the Brighton Beach area. Most of them came from Odessa, and in their honor the neighborhood was jokingly referred to as Odessa Beach. Boris, our benefactor, talked us out of following their example.

"I wouldn't advise you to live there. Brighton Beach is not for people of your kind. Why should you go there? They all live the way they did in Russia, speaking only Russian, eating only Russian food, reading only Russian-language newspapers, watching only Russian movies. Have you come to America to dwell in your past?"

Of course he was right. We came to America to become Americans. The last thing we wanted was to impede our adaptation to the new country by clinging to traditions and customs. So we refused to move to Brighton Beach and did not even bother to go there for a peek.

We went to Queens to visit a couple we had known in Moscow. Old-timers of three years' standing, they had much experience to give us. Also, the husband was a physician about to complete residency training. That was particularly important, because so far I had had no opportunity to talk to a single colleague with professional experience in America.

Faced with another subway trip, we could not help being wary, particularly Irina, who had not yet overcome her fright. Besides, we did not know the route, and it was impossible to read station names on dimly lit platforms through the dirty car windows. A subway map was on display in the car but graffiti covered it so solidly that we could discern nothing of value. I was edgy; Vladimir, Jr., grew noticeably glum; Irina was close to hysteria—I could plainly see the symptoms.

At the Fifty-ninth Street station, Columbus Circle, we went out on the platform to change trains and looked about helplessly, trying to figure out which way to go. All signs were nearly illegible and totally confusing. We asked several passersby for directions, but the crowd moved so swiftly that no one could hear our timid "Excuse me, please." Rapidly losing the remnants of patience, Irina threatened to bolt and walk home. I tried to reassure her, saying that we certainly would find someone of whom we could ask directions and sooner or later we would get to Queens.

"No, I can't stand this place any longer!"

"But we promised we would come. Those people are waiting for us."

"I don't care. I'm not feeling well."

"Please, Irina, please . . ."

At that crucial instant, someone addressed us in polite Russian, though the accent betrayed the speaker as an American.

"Pardon me, but could I be of any help?"

I looked at the most welcome intruder and saw a man of exactly the type I had pictured in my imagination: tall, blond, with a handsome, rugged face, well dressed and well mannered.

"Thank you," I said. "This is our first trip in this direction and we seem to have lost our way. How can we get to Forest Hills, Queens?"

He told us very clearly where to change trains. Irina regained her composure and started talking to him in English. He complimented her on her pronunciation.

"How come you speak Russian?" I asked.

"Simply because I've learned that language."

"Do you need Russian in your line of work?"

"Oh, no, it's for my own sake. I'm a lawyer and have nothing to do with any Russian business. But my ancestors hailed from Russia so I set myself the task of mastering their language."

"Have you ever been to Russia?"

"Yes, on two occasions. I liked it very much there."

"Sure, it's great to be a tourist wherever you go," I said.

"Yes, of course, you're absolutely right," he replied with another smile. I was positively falling in love with those American smiles.

Before saying good-bye, he gave us his card. "Please call me one of these days. Make sure you do."

Irina and I thanked him; he gave us a pleasant smile out of the window of the train that took him away. I read his name on the card: Allan Prince. He had been steered to us by providence.

6

The Moscow couple gave us a cordial welcome. I wanted to seek guidance about how to start a new life—but above all, how to start a career in American medicine. The man was completing the last year of residency training, which was an unattainable pinnacle of success in my eyes. I was fully aware that the quarter of a century of my past experience as a Russian doctor and all my academic kudos were of little worth here in America. In any case, first I was to take a medical exam and also an exam in English—a standard requirement for all graduates of foreign medical schools.

I felt no false pride on account of my past achievements. The very first day after leaving Russia, in Vienna waiting for the next leg of our trip, I had a mystic experience. Suddenly I felt as if part of my soul detached itself and flew away; I even found it easier to breathe afterward. I did not know what to make of that episode, but I remember telling Irina that my past life had just taken leave of me. Since then I had really changed and never looked back on my previous status. In a new environment, I became a new man.

And so I diligently listened to my colleague, as a greenhorn should. I even took notes on much of what he was saying about the textbooks, the ECFMG exam (Educational Council for Foreign Medical Graduates, although I did not know yet what that acronym stood for), the best ways of seeking a position on a residency program or a job related to the medical field. Irina also listened attentively. After all, the fate of the whole family depended on my future. He gave me a great deal of valuable advice and a few practical pointers to go by in the new life. I committed them to memory.

"In this country, no one turns down a job," he told me.

That was exactly the precept I had decided to embrace from the start. If need be, I would take any job, even that of a nurse's assistant, as the first step toward the top. But how high was that?

"In Russia, you were like a general (or a colonel, at the very least)," he said. "Forget about ever attaining a comparable rank in this country. Now you are a private, at best a sergeant. But you can rise to become a captain or even a major. Only this time around you won't need as much time to get your promotion."

Well, at least his description of the past and future chances, couched in military terms, conformed to reality. At any rate, it made life clear and comprehensible.

"At first you, and in fact all of your family, will have plenty of reasons for whining," he continued. "No one, but no one, has it easy from the start in this country. I've seen Russian immigrants who were really pathetic—so crushed were they by their initial hardships. But later on, whatever the degree of misery at the beginning, each of them found a niche in life and began making money—and everything was fine again."

Those were exactly the confidence-building words I had already heard at the NYANA briefing. But Irina, a doubting and emotional person, peppered our host with questions.

"Both my husband and I held important positions in Moscow. For instance, I was a researcher with a job first at an allergology lab and later at a microbiological institute. Can I count on a comparable job here?"

"In this country, all research is financed by grants," our friend replied. "And any grant is temporary. Besides, only really major researchers can count on such financing. So, as you see, scientific research is not a sure thing; far from it. You work only as long as grant money is available."

His words scared Irina, and her mood soured.

"I thought so," she said. "I knew I would never be able to work here."

"Hey, don't get discouraged prematurely," I said reassuringly. "Wait till we look around and get our bearings."

Our son's future was one of the topics of conversation. Our hosts had a daughter of the same age who was already in college. Judging by the collective immigrant experience, Vladimir, Jr., faced the inevitable prospect of first going to college and then trying to enroll in medical school—an all but impossible task, although he had left Moscow as a third-year medical student (at a six-year medical school). No matter what happened, he stood to lose at least six to seven years. This information upset both Junior and his mother—so many years would be spent, with no certainty of a happy end.

Another Russian immigrant couple dropped by, the husband was a surgeon who had passed the exam and entered a surgical residency program. He talked about the unbearable physical and mental stresses resident physicians were required to endure: night duty every third day and twelve- and fourteen-hour working days. Under the onslaught of discouraging information even my composure was shaken.

"I don't think you'll cope with such a load," Irina told me with desperation.

"Why don't you forget about surgery and take residency training in, say, pathology or psychiatry?" our host suggested. "They're far less demanding fields."

"Good idea," Irina concurred.

All my life I had a love affair with orthopedic surgery. If I were forced to part with my vocation, I would suffer real pain, comparable to the suffering brought by the loss of a true love. I realized that at my age it was much too late to embark, all over again, upon a surgical career at the entry level. And yet I made a resolution that I would give it a try. I would surrender only when the last of my stamina gave out. But to yield in advance, without a fight? Never. It was contrary to my rules. What made me particularly mad was Irina's attitude. Who else should have known that I was totally addicted to my specialty and temperamentally unsuited to compromises on points of principle? Why then was she prodding me to capitulation?

"I was born a surgeon and intend to die as one," I told her testily. "I vastly prefer to collapse at the operating table rather than suffer through interminable sessions with crazies."

We were angry with each other.

7

The next morning, I went to mid-Manhattan alone. I wanted to have a one-on-one rendez-vous with my new town. Besides, there was a lot to mull over. The new—good and bad—that had come tumbling down on our heads within those first few days, created psychological stress and needed sorting out.

I had no inkling of the city geography and walked like Tarzan prowling the jungle—guided by intuition. My wanderings led me to a skyscraper-rimmed square with an artificial skating rink in the middle, surrounded by a fence of national flags. I walked with a permanent crick in my neck, admiring the stupendous monoliths. America, with its power and drive, is best epitomized by the architecture of its skyscrapers—as mighty and as aspiring to great heights as the country itself. Roaming agape around the square, I finally found out its name— Rockefeller Plaza. From then on I went to Fifth Avenue and farther on to Park Avenue. The skyscrapers there were even more numerous and more modern in design; besides, they looked even more imposing from across the wide street. They were not beautiful in the conventional sense, but their huge proportions and revolutionary design had an overwhelming effect on my imagination. I felt a surge of energy and optimism, thrilled by the thought that all that novelty and originality would henceforth become part of my natural, day-by-day surroundings.

In such buoyant spirits I wanted to think over my immediate plans. But where? No suitable spot to sit down and concentrate in solitude was in sight. I continued walking, still craning my neck, when all of a sudden the expanse of a park opened up before me, with yet another marvelous skyscraper in the distance. There could be no mistaking the United Nations building I had admired in so many photographs. I came up to the fence surrounding the park and saw a guard. Unsure of whether or not one was allowed to enter the park and have a stroll, I asked the guard for permission.

He shrugged in some surprise. "Sure, go ahead."

How was he supposed to know that I came from a country where all administrative territory was off limits to all but authorized personnel, and where in general just about everything was forbidden to common people?

It was peaceful and beautiful inside: trees in bloom; masses of flowers; a fresh, moisture-laden wind blowing from the East River; empty alleys and benches in quiet, secluded spots—exactly what I craved to sit and think.

So, it will take me at least two years to study English and get prepared for the ECFMG exam, plus another three years at the very least for residency training (even if I am lucky enough to get partial credit for my past professional experience). It adds up to five or six years. Thus I will be about fifty-five when the training is over—a bit too late to start in private practice. And yes, this time frame will hold if, and only if, I remain in good health.

Now then, while studying I won't be able to earn a living, which means that my family will have only Irina's earnings to count on, and no matter how lucky she may get, she won't be paid much. Junior must become a student and hence we will have somehow to support him—this is a paramount concern.

But what sources of income are available to me? When

our valuables, which I managed to smuggle with the help of my friend from Holland, arrive from Europe, I will sell them; but surely it will be unrealistic to hope that the proceeds from their sale will last us a long time—twelve to eighteen months at best, if I am lucky. Another two standby options: I might land a job at a hospital—not as a physician, of course, but maybe as a plaster technician or as a surgeon's assistant. In such a case my studies will be deferred, but on the plus side, I will be able to feed my family. Finally, if I write a book about my past experience and find a publisher willing to give it a try, the book might bring me enough money to end our immediate worries.

Unseen birds were flying and chirping above my head. The din of the enormous city was partially screened by the trees. The glass walls of the skyscrapers glistened in the sun. The more I deliberated, the clearer and the more tangibly I realized that the road ahead was strewn with obstacles and I was facing a long and hard fight for survival in a totally unfamiliar environment. Well, so be it; if there was to be a fight, fight I would.

I stood up and went to NYANA to seek referral to an English-language school.

NYANA was always crowded with hundreds of Russian immigrants seeking help—with an apartment, a job, or a referral to the doctor. Many needed financial assistance to claim their belongings shipped in containers from Israel and released only upon payment of a considerable sum. Others wanted to be enrolled in a language school or some vocational course. Social workers talked to their wards through interpreters. Sometimes the demand for interpreters exceeded the supply, in which case social workers tried to communicate with immigrants in English in the belief that such language practice was beneficial to the Russian newcomers. Patiently and methodically they spoke, but in most cases the immigrants did not understand a word and either flew into a rage or sank into gloom.

"Oy, what is it she is saying? It's all Greek to me!" a young woman from Odessa wailed hysterically.

"I see, I see," an old woman from Kishinev nodded know-
ingly, and then commented aside: "Do you really think I
understood a single word? Nothing! Zero! Zilch!"

"Take your English and shove it, dammit!" a confused man
mumbled in a hoarse angry voice under his breath. I was surprised to learn he was a physician and used to be deputy head
doctor of one of the biggest Moscow hospitals. The administrative positions were usually filled by party members and ac-
tivists. How could he manage to emigrate?

I watched and heard scenes like this with distaste while
waiting for my turn for an interview. I belonged to that mass
of immigrants and shared the stigma of their maladjustment to
the new world. At the first two or three interviews, a young
volunteer named Daniel helped out, but later on, my caseworker dispensed with his services. I could understand her fairly
well, but speaking was a far more difficult proposition. I tried
to prepare my presentations in advance and rehearsed the words
so as to pronounce them correctly, but nothing helped. Whenever I was called upon to speak, my tongue stuck to the roof
of my mouth. I felt as if every single word, before finally
bursting forth and falling in a lump off my tongue, passed with
the bloodstream through my entire circulation system—from
the brain to the heel via the stomach and back to the mouth.
I strained to the limit and sweated profusely. A brief interview
sapped my strength like the most extensive and demanding
orthopedic surgical procedure. My fatigue was compounded
by exasperation born of inability to express myself adequately.
I used to be a poet, author of books and learned articles, lec-
turing professor, and a speaker at scientific conferences. And
now I could barely manage a few elementary words—just
enough to be understood.

I relied on my strong nervous system not to betray my
frustration as I saw in other immigrants, but pity and compassion were clearly written in the caseworker's face, and she
eventually handed me a referral slip to the Cambridge School
on East Forty-second Street.

I went to the school on foot. The expense of several bus
or subway trips a day was beyond my meager means. At the

Cambridge School, the secretary took my referral slip and issued me forms for a written test to determine the language
level at which I was to start. Having no idea that an exam was
in store, I was unprepared and decided that all I could count
on was the beginners' level 1. The secretary applied a card-
board stencil onto my answer sheet and immediately came up
with the result. To my surprise, I qualified for level 3. This
gave me such a lift that I walked another fifty blocks, through
Central Park, to the hotel. Irina was worried, of course—maybe
something had happened to me in this awful town.

"I am a third-level student and demand respect befitting
such an exalted station in life," I told her importantly.

Laughing, we embraced.

Irina was the first in our family
to strike pay dirt. She found a job a mere three weeks after
our arrival in the country—an incredibly short time considering that usually it took immigrants months to find employment.

At NYANA's recommendation, a physician with an office
on Fifth Avenue employed Irina as his assistant at $190 per
week. After deductions, her take-home pay was $150—a royal
sum in our eyes. Irina was overjoyed, while Junior and I took
over her household duties and prepared to live on her salary,
particularly insofar as NYANA promptly struck us off its financial assistance list.

News of Irina's good luck spread through the Greystone

rapidly. Boris and the rest of the old-timers heaped congratulations on her. Boris beamed with pride, much as a sports coach proudly rejoices in the triumph of his athlete.

"Like I said," he repeated to all and sundry, "little by little, everything will work out all right. Today you are making a hundred fifty dollars, tomorrow you'll be making two hundred fifty, and in no time soon you'll graduate to five hundred. This is America!"

Junior continued his extended daily strolls about the city, but he no longer concentrated exclusively on window shopping. He also earned some money, helping with cargo handling at downtown stores. He was a sturdy fellow, and store owners readily hired him for a couple of hours at a time, paying him twenty to twenty-five dollars.

Two weeks later he, too, landed a permanent job as a helper at a watch company in mid-Manhattan. His first job paid $110 a week. Simultaneously, he applied to Hunter College on Park Avenue. As the college was run by the city, tuition was very cheap for city residents, which was the paramount reason that Junior chose it.

I spent afternoon hours at the English school, devoting mornings to homework and apartment hunting. I also had to take care of my elderly parents' affairs, so that they could start drawing Social Security, Medicaid, food stamps, reduced transit fare, and other benefits due senior citizens. In addition, I had to look for an apartment for them as well. Father's condition deteriorated; he urgently needed professional advice and treatment.

I still walked to and from my English school on East Forty-second Street, a hundred-plus blocks a day. Irina and Junior also moved about exclusively on foot.

Altogether, walking saved us three dollars daily, a not insignificant portion of our budget. But Irina's work took a heavy toll of her energy and I insisted that she should take the bus at least one way—returning home from work.

The single most taxing duty for her was the need to speak English all the time. Her fluency improved day to day, but she paid dearly in nervous tension. Straining her ears trying to grasp the meaning of words uttered in an unfamiliar fashion, and the constant fear of misunderstanding or being misunderstood, cost her a great deal of energy, and as a result she came home exhausted. Besides, her job was new to her, and she had to learn from scratch how to take an electrocardiogram, how to prepare the instruments for surgical procedures, even how to talk to patients on the telephone. The Fifth Avenue patients, too, were a novelty to her.

The office was frequented by affluent patients, mostly women, whose health problems were by and large imaginary. They arrived attired in expensive furs and diamonds, their faces masked by makeup. Many of them brought tiny dogs, carried in their arms or held on leashes, always clean and beribboned. Irina's duty was to welcome them at the door and show them attention.

"How are you today, Mrs. Smith?"

"Oh, horrible, my dear, perfectly horrible!" The patient's eyes would roll in her head. "I'm a total mess! Last night I had absolutely no sleep, not one minute! That is why I want to be examined."

"I feel so sorry for you!" Irina was expected to respond. "Please be seated, the doctor will be with you in a minute."

Then Irina would help the doctor examine the patient, to wrap the blood pressure cuff around her arm, install suction electrodes for electrocardiography, or apply a tourniquet, if a blood sample was to be drawn from the vein.

Irina, who had worked all her life and had a Ph.D. in biology and who until recently had been herself a part of Moscow's intellectual elite, felt like a Cinderella at the office. But what really galled her and made her work so tiresome was the need to humor rich loafers—a species she had never cared for.

The doctor made it a point to introduce Irina to some of his lady patients as a special attraction of his office, telling them that his assistant was a recent Russian immigrant and herself the wife of a physician. The response was always the same:

"Oh, really? How perfectly wonderful!" To while away the time, some of them asked Irina about her family, about

Russia, about our current circumstances. Irina did her best to answer simply, courteously, and in a dignified manner. Her replies never failed to elicit an enthusiastic response, always the same: "Really? How interesting!"

Some of them went so far as to promise to invite Irina with her husband to dinner, some vowed to tell our story to their husbands or some highly placed friends to try to help us. Irina never asked them for any kind of help, but naturally thanked them for their kindness. But their good intentions always evaporated the minute they stepped out of the office.

Irina didn't much care. However humble her new station in life, a weekly check for $150 made up for it every Friday.

9

I remembered that Mr. Allan Prince, the gentleman we met on a subway platform, had asked us to call. Irina and I discussed his offer several times but could not get the courage to do it. Not knowing Americans, we were not sure that he had meant what he said; maybe it was just a formality to be promptly forgotten? Finally, I took the matter to Boris.

"Of course you should call," he said. "And why not? Besides, you should know that no American would waste his card on someone he did not want to see again. In other words, he actually did mean what he said. Did you say he is a lawyer? Fine, it's even better; now you'll have a lawyer among your acquaintances. Where does this guy live?"

I showed him the card. Boris read the address and was impressed.

"He must be important because he lives in a really swanky house. I should know, I sold newspapers in the vicinity. Unquestionably, you should give him a call; it seems like a very good connection. Like I said, little by little, you'll have everything. Maybe in a few years' time you will be his neighbors, who knows? And why not? Remember this is America."

Irina had to make the call because I could not bring myself to speak English on the phone. No sooner did Irina start explaining who she was and why she was calling, than the woman on the other end of the line exclaimed effusively: "Oh, I know who you are; you must be the Russians my husband met recently in the subway. He told me you are a very nice couple with a wonderful son. Why on earth haven't you called earlier?"

"We have been busy, you know, so much to do," Irina explained.

"We would be glad, both of us, to see you all at our place. Would tomorrow be a convenient time for you?"

"Thank you, I am sure we will enjoy it."

"Fine, we'll be expecting you for dinner tomorrow at six."

Precisely at the time we were to set out for the Princes', a downpour began. But the elements did not deter us; we heroically waded through the puddles and, drenched, arrived at a magnificent old-fashioned building on West Eighty-first Street. The door was opened by a liveried doorman, and a liveried elevator attendant took us upstairs. The elevator was bedecked in bronze and mirrors so we could watch our funny, wet images.

The door of the apartment opened and we found ourselves in a hall so huge one could use it for bicycle practice. Allan and his wife, Margaret, did not wear formal clothes; he was tieless, she wore a plain dress. Somewhat ill at ease, we lingered at the door because we were still dripping and could not bring ourselves to move further. Laughing, they dragged us inside and forced us to change into dry clothes and shoes from their wardrobe. While this was happening, amid talk, laughter, apologies, and clothes changing, a friendly atmosphere was created all by itself, and when the initial commotion was over we felt completely at home with our hosts.

We had never seen an apartment that vast: three bedrooms of a size dictated by bygone standards, a huge living room, a hall, a dining room, and a kitchen with an adjoining maid's room. The Princes had bought the apartment a short time before and were in the process of redecorating it themselves, working with loving care. The way they enthusiastically described their project made it clear that no kind of work was regarded beneath their dignity, although they were rich enough to stay away from manual labor. I was greatly impressed by that typically American trait—not to be afraid to work—that I had heard about and now could witness. It was an interesting experience for us to study the unfamiliar day-to-day habits of an American family.

We took our drinks in the living room and ate, for the first time in our lives, fresh vegetables served with a thick dip. Then we had dinner in the candlelit dining room—another novelty. The way food was served and the selection of dishes fascinated us. Then we moved to the library/studio for coffee and brandy. It was my first glimpse of an American book collection—all I had seen before were a handful of American editions, and paperbacks at that. Allan owned a wonderful library of lavishly printed and bound books, which I found totally irresistible; after all, I, too, was a bibliophile and had once owned a respectable library—in my past life. Someday I would also be able to read English and start my own library anew, I was thinking. But when?

I sighed involuntarily—my dream would take a long, long time to come true, if it ever did. Allan noticed my gloom and, an intelligent and shrewd man, correctly read my mood. He started talking about the Russian books that stood on the shelves next to local editions. I was struck by Allan's wide range of reading; he had read all his Russian books in the original and remembered a lot.

Allan and Marge encouraged us in our ambition to regain

our past standing in the new society. For our part, we peppered them with questions and doubts. Thus we spent the evening interspersing serious talk with stories, recollections, and jokes. We felt so comfortable with the hosts that even my English thawed a bit.

Allan had no doubt that Vladimir, Jr., had an excellent chance of making it to medical school in America.

"Your knowledge of Russian and your general cultural background from Russia will always be a plus for you," he told Junior, who listened attentively to the opinion of an obviously knowledgeable person. Then Allan turned to Irina.

"I disagree with those people who told you that your chances of finding a research position are negligible. There are so many scientific centers and laboratories in this city that you should find a vacant spot, particularly considering your experience and good English. I'll try to talk to a few friends; maybe we'll be able to do something for you. After all, you wouldn't want to die a physician's assistant, would you?"

His reasoning and friendly tone had a beneficial effect on Irina. For the first time in a long while she relaxed, laughed a lot, and chattered unstoppably. I was happy to see her old self reemerge.

Allan managed to find something encouraging to say even to me:

"I have no idea of your past professional standing," he said, "but I am certain that, given the extent of your experience, you'll have no trouble finding a residency position. Nothing is valued in this country as highly as experience and initiative. If you were a good specialist, you'll be okay here."

Of course, he had no idea of my professional reputation in Russia, if only because I was reluctant to talk of it. I did not want to mention my academic achievements and the names of my celebrity patients, from Boris Pasternak to Maya Plysetskaya, lest he think that I was boasting. So I preferred to keep silent about my stature in the old country—I was a physician, an orthopedic surgeon, and that was that.

However, I felt an urge to share my literary plans with Allan. I had not discussed the problem with a single person, but here was a golden opportunity—a highly educated American, versed in Russian as well as American letters, in short, a top-notch reader.

"I'd like to write a book about my experiences that would give American readers an insight into Russia today. Over the course of my professional career I passed all the hierarchical rungs—from a green doctor in the countryside to a professor at a Moscow medical school. I treated a lot of people, some of whom are household names the world over. What do you think of my plan?" I asked.

Allan was clearly intrigued: "American readers love real-life stories about Russia. I know nothing of your writing talents, but the idea is certainly interesting, and I wish you the best of luck. And when you have a draft contract with a publishing house, be sure to consult me before signing. I'm something of an expert in legal matters, after all, and could be of help to you."

That unforgettable night in the company of our first American friends was the first time, after a long hiatus, that we could immerse ourselves in the intellectual milieu to which we had always belonged, but which we had temporarily lost. We had no way of knowing whether or not we would reach the level of the Princes, but at least we had found a model to emulate. That night we experienced at firsthand that Americans were cordial and genuinely democratic people.

10

Ⓐnd then we were again carried by the swift current of everyday cares and concerns of adaptation to the new. The paramount problem was renting an apartment. NYANA cut off financial assistance, and we could not afford the hotel any longer. Circumstances bound us to Manhattan: Irina's job, Junior's job and college, even my language school—all were within walking distance. Furthermore, I could not live too far from my elderly parents who, for their parts, hoped to remain with Aunt Lyuba, who was expecting to move shortly into a co-op apartment on West Ninety-sixth Street with them. But then, given our limited means, it was all but improbable that we would find a suitable apartment on the Upper West Side of Manhattan. My valuables were to arrive from Holland any day and I planned to sell them. But it all required time, energy, and patience. Three months of living in cheap immigrant hotels was finally getting to us, particularly to Irina. The endless immigrant talk in the hotel—reminiscences and complaints, complaints and reminiscences—tired and infuriated her.

I hoped that the privacy of our own apartment, the chance to avoid unwanted socializing, and some elementary comforts would combine to produce a therapeutic effect. We visited several buildings on the Upper West Side, but they turned out to be slums. To take an apartment in them would be tantamount to moral and physical suicide. However humble our circumstances, we had still not sunk so low as to live on the bottom of society, side by side with its dregs—prostitutes, bandits, and junkies. One of the slum buildings was across the street from our hotel. One night we heard the noise of a loud scene there, yells and wails, then a desperate piercing scream— a woman was thrown out of the window from one of the top floors. In no time police cars arrived, their sirens wailing. Gunshots boomed, a crowd gathered, all our fellow immigrants rushed outside to see what had happened. My poor Irina was terrified.

In desperation she kept saying: "We must go away, we must!"

I succeeded in cheering her up a bit and went downstairs to find out, for the umpteenth time, if anything new had transpired with regard to housing. As always, the Kharkov watchmaker dominated the discussion in the lobby.

"What kind of country is this? You call them people? I call them animals!" he was screaming. "Criminals, all of them. All one hears about is mugging and killing, killing and mugging."

"Come on," Boris interjected ironically. "Do you mean there was no crime in Russia?"

"Of course there was, but not as much. Look—they've just killed a woman. And tomorrow the papers will tell us of other murders. One can get crazy reading this stuff every day!"

"And what did the papers write about in Russia?"

"The papers there are such trash that nobody reads them," chuckled the watchmaker.

"But what exactly did they write about? Give me an example."

"Socialist competition, overfulfillment of production quotas, industrial triumphs, how the country thrives and prospers. In a word, lies!"

"And what about Gulag Archipelago? Did they write about it?"

"No, of course not."

"Now try to imagine what would happen if the Russian papers covered all KGB arrests."

"Then, of course, they would run out of space." The watchmaker was amused by the thought.

"So? You said it, I didn't. Now, collect yourself and try to be calm. Little by little, you'll get used to this country and its ways."

"But you can't compare. Those people were arrested by the state."

"Do you mean to say that state crime is better than private crime?"

"No, I wouldn't say that, but there's a difference. Here I'm afraid to go out into the street."

"And there people were afraid to stay at home. KGB agents came at night and dragged people out of bed. Then they were gone for good—millions of them," Boris pressed his attack relentlessly.

"That was a long time ago, when Stalin was alive," the watchmaker replied.

"And later on things improved?"

"At least people were not arrested on such a scale."

"Why then did you leave Russia?" insisted Boris.

"Because I was a fool, that's why!" the watchmaker screamed in sudden fury. "All the Jews started yapping: time to move, time to leave. My children, too. The Jews must leave. And they left, and so did I. On account of my wife, who cried that she couldn't live away from her kids. So, we are here. America, Shmamerica," the malcontent grumbled. "Had I known what it's like, nothing would have lured me here. What kind of country is it? Savages, that's what they are!"

Boris left his side. "He's a very sick person," he told me. "But you can bet that as soon as he starts earning more money, he'll love everything around him. I know the type. Little by little, everybody settles down and finds a niche in life."

"Do you think I have a chance of finding a decent apartment on the Upper West Side?" I asked Boris.

"Why not?" he replied. "All it takes is the right connections. What kind of relationship do you have with that tall, bearded Jew from the synagogue?"

"Excellent."

"Good. Take your case to him. I hear an apartment is going to be vacated soon in a building nearby. He knows the landlord and can help."

About that time, my cousin came to visit from Europe and brought our valuables from our Dutch friends, the Sinitskys: diamond earrings, a lady's watch with a diamond-studded bracelet, and several Czarist gold coins. I had bought the lot not long before leaving Russia for 22,000 rubles (about $30,000 at that time). I planned to sell them and use the proceeds to supplement our income in order to rent a decent apartment and buy some furniture. But I was totally in the dark as to the real value of my jewels and gold here in America.

The next Saturday, I went to the synagogue to discuss the apartment problem with my friend. He was in his customary place, worshiping with fervor, his tall, gangly body rocking so violently that his long beard whipped back and forth. I put on a tallith and stationed myself nearby.

As soon as the prayer was over, I whispered to him, "I have some business to discuss with you."

"Shoot. I'm all ears."

"But isn't it unseemly to conduct business in the synagogue? Let's step outside."

"No, you don't understand," he told me. "The synagogue is the best place for any kind of business deals."

"Okay, I need an apartment in this area."

"If you need it, you'll get it," the bearded worshiper said. "Do you have money?"

"I have some jewels."

My statement produced an electric effect; he immediately closed the prayer book and pricked his ears.

"What kind of jewels?"

"A diamond-studded watch, antique, excellent workmanship." I decided not to mention the others.

"Do you have it on you?"

"Of course not. Why should I carry it around?"

"That's right. I can see you're a businessman. What else do you have?"

"That's all."

"That's all?"

"Right, that's all."

"Come on, who are you kidding? I know you must have something else. But it's up to you; if you prefer to keep it to yourself, it's none of my business. All Jews from Russia come here poor, but then it transpires that almost each of them has brought a little something. They manage to hide their jewels and smuggle them out; some of them even drill holes in their furniture and hide valuables there. How much do you want for your watch?"

"I don't know the going prices."

"Show it to me, I'll give you the best price. Nobody will beat my price."

"I'd like to have a professional estimate."

"I know some people on Forty-seventh Street," he said. "I'll take you there. I have good connections among the right people. I'll ask them to inspect your diamonds and name the right price. Then I'll buy your watch on the spot. But don't make a fool of yourself by selling to somebody else. Nobody, but nobody, will give you the right price. I alone will, trust me."

"I trust you. And what about the apartment?"

"What about it?" he asked, obviously oblivious to my request.

"I need an apartment on the Upper West Side, somewhere in this area."

"If you need it, you'll get it," he said, and promptly added, "I can do anything, and I'll do anything for you. Just don't sell your jewels to anybody else."

11

The student body at the Cambridge School was made up of immigrants from all over the world. The dominant group was Latin American. For the first time in my life, I had an opportunity to find out what people from Haiti, the Dominican Republic, Bolivia, Venezuela, and Peru looked like. There were also many Filipinos, Koreans, and Israelis. Alongside of them sat French Canadians, Italians, and Spaniards. And, of course, a lot of my brethren, Russian immigrants.

I could see with my own eyes the tremendous diversity of people my new country was ready to accept and absorb. Most immigrants were young, from seventeen to thirty. They came to America looking for jobs and success, with no intention of saying good-bye for good to their homeland or families. Many had a fair command of spoken English, but they could not read or write. Most of them, belonging to different races, religions, and nationalities, were easygoing, amiable, and merry. American life presented no mysteries to them for they had had extensive exposure to American goods, magazines, movies, and household appliances at the preimmigration stage. For this reason, they felt entirely at home in New York.

But the Russian immigrants were a different breed. Most of us were mature adults—past forty, and some of us past fifty. All of us had left our country for good, leaving friends and relatives behind, going through the tragedy of parting forever. Most of us spoke almost no English. We felt lost, because our life in Russia had been all but totally insulated from all things American. Thus the Russians were ill at ease, banded together, and kept at a distance from their fellow students.

I was distressed by our self-imposed isolation. "My God, here is what the Iron Curtain brought us!" I thought. "Just to think that an illiterate kid from Haiti feels more at home and behaves more sociably than Russian physicians, teachers, or engineers!"

Once, during a recess, I felt hungry and decided to buy a sandwich from a coin-operated machine. A whole dollar was a major expense for me and I preferred to bring homemade sandwiches. But that time it so happened that I had no other choice. Also, it was interesting to find out how the vending machine worked. There was a plate attached to the front of the machine with operating instructions, but to read and understand them was difficult for me. The prospect of demonstrating my ignorance publicly did not appeal to me either. So I spent some time watching others use the machine and then hesitantly approached myself—only to find out that I did not have enough change. Where could I change a dollar bill? Another Russian immigrant, a fifty-year-old engineer from Leningrad, came over. He was not familiar with the self-service technology either, and we started discussing the complicated problem. Apparently we looked quite funny in our bewilderment.

A young black girl asked me with a warm smile if she could be of any help.

"Thanks," I said in embarrassment, "I don't know where to change a dollar bill."

"But here is a money-changing machine," she pointed out.

"Oh, thank you so much!"

I had not noticed that machine and, again, did not know how to coax it into giving me coins. Obviously the girl realized my predicament, for she dazzled me with another smile and offered to help.

She took my dollar, turned it face up, and fed the bill into the machine, which chomped it up and produced several quarters. The girl picked up the coins and asked me which sandwich I wanted. I watched her manipulations as though charmed. She dropped in the coins and pressed the button opposite the sandwich I indicated. The machine set in motion its shelves, and my choice appeared in the window, but I did not even know how to open it. The girl smiled and took the sandwich out. Miracles!

I thanked her profusely.

"What country are you from?" she asked.

"Russia. My name is Vladimir."

"Say it again."

"Vlad-i-mir."

"Hello, Vladimir. My name is Dorel, I am from Costa Rica. I don't know anything about Russia except that it is supposed to be very cold there."

"Yes, in winter there is much snow," I put together the sentence with some difficulty.

"I've never seen genuine snow except in the movies," she laughed and walked away.

"All those blacks are savages," my fellow Russian student said.

I felt an urge to retort that, conversely, we, two middle-aged Russians, must have struck her as savages, but I was reluctant to get involved in a debate. I knew that Russians had a hard time getting accustomed to black skins.

Watching my black fellow students, I was surprised to discover quite a few likable faces, with keenly intelligent features and handsome smiles. Young black girls—graceful, lithe, and vivacious—were particularly attractive. They were always smiling and affable, a stark contrast to my fellow Russians, including pretty women, who wore surly expressions almost all the time.

Dorel and I became friends. I told her stories about Russia and myself. It was a good way to improve my fluency. I think she had difficulty understanding me, but she was polite and never showed it.

"When are you going to return to Russia?" she asked me.

"Never."

"Why? Don't you like it there?"

I replied concisely, "Communists, piff-puff, piff-puff. Siberia." And we both laughed.

I presented her with a gift, a Russian wooden *matryoshka* doll. Broken apart, it contained a smaller replica of itself which, broken apart, contained yet a third doll. Delighted, Dorel kissed me and then spent the recess running around in the corridor and showing off her gift and the way it could be taken apart.

The Russian immigrants watched her disapprovingly.

"I don't see why you should play democrat," the engineer from Leningrad told me. "Don't you see she's a savage?"

These black youngsters proved far more adept at language studies than we Russian immigrants. Naturally, we were hampered by age, but it also indicated that we had no special intellectual advantages over our black fellow students of either sex.

12

The housing problem was foremost in my mind—I needed an apartment badly.

"You'll have to wait," the bearded worshiper from the synagogue told me every day. "I've lined up an apartment for you. Don't be jumpy; I told you I would do it, and I will. I can do anything."

On a designated day, we took the M104 bus to Forty-seventh Street to have my watch with its diamond band evaluated. I put the watch in my breast pocket and tried to feel its reassuring presence all the time.

It was my first visit to the diamond center, but I still remembered the atmosphere of mystery and danger surrounding all diamond deals in Russia. Private sale or purchase of diamonds in Russia was a criminal offense punishable by a stiff sentence—anywhere from five to ten years of imprisonment. The law demanded that diamonds only be sold to state-owned stores that bought them at a fraction of the true price—from one-third to one-fifth—and then resold them for twice or thrice what they were really worth. The Soviet government itself speculated in diamonds. Needless to say, people did everything they could to bypass the idiotic law, but they did it on the sly.

The window displays on Forty-seventh Street, glittering with thousands upon thousands of diamonds, struck me forcibly. I stood paralyzed and speechless. I had figured that the diamond business in America would be conducted differently from Russia, but I had never imagined that the difference was that great.

I stood transfixed at the window display of Kaplan Jewelers' store, watching mounds of diamonds being bought and sold absolutely openly. "Good God, what a gap between two worlds!" I thought. "What a difference!"

My companion was chattering away. "You see now? I've brought you to the right place, haven't I? I have many friends here; they would tell you the real price. Nobody but me can do it. I can do anything."

He dived into a doorway. Still dazed, I followed and saw a multitude of separate counters, actually a conglomeration of small stores under one roof. We came up to a counter behind which sat a Jew in a yarmulke. My companion started talking to him in a mixture of English and Yiddish. I did not understand what they were saying but I could plainly see that the jeweler treated my companion with total indifference, not as one seeing an old friend. He took my watch and inspected it through his eyepiece. Then he said something.

"He is willing to give you a thousand dollars," my companion said.

I had bought the watch for 7,000 rubles back in Russia. It would be better to get a couple of other opinions, I thought.

"No, let's go to somebody else," I said.

We left the store.

"You know what?" he asked. "I'm prepared to pay you twelve hundred dollars—ready cash on the spot."

"No, let's get the opinion of another jeweler."

He took me to another store where there were even more counters. He found his man and again started conversing with him in his incomprehensible combination of languages. Another inspection, and the jeweler named the price: $1,500. Careful, I said to myself. Just a few steps and the price jumps fifty percent. Haste is counterproductive. We visited yet another store, and I was offered still more: $1,700. Finally my companion said:

"Two thousand dollars right here. A deal?"

"Let me sleep on it," I replied.

13

All of a sudden I had a stroke of good luck—an American acquaintance of Russian ancestry recommended me to an orthopedic surgeon at a Bronx hospital, and I was invited for an interview. The surgeon was in a position to offer me a job and I rejoiced in advance. But my poor English made me anxious. Why would he be willing to employ a person barely able to utter a few words? To improve my chances, I rehearsed with Irina several key words and even short sentences, anticipating possible questions. My acquaintance told me that Dr. S. was a prominent physician on the staff of the orthopedic surgery department, that he was Jewish, and that his parents had come to America from Russia. You can count on his total benevolence, he reassured me. Cheered up a little, I took samples of the wrist, elbow, and shoulder prostheses I had designed in Russia—what could be a better recommendation of my orthopedic skills?—and at the appointed time appeared at the secretary's desk.

"Good morning. My name is Doctor Golyakhovsky. I have an appointment with Dr. S."

"Have a seat, please, the doctor will be with you in a minute."

"Thank you."

Ugh. But the secretary did understand me! I thought and wiped beads of sweat off my forehead.

The doctor was a few years my junior. He looked tired and showed little, if any, interest in me. He introduced me to another physician in his office, a Polish resident, who spoke some Russian and could help as an interpreter. But we spoke by and large in English.

"Why have you left Russia?" Dr. S. asked.

I was taken aback by the question, coming as it did from a Jew whose parents had emigrated themselves. The real answer was clear: People are leaving that country because they cannot stand it.

"I was tired of living there; I paid too high a price for the few necessities I managed to obtain, and even they were not enough."

"Did you have a good position?"

"Yes, I was a professor and head of a chair of orthopedic surgery in Moscow."

"Maybe you had a nasty temper and quarreled with your subordinates? What kind of disposition do you have?"

"Good enough, I think. And I never had any quarrels with my people."

After the initial questions, Dr. S. led me to an X-ray film viewer displaying several pictures of a rather complicated fracture compounded by the dislocation of the shoulder joint.

"Well, doctor," he addressed me, "let's see what you would do in this case."

49

The picture was clear in an instant.

"Whatever one does, the prognosis is not good," I said.

"Agreed," Dr. S. nodded. "But still, what would your strategy be if the patient insisted on surgical intervention?"

"I would choose between fusion or prosthetic replacement."

"What kind of prosthesis?"

"I have a prosthesis of my original design for just such an operation."

"Can I see it?"

"Sure," and I took it from my attaché case.

'Hmm, interesting, very interesting," Dr. S. said. He and the resident bombarded me with questions as to the technique of such an operation and postoperative treatment, how many procedures of this kind I had performed, and with what results. I answered all their questions.

"Have you patented this prosthesis?" Dr. S. asked.

"Yes, in five countries," I replied.

"Interesting, very interesting." He sighed. "Okay, let's go see some of my patients. I'd like to have your opinion."

After the conversation, I felt somewhat more confident.

How an American orthopedic surgeon makes the rounds of his patients, what kinds of rooms they have in an American hospital, what kind of equipment they use—these and other questions intrigued me to such an extent that I all but sang as I followed Dr. S. down the corridor. The diffident way the Polish resident made way for me and addressed me clearly showed how impressed he was by my explanations and the prosthesis. As for Dr. S., he exhibited no visible reaction at all. I kept my eyes open, trying not to miss anything of significance. In Russia I had never seen such excellent single- and double-occupancy rooms, except in the exclusive Kremlin Hospital for the supreme rulers. But the equipment here was even better. Dr. S. examined his patients brusquely, exchanging few words with them. Once out of the room, he informed me of the diagnosis and treatment strategy for each patient. I understood a lot, though naturally not everything. But I could not muster the courage to ask for clarifications.

We returned to Dr. S.'s office.

"So in what way can I be of use to you?" he asked.

"I'd like to get a job."

"What kind of job?"

"I realize that I cannot hope for a physician's position before I pass the required exam. But maybe you have some sort of auxiliary position for me? I am sorry, but the structure of an American medical institution is unfamiliar to me."

"Well then, I think we'll be able to do something for you," Dr. S. said. "Say, what about a surgeon's assistant? In this state you can fill it without a license. Any comment?"

"That would be wonderful!" I blurted out in delight.

For several days afterward I lived in a state of joyous anticipation. I was about to get a job! But I had to wait till Dr. S. completed negotiations with the hospital management.

I told Boris about my good fortune.

"You see, like I said—little by little, you'll have everything. But is that surgeon a reliable person? Is he trustworthy?"

"I don't know much about him, but do you think it possible for an American Jewish doctor to deceive his immigrant colleague?"

Boris shrugged. "How should I know? There are all kinds of people here in America."

But I had no doubts whatsoever; I believed that an American physician was implicitly benevolent, honest, and decent.

All my family shared my optimism. Along with the obvious importance of an extra salary, Irina saw another benefit in my coming employment. She thought that daily intercourse with colleagues would be the most effective way for me to master English. My parents believed that I was about to step on the first rung of a new career destined to be as successful as the one I had left behind. Aunt Lyuba contributed by finding out that the hospital in question was known for an excellent pay scale.

In the course of our nighttime discussions, Irina told me, "You must steel yourself; you will be dog tired at all times. I know it from my own experience. The need to speak an unfamiliar language all day long produces a lot of stress. I can't imagine how you'll manage to combine work with studies for the exam. At your age, will you be able to stand such a load?"

I could not imagine it either, but I was sure that once I settled into the work, I would carve out some time to devote to academic pursuits.

"Don't worry, everything will be fine," I assured her.

14

The tall, bearded worshiper from the synagogue stalked me with a standard question: "Have you made up your mind about the watch?"

I gave him a standard reply that I had to think it over some more and asked him in turn about the apartment.

"It will be vacated any day now," he would tell me.

Thus we became linked by a mutual business interest, though I could see that he planned to buy my jewels on the cheap, taking advantage of my incompetence, immigrant ignorance, and my burning need for an apartment. I had always disliked shady deals and tried to stay away from people of his sort, but I had no alternative now.

Irina was not pleased.

"You've made a mistake by going to him. You shouldn't have told him about your jewels. He is a crook who'll get you in trouble. This country is full of crooks," she said.

"Name me one country free of crooks," I rejoined. "He's the only one who can help us find an apartment of the kind we're looking for. I promise to be on my guard."

Still, Irina was nervous. In general, she was getting increasingly frightened, and I was at a loss as to how to deal with her. No sooner did I manage to distract her from one specter of trouble than she would immediately find another. Now she was apprehensive about my business connection with the bearded Jew.

At last he took us all—Irina, Junior, and me—to inspect a vacant apartment in a stately old building on West Ninety-first Street. A doorman guarded the entrance, the lobby was bedecked with vases and mirrors. We were impressed by these emblems of luxury. We took the elevator to the tenth floor. The door of the apartment was open, giving us a view of a glistening parquet floor, a large living room, two bedrooms with adjoining bathrooms, a dining room, and a kitchen. Our hearts raced.

"Aha, I can see you like it. I alone can find such a gorgeous apartment. I can do anything."

"What's the rent?" I asked. That was the most important point.

"How much would you be willing to pay?"

"I've no experience, but I would say the rent should be in the neighborhood of three hundred dollars a month." I based my guess on the known fact that the worse apartments in worse neighborhoods rented for $180 to $250.

"Are you crazy?" he exclaimed. "You'll never find anyone willing to rent an apartment of this class for a mere three hundred dollars. Listen, I know the landlord. He's a millionaire. You can't imagine how rich he is. He owns fifty buildings like this one all over the city. And look at him on a Saturday in the synagogue: a pauper, a veritable beggar. Believe me, he's so tightfisted, he'll never go down a lousy five bucks. But you needn't worry; I will talk to him personally. For me he will make an exception."

"Thank you."

"Keep your thanks to yourself; you'll have plenty of time to show your gratitude later. The most important thing is to make him trust you. You are without a job yet, your wife earns little. He is likely to doubt that you would pay rent reglarly, though it will be beyond his power to evict you. So why should he bother? Each landlord looks for employed tenants who have a permanent income. This is the crux of the problem. It will take a lot of persuading. No one can do it except me. I will do it. You'll see, I can do anything."

For some reason or other, the doorman came up, surprised to catch us inspecting the apartment.

"I told you, it's not this apartment, but the one on the opposite side," he reproached our benefactor.

The tenant in the apartment across the corridor opened the door. She was making preparations for moving out, and the apartment was in total disarray. It had just one bedroom, a living room, a dining room, and a kitchen. The apartment was smaller, but I liked it more since it was clear that it was cheaper.

Irina took an immediate dislike to the apartment. Junior asked which room was designated for him and was satisfied to find that he would have the bedroom that was far from ours; he wanted to be as removed from us as possible.

Our guide had obviously planned to take advantage of us. Still, I was grateful to him for leading us, if inadvertently, to an apartment I liked. Now it only remained for me to win over Irina and the landlord.

Several weeks passed but Dr. S. was still not forthcoming about my job. We called him on the days he himself named, Irina representing me in telephone conversations because I couldn't talk fluently without visual contact. Each time we called, Dr. S. dodged the definitive reply, insisting that the question had not been settled, that he had to talk to yet somebody else, and that the hospital management was procrastinating.

"Call me again in a week," he would invariably say at the end of the brief conversation.

Finally, his evasive tactics aroused doubt in Irina's mind.

"Judging by the way his tone of voice has changed over the past few weeks, I don't think he seriously wants to help you," she told me. "So far as I can see, he's a liar and a windbag. Whether you like it or not, I'm not going to call him again."

"Do you really believe that a serious man would be that flippant with his promises?" I asked. "Try to put yourself in his shoes. I know from personal experience. When I was a director, many people came to me seeking jobs, and I never led them by the nose—I either employed them or turned them down, as circumstances dictated. But I never kept them in the dark. No, there's no way an American physician would stoop so low. You know well enough that Americans are cordial and democratic people—remember our friends the Princes?"

"In my opinion, you idealize Americans."

"Okay, maybe I do. But in my case Dr. S. should simply sympathize with the plight of an immigrant physician from Russia, the country his own parents had come from. Also, he's a fellow Jew. Let's call him at least one more time."

The tall worshiper tried to persuade me that he had talked to the landlord on several occasions but so far failed to elicit a decision out of him. Meanwhile, I made my best effort to talk Irina into liking the apartment (if only we were lucky enough to get it!).

"We'll never find a better location," I said. "Besides, if you keep on disliking it, we'll be able to find another one after a while. It's not Russia where a multigenerational family is stuck for life in a poor apartment. This is America. Everybody moves from one place to another, everybody moves upward. And so will we some day."

Finally Irina saw that we had no alternative and agreed with me.

Then I went to talk to the landlord. For a big-time operator, with fifty large apartment buildings in New York, he was in fact very unpretentiously, even poorly, dressed. All his family, including his elderly mother, worked for him.

I explained our circumstances to him as best I could. He listened without the flame of sympathy in his eyes, suggesting that I should abandon all hope for a discount.

"The rent is three seventy-five per month plus utilities," he told me in a businesslike manner. "The lease should be at least two years, within which period you will have to pay me nine thousand dollars. If you are able to pay three months rent in advance and a month's deposit—today and in cash—the apartment is yours. Agreed?"

I made feverish mental calculations. Irina's monthly salary is $650; Junior will have to study and cannot be counted on for additional income; as for my earning potential, it's too early to evaluate. So, assuming we'll have to pay $50 a month for gas and electricity, the apartment will cost $425, leaving some $200 for us to live on. But I will sell my jewels. How much can I get for them? Let's say between $7,000 and $8,000— almost the entire amount of two years' rent. I can't turn it down, we won't be able to find a better apartment anyway, while so much will depend on the right place to live. I'll take it. And yes, I'll have to borrow the cash today.

I said okay and ran to Aunt Lyuba to borrow the required sum. She led me to her bank, wherefrom I returned to the renting office, still deep in calculations. But there was no alternative. I gave him the money in exchange for a receipt and a draft lease.

Although that day I had already covered at least one-hundred blocks on foot, I breezed to the hotel as if on air. At least we had a place of our own! Near the hotel I was inter-

cepted by the bearded worshiper, who started without prelim-
inaries:

"Listen, I've had another talk with the landlord, he promised to think it over."

"Don't worry, I already have a lease," I told him triumphantly. He was taken aback but quickly recovered.

"You see now, he gave me his word and he kept it. Do
you appreciate what I've done for you? I can do anything. Hey,
and another thing, when are you going to decide about your
watch?"

But I was in no mood to go on talking to him. Burning
with a desire to tell Irina without delay, I went to meet her
after work—another thirty blocks one way. I came a little too
early and waited across Fifth Avenue from the gorgeous Temple Emmanu-El. Irina came out into the street.

"What happened, why aren't you at school?" she asked
me anxiously.

"We have an apartment!"

"Really?"

"Really."

"Thank God, one less thing to worry about."

Hand in hand, we walked through Central Park. We made
it a point to pass "our" building and stopped to admire it. Now
we had a different, proprietary, attitude toward it: It was our
first American home.

16

The next time Irina called Dr. S., he told her, "Tomorrow I'm having a special appointment with the dean regarding your husband. Call me the day after tomorrow after lunch, and I'll be able to give you a definite answer."

"You see how wrong you were about him," I said. "I've known all along that Americans mean business. Maybe the day after tomorrow we'll know something about my job."

Two days passed in anxious anticipation. My God, how long had I waited since the fateful day of filing for emigration from Russia! But the wait, it seemed to me, was coming to an end. If I got a job, any job at all, we would survive. And if we survived, sooner or later I would overcome all difficulties and become a physician again.

Irina made the call from the pay phone in the hotel lobby. I stood behind her with bated breath.

"Good afternoon, I am Dr. Golyakhovsky's wife," Irina told the secretary. "May I speak to Dr. S.? He has left? On vacation? For three weeks? Has he left any message for my husband? No? Maybe you know if he saw the dean yesterday . . . ? Oh, he left the day before yesterday. . . ." She hung up.

I was thunderstruck, barely able to move. Nearby a crowd of hotel residents milled around as usual, with Boris in habitual attendance.

"What's the matter?" he asked Irina.

Tears welling in her eyes, she explained.

"I think he is just a no-good guy, this doctor of yours. So what? There are rotten apples among Americans, too. But don't worry, little by little, everything will be okay, your husband will find another job. Remember, this is America."

I could barely make out his words. It was as if my ears were stopped with cotton.

17

My first unhappy business contact with an American counterpart shook me badly, and it took me a long time to recover. What really galled me was not that a job far below my level of skill had eluded me, but that Dr. S. had treated me like trash and deceived me so blatantly. I realized that in his eyes I was nobody. I also realized that I had better be prepared for more of the same, because in truth that was exactly what I was in this country. Professionally a nobody. Not only did I lack a physician's license, but I had not even passed a qualifying exam and could not speak English.

Irina and Vladimir, Jr., were also deeply shaken by my defeat. But for them it was primarily a threat to our material well-being rather than a slap in the face, which it was above all for me.

Irina told me irritably, "You yourself are partially to blame. It happened that way because of your unpreparedness. Had you wasted less time on empty babble with immigrants and studied English more, you would be able to speak decently, and people would treat you differently. Who needs all your observations of the immigrant masses?—Nobody. It's all your poetic nature."

A wife is always right. Yes, indeed, I did "waste time." Yes, indeed, I had a "poetic nature." But I had been that way all my life. And prior to emigration I had been in a depression and now needed to relax. Why was she angry with me instead of trying to show some sensitivity to my feelings? I resented Irina's attitude, particularly because our son copies her mood. He was sinking deeper and deeper into gloom and studiously avoiding talking to me.

Thus, one setback brought about other complications. Our family tottered on the brink of collapse.

Still, Irina not only pouted but also tried to help me as best she could. Someone advised her to consult the rabbi from the synagogue nearby, reputedly a very cultivated, compassionate, and influential man. Irina secretly called him and arranged for an appointment. The rabbi's amiable manners impressed her favorably. She told him what a richly endowed person I was—physician, professor, writer, inventor—how desperately I yearned to be of use to my new country. She implored him to help me find a job and lend me some support lest I lose faith in myself and miss a chance to regain my self-respect and vigor. The rabbi pledged to do something for me. He even wanted to invite both of us to dinner and introduce us to his wife. Moreover, he planned to help Irina as well in finding a job in research.

Buoyed by his promises, Irina shared her joy with me and we set about waiting for practical results. This time Irina was the optimist and tried hard to dispel my skepticism.

"I can't believe that the rabbi will follow the example of your surgeon and do nothing for you. As distinct from you, I told him everything exactly the right way. The whole tenor of our talk suggested that he took considerable interest in you and was eager to help."

"We'll see," I replied.

Time after time, Irina called the rabbi, talked to his wife, and waited, waited, her enthusiasm and faith gradually dissipating. After five or six futile telephone conversations, she realized that her high hopes were in vain and stopped calling. The invitation to dinner did not materialize either.

To distract myself, I started jogging in Central Park every morning. Summer was just beginning, the weather was wonderful, the mornings were fresh. The lush young greenery silhouetted against the bright blue sky was strikingly beautiful. I enjoyed communal jogging; it gave me the feeling of being assimilated into the new life-style. I struck up a few nodding acquaintances; we would greet each other without stopping and exchange a couple of words.

All this was a novelty for me. In Russia, jogging was not popular; leaden-gray clouds hung overhead instead of the blue sky; people were glum and surly.

Four months had passed since we left Moscow, and I often recalled Russia. It was not nostalgia; not for a single instant did I have an urge to go back or even sneak another glance at the "old country." But the burden of new impressions and experiences was so heavy that all of us instinctively sought refuge in old, cozy memories.

Even nature was entirely different in New York, far more graphic and powerful. I had always been fond of trees and now took delight in admiring Central Park's arboreal beauties. One tree attracted me in particular, a giant plane tree on the north shore of the pond. Jogging by, I always stopped and stroked its smooth, gray bark. I remembered Russia's trees, her white-trunked birch trees, but no, there were no nostalgic stirrings in my soul. The American plane tree was more to my liking.

Whether because of my mental turmoil or physical exercise, I lost ten pounds and looked rejuvenated. As I ran out of the hotel every morning wearing nothing but shorts and a T-shirt, Boris, who seemed never to leave his position in the lobby, always commented, "Hey, you're a real Yankee now, running all the time. And you look well, too, knock wood."

"Thanks," I would reply. "The more dismal the circumstances, the wider the smile should be."

"Don't worry, little by little, everything will be okay."

The lobby was now quiet; the querulous watchmaker was gone and there was nobody left to rebel at American ways. I asked Boris what had happened to the watchmaker.

"He's found a job and now can't find fault with America. You wouldn't recognize him."

Yet I saw the watchmaker one more time in the hotel lobby. It was Saturday, and he had a day off. As always, he was in a loudly sour mood, but for a different reason.

"Why can't I work Saturdays if that's what I want?" he said. "Every damn Saturday costs me fifty bucks! I told my boss that I wanted to work Saturdays, but the son of a bitch said that we Jews are not allowed to do that. If it goes on like this, you bet I'll quit and start my own business."

Having vented his indignation, he proceeded to discuss with the old-timers what kind of car he should buy.

"For starters, I'd like to buy a used car," he was saying. "And after I learn to drive, I'll buy myself a new car, and let my wife drive the old one."

"Can you see the transformation this guy has undergone?" Boris asked me. "This is America for you."

Soon repairs were complete in our apartment and we could move in. Irina still hated it. Or maybe her attitude was to hate everything around her. The apartment was totally empty—we had no furniture whatsoever. Thank God, Aunt Lyuba had had the foresight to save a few pieces of furniture belonging to her late husband: a bed, a desk, and a chest of drawers. That was all we had, plus half a thousand books from my Russian library that I had mailed to myself before leaving Russia. We badly needed money to buy furniture, any kind of furniture.

My synagogue acquaintance was still waiting for me to sell him my jewels. However, I was in no mood for business negotiations and not a little nettled by his insistent reminders.

"Listen, when are you going to talk business? I am giving you a good price," he badgered me. To show my gratitude for his apartment-hunting services—and also to get rid of him—I gave him a gift of several gold coins and an antique brooch for his wife. As for jewels, I sold them for $7,000, at Aunt Lyuba's recommendation, to her late husband's nephew, a respectable and totally trustworthy man. Now I had the money to furnish my apartment.

Irina and I went to the nearest discount furniture store and bought a cheap bedroom set whose pseudo-Spanish styling was not much to our liking but more than offset by the attractive price. And I also bought an Admiral color TV set with a remote control—a marvel of esoteric technology by our lights. I reasoned that no matter how limited our resources and viewing time, we needed to watch TV—both as a language aid and as a means for getting our bearings in the new country. Irina disagreed and viewed the TV as a luxury.

For my own needs, I bought a plain, unpainted wooden desk topped by a set of shelves for my most indispensable books. I put it in the dining room and earmarked the desk for my medical and English studies. A writer's career became my idée fixe: I dreamed of writing. Having been slapped in the face as a prospective doctor, I pinned more and more hope on seeking success and financial security in the literary field. I did not intend to give up medicine, but I believed that many of my observations of Russia and whatever literary talent I possessed were more valuable than my medical experience. If I succeeded in writing a book and having it published in English, I thought all my problems would be taken care of. The book would bring me some money, catapult me into public prominence, and even restore my dwindling stature in my own family.

But it was clear that the path to the book was at first to run through magazine articles. Therefore, the first thing I wrote at my new desk was a short letter introducing myself and offering material based on my experience. The letter was crafted with an eye on popular medical magazines. But the letter had to be translated into English and I had no choice but to appeal to Irina for help.

"Please do it for me," I said. "I know only too well your attitude toward my literary endeavors, but forget your resentment for a moment. Otherwise, I'll be forced to seek the services of a paid translator."

Irina had to overcome her disgust to comply with my request. She believed that I ought to concentrate totally on English and medical studies to the exclusion of everything else. By this time, we had begun to quietly hate each other, each considering himself (or herself) in the right and bitterly resenting the other's attitude—family quarrels! Still, she clenched her teeth and did the translation. I had ten Xerox copies of the letter made, paying a dollar for the job. God, did I hate to part with a whole dollar! And I also had to buy postage stamps. But I hoped the payoff from the letter would be worth the expense.

I satisfied my Jewish pride at a parade in honor of Israel's thirtieth anniversary. It was the first parade we saw on Fifth Avenue in New York.

Irina and I arrived well in advance and stood in a very dense crowd near Temple Emmanu-El. Numerous volunteers collected money for Israel. I eagerly gave them almost all the money I had on me—after all, it was for that special country! For once, Irina took no exception to my generosity; we shared feelings of joy and harmony.

We expected to see only Jewish organizations among parade participants and were astonished at the sight of marching policemen, firefighters, clerks, hospital workers, professors, and students of almost all local colleges and universities, many school children and representatives of hundreds upon hundreds of organizations who all came to celebrate Israel's holiday.

The most pleasant surprise for us was the festive atmosphere: celebration, merriment, friendliness. There could be no doubt that the marchers and spectators were really enjoying themselves.

In Russia, all of us had been forced, on pain of punishment, to attend parades and demonstrations. There, too, music blared; people thronged. But the attributes were propaganda slogans and portraits of the rulers; the music consisted of sickeningly familiar military marches; the people made an unconvincing show of merriment that could not deceive anyone.

But here—what a contrast! How pretty were the girls

marching to the beat of uplifting music! How dashing were the veterans in combat uniforms! What a pleasure it was to watch columns of young athletes demonstrating martial arts techniques on the go.

And there were funny things, too. Someone carried a placard saying "Excuse Me for Having Voted for Carter" (the Camp David Accords did not come until later in the year). Needless to say, such a novel form of democratic expression—to criticize the president of the United States of America, and to do it publicly—was an eye-opener for us. All we had been entitled to carry on parades in Russia were portraits of the rulers—nothing else.

But our predominant feeling was that of pride in the country, the people whose jubilee was being celebrated so joyously, so sincerely. We were happy.

18

I loved our apartment. It was a pleasure for me to come home. Sometimes I woke up in the middle of the night and wandered around the rooms. I felt completely *at home*—an all but forgotten feeling. I derived particular pleasure from being home alone in the morning, when my wife and son left for work and I sat down at my desk to study English or write notes for my book-to-be. My progress in both areas was slow, but somehow or other I did manage to graduate to the fourth level at school and to write several short stories.

I loved watching TV, although for all practical purposes I

did not understand the hosts and performers in movies and commercials. In Russia, I had been only an occasional viewer, for the two available channels rarely carried anything of interest; all news was filled with propaganda, while the quality of other entertainment was generally inferior and marred by primitive production techniques.

But here, television introduced me to the whole world and, above all, to American life. Though the narration was beyond me, I did grasp the meaning of all major international and domestic news from the documentary footage. The instantaneous, dynamic, and comprehensive nature of news shows astonished me. I could hardly believe that I watched live telecasts from Paris, Tokyo, Jerusalem—from all over the globe.

I even liked the commercials. I enjoyed their excellent technical quality and the enormous amount of information they carried. Through television advertising I got to know a lot of new products, goods, and automobiles, complete with prices. It was an absolute novelty for me.

Weather forecasts were also a pleasure to watch, if only because the text was basically always the same and thus easier to understand. But I also liked the natural manners of the forecasters. They handled their audience in such a pleasant way that even gloomy weather predictions never failed to cheer me up—and cheerfulness was one thing I sorely lacked.

In the evening, the TV set was taken over by Irina and Junior, who were equally smitten by American television entertainment. They had a better command of English and preferred movies. The world of Hollywood, which we had known only by hearsay and from critical barbs in Communist papers, unfolded before their eyes. They watched indiscriminately all movie fare—from silent movies of the 1910s to the latest productions. Some of the films did not win their approval.

Once Irina told me with a sigh, "Yesterday I watched a movie made in 1937. What a piece of junk, as in fact almost all Hollywood creations are. And yet I could not but think that it's immeasurably better to make people watch this garbage than to deport them in thousands to Gulag concentration camps, as was the case in Russia that very same year."

I roared at her unexpected comparison and indisputable conclusion; at long last she was forced to admit that America was better than Russia. She also laughed, realizing how naïve her pronouncement sounded. For a short while we regained our good spirits and mutual affection. But such instances occurred with decreasing frequency.

A building on East Forty-second Street, not far from the Cambridge School, housed Radio Free Europe/Radio Liberty. One of its units beamed Russian-language broadcasts into Russia. I believed there were a lot of new and interesting things I could tell my former compatriots over the radio. And so I called Radio Liberty and arranged for an appointment with one of the managers, a Russian immigrant named Ras. For starters, Ras, a man of about sixty, suggested that I speak before his staff, adding that I would be paid a hundred dollars for the lecture and eighty dollars for each broadcast. Not bad, not bad at all!

About fifteen people came to hear my reminiscences. Most of them were Russians who had left their home country shortly after World War II, and they were eager to listen to a doctor who, a short while before, had treated some of the Soviet big wheels and celebrities.

Several days later I brought my first script to Radio Liberty. The science editor, a man named Ghen who had been at my lecture, quickly looked through the four pages of the script, transposed a few sentences, changed a few insignificant words, and asked me, "Any objections to my editing?"

"Of course not. As a matter of fact, you haven't changed anything of substance."

"I didn't have to, the script is good enough as it is. Let's go now to the studio and record your narration of it."

"Right now?"

"That's right, now."

"But isn't anyone of the higher-ups going to check the script?"

"What for? You will narrate it, we'll mail the tape to Munich and it will be broadcast from there."

"Without any checking?" I asked in surprise.

He smiled, crinkling his eyes, "None whatsoever. I know what you mean—something along the lines of censorship. But we don't have it here, forget about it."

I knew, of course, that there was no censorship in the West, but that was my first personal encounter with creative freedom. After all the restrictions I had been accustomed to in Russia, I felt like a man taken into the bright sunlight after a prolonged stay in the darkness—I was all but rubbing my eyes, shocked by the unusual brightness.

Ghen took me to the studio and introduced me to a young woman. "And this is Anya, our recording engineer; she will handle your broadcasts," he told me. I was thunderstruck. She was a true beauty, straight out of a Russian fairy tale, with a long, light brown plait, gorgeous black eyelashes, and blue eyes of enormous size and depth.

"Where are you from, Anya?" I asked her.

"From Moscow," she sang melodiously.

Anya cast down her blue eyes and blushed.

Thus I started a broadcasting career that lasted two years. In the absence of censorship my author's personality was gradually unfettered. At long last, I had an opportunity to write what and how I pleased.

Beautiful Anya often told me, "I really enjoy your scripts, Doctor," and lowered her luxuriant eyelashes.

"You're doing just fine, old boy," Ghen said time and again. "You have a knack for combining the interesting with the understandable. The bosses in Munich heap praises on you, and, according to our intelligence, our listeners in Russia like your program."

Ghen was a talkative man who brimmed with all manner of bold ideas and imaginative plans. I enjoyed his company and tried to profit from his immigrant experience. He was an American of three years' standing, his wife worked, his daughter attended college. In short, the Ghens were solidly on their feet. They owned a car, a credit card and all sorts of appliances. It was in their apartment that I noticed, for the first time in my life, an air-conditioning unit. But so far as I was concerned, Ghen's biggest accomplishment was a fairly good command of English and an ability to read American periodicals. He often shared with me bits of wisdom gleaned from his reading and cited interesting examples of the new life that seethed around me but so far eluded my grasp.

"In this country," he liked to instruct me, "one must read *The Wall Street Journal* every day and follow the stock exchange. And every Sunday, of course, *The New York Times*. For instance, yesterday I read my way through three pounds of newspapers, primarily business and real estate sections. So long as one lives in this country, one must know what's going on here."

I listened to him enviously, like a child at the knee of an adult, although we were the same age, and dreamed of the moment when I, too, would be able to read the *Times*.

19

One day Irina answered the doorbell of her doctor's office and saw a young fellow who doffed his uniform cap and said, "Con Edison."

"Good morning, Mr. Con Edison," she welcomed him. "Come on in."

"Con Edison," the visitor said emphatically, evincing some surprise and standing his ground.

"Very good, Mr. Con Edison," Irina replied even more courteously. "Come in, please."

The boy looked at her as if she was crazy, while she thought: What's the matter with him? Why is he looking at me this way?

Fortunately, her boss arrived on the scene and solved the puzzle. How was Irina supposed to know what Con Edison meant when we were just starting our life in New York?

That night she told me the story with a mixture of laughter and frustration—how maladjusted we still were! Her work load increased steadily. Now the doctor demanded that she perform blood tests, making blood cell counts under the microscope. The procedure was new to her, and she was afraid of making mistakes. Her boss also assigned her, with increasing frequency, to administer medicines intravenously. But she had neither the background nor the practical experience of a nurse. She thought it was wrong on the doctor's part to make her perform such procedures, but she was afraid to protest and vented her feelings only at home. We had no idea that she was not allowed by law to perform the duties of a nurse without a license.

I was still waiting for replies to the letters I had sent to medical newspapers and popular magazines. In the meantime, I went to the Russian daily, *Novoye Russkoye Slovo,* and offered some of my articles and poems to its editor-in-chief. The editor was an old immigrant who had left Russia as far back as 1919, a veteran of Russian literature in exile. Himself a writer and one who had known hundreds of Russian writers, he was a hard man to please. So I did not expect to dazzle him, but his opinion was very valuable to me. I had no idea of the importance, if any, of a Russian newspaper in America's public life. But it seemed to me that a periodical with a circulation of some thirty thousand should pull some weight, and not only among Russian readership.

The editor told me, "Don't underestimate us—the elite media and even the administration in Washington keep an eye on the materials we print."

And so, on August 6, 1978, the Russian daily carried my versified poetic fable "The Carrion-Crow Kingdom," which had been banned from publication in Russia because it was a kind of political satire. It was followed, once every week, by my articles on Russian medicine under the general rubric "This so-called free and accessible medicine." Here is how the series opened:

> Health is the most individual of all forms of human property. One would think that there is no way to nationalize health. Yet the Soviet partocracy has managed to do just that and deprive its subjects of any possibility of fully preventing or treating diseases. Soviet poverty-level health care—that's what a right advocate, Dr. Andrei Sakharov, called it. The myth of Russia's free and totally accessible health care is a propaganda ploy aimed at the gullible and misinformed Western public. Having physically destroyed tens of millions of its citizens, the Soviet authorities try to persuade public opinion in the West that their subjects' health is a matter of great concern to them. . . .

From the start Irina was adamantly opposed to my radio and newspaper endeavors for the simple reason that she was afraid that KGB agents might harass or even kill me. She dreaded the thought that they might stalk our son as well. She failed to see any reason for my literary effort, particularly insofar as it brought me very little money—between $200 and $250 a month—while distracting me from language and medical studies. We had frequent heated arguments. I did not think that my articles were so important as to warrant KGB persecution; they had a lot more important business in America than to bother about me. Having the chance, for the first time in my life, to unburden my soul without any restraints was magnetic. In consequence, our arguments developed with increasing frequency into open quarrels; Irina and I were gradually drifting apart.

Precisely at that time, Senator Edward Kennedy went to Moscow on a private visit. He planned to gain insight into the Russian health-care system in order to improve the American system. The media covered his trip extensively, showing Senator Kennedy in the Kremlin where Brezhnev received him, and then on a tour of several Moscow hospitals. I knew full well that the Russians would try to set up Potemkin villages for the visitor, because there was actually nothing to show off there.

"Look how important it is to write the truth about Russian health care," I told Irina. "If a man of Senator Kennedy's stature is able to hold a deeply mistaken opinion, what will the average person know of Russian medicine? The answer is nothing at all. My articles and my future book will be an eye-opener for them in the true sense of the word. I think that had Kennedy known of my articles, he would certainly have read them or even talked to me before going to Moscow."

"The hell he would!" Irina replied heatedly. "How naïve can you be? All politicians here are shrewd and corrupt businessmen. Haven't you watched on TV how senators take bribes in the tens of thousands of dollars? Do you seriously believe he needed your advice? For him it's a purely political trip."

"Come on, Irina, don't exaggerate. Not all of them are corrupt. Anyway, corruption here can't be as rampant as it is in Russia. But I don't give a damn about politics. I only want Americans to learn the truth about Russian medicine. And I know that truth and can tell it as well as anybody. I feel it in my guts that my time has come!"

My poor Irina was torn asunder by apprehension about our present and future. She looked at me and said, "You think so? All right, I trust you. I have always trusted you. But how long do we have to wait?"

I pulled her to me and we froze in an embrace.

And soon it so happened that a high-ranking Soviet diplomat at the UN defected. All newspapers, magazines, TV, and radio channels overflowed with reporting about the defector, and his wife who returned to Russia. Several days later a new bombshell, and what a bombshell! A New York hooker had spent several nights with the defector and planned to write a book about her experience: what he had told her in drunken revelries and how he had failed in bed. The hooker called a press conference at one of the best hotels, TV crews were invited, she appeared before the journalists accompanied by her agent, lawyer, and publisher and strutted like a literary star. I don't think any Nobel laureate has ever had better publicity or spoken with such aplomb.

I was completely crushed by that story. I could never imagine such things were possible. Well, okay, that a prostitute could have a book ghostwritten by a professional of a related trade was conceivable. That the media could sensationalize it was also within the realm of the possible—they wanted to dress up shit as candy and did. But what I could not imagine was of what value were her recollections of their short time together, with the defector drunk all the time. What was so hot about his drunken blabber? The only conclusion I was able to draw was that just about any material related to Russia was fit for a book.

This spurred me on in my resolve to write. And while the heroine received correspondents (not in her main line of business) at her luxury East Side apartment and briefed them on her literary plans, I sat in my poor and almost bare West Side apartment, writing about my dinner with Khrushchev and Brezhnev, my visit to the Soviet army general staff, my involvement in the treatment of the world's very first cosmonaut to be.

I told Irina in excitement, "Don't you see now how much interest should be aroused by my material? Just look at that defector story. But what is this thing called a 'literary agent'?"

Irina did not know that either. There had been no agents in Russia. I had written eight books and sold two and a half million copies without ever suspecting the existence of such a trade—literary agent. Where could I find one?

20

H umid summer came to New York. Moscow has a Continental climate—much cooler and drier—and we had never imagined weather could be this bad. When the first heat wave hit, we had a tough time, particularly at night. Irina suffered the most; she could not sleep and was really miserable. We had to think of buying an air-conditioner, though in cooler times we regarded climate control as the height of extravagance. But now we paid $400 for two units almost without compunction and even regarded that expense as well-advised. When our units began buzzing at home, we felt like genuine Americans. True, we paid a price for comfort in the form of frequent colds, but then genuine Americans were similarly afflicted.

Once I walked from my language school down the west side of Central Park, preoccupied by my numerous thoughts. Cars were gliding by, pedestrians were streaming past me, the pulse of a strange life was beating, reminding me of the need for adaptation. Under the onslaught of fatigue and heat, I walked slowly and my thinking process was equally sluggish. And then, all of a sudden, I realized that I was thinking—in English. For the first time I was thinking in English! I all but jumped at the enormity of my discovery. It meant that some sea change was under way. I had dreamed of that moment, and at last it did happen. I stepped up my tempo and rushed into my air-conditioned apartment bursting with joy. Irina looked at me in anxious surprise. She was forever ready for the worst.

"What's the matter?" she asked apprehensively. "Anything happened?"

"It certainly did. I have just thought in English. It happened all by itself, I can hardly believe it."

"Thank God," Irina sighed with relief. "Maybe this letter is a form of congratulation." She handed it to me.

"From whom?"

"Someone from Washington, D.C."

I did not know anyone in the nation's capital and was surprised. The letter was composed in Russian but contained so many mistakes that it became immediately apparent its author's command of the language was limited. He wrote that he had read my articles and short stories in the Russian newspaper and liked them, and offered to translate them into English free of charge and try to sell them to a magazine. If his plan worked, and he had no doubts on that score, we would split the royalties fifty-fifty.

"Aha!" I told Irina. "You see now—it's the beginning of exactly what I expected all along. I only hope his English is better than his Russian, for otherwise who would understand what I tried to say? Anyway, one thing is marvelous—that he does not demand money in advance."

Without further delay, I sat down and wrote him that I agreed to his proposal and terms.

Letters started to come. The magazines that I had approached with my writings sent polite notes of rejection. I also received mail from readers of the Russian newspaper. Some of them, particularly old immigrants who had left Russia fifty or sixty years previously, liked my articles. They wrote to thank me for telling them the truth about Russian health care. By contrast, some of the new immigrants, fresh out of Russia, wrote hate letters. My Russian colleagues were particularly acerbic. One woman doctor wrote,

> Yes, we worked in appalling conditions; no, we didn't have enough medicines; no, we didn't have enough instruments; and yes, sometimes we had nothing with which to treat our patients—yet, we managed to treat them better

than American patients are treated. What is your goal in criticizing Russian health care? I'll tell you: to make Americans suspicious of us Russian physicians. Exactly what we need on top of their inhuman requirement that a physician with thirty years of unblemished experience should take an exam if he or she is to count on a job. And forget about passing that exam, it's impossible.

What could I write in response? I realized the source of her spleen—she could not speak English, she could not hope to pass the exam and find a job. Without a single day at a doctor's office or a hospital to her credit, she condemned and negated everything sight unseen. It was actually a hysterical response to an unfamiliar environment.

I showed Irina her letter.

"Look at the kind of nonsense people are capable of writing," I said.

Irina read the letter, and her face darkened.

"I told you," she said. "You are going to have no end of trouble because of your writings."

However, editor Ghen and sound engineer Anya were still my admirers, and since it is only human to like those who like us, I spent more and more time at Radio Liberty.

I walked to the radio station past the public library on Fifth Avenue. I liked its beautiful architecture. Once I wanted to have a better look at the building and decided to walk around it. Wandering through the park behind it, I saw small groups of people standing on the paths or lounging on the benches— lovers of literature or readers taking a break, I thought. Deeply engrossed in the contemplation of the architectural proportions, I passed unseeing one such group and was startled to hear a man addressing me.

"Excuse me," I said. "Are you talking to me?"

"Smoke-smoke-smoke," a black youngster of about twenty half whispered.

"Beg your pardon?" Baffled, I stared at him.

"Smoke-smoke-smoke," he repeated. He came up and showed me a self-rolled cigarette deftly hidden in his fist. Only then did I realize that apparently he was offering me marijuana. I had a better look at the people in the square and saw that they in no way resembled bookworms. I left quickly, but as I walked toward the exit, even at the very door of the library, voices behind my back whispered: "Smoke-smoke-smoke . . ."

At the radio station, I told Anya about the park behind the library.

"I know," she said. "As a matter of fact, I myself go there to buy a joint now and then."

"You?"

"What's so surprising about it? Nearly everyone in this town smokes pot, and we've lived in New York for six years now. Incidentally, yesterday I became a U.S. citizen."

I felt a touch of envy. "Congratulations."

"Thanks. We are going to have a little party here, and you're invited."

For me, to become a U.S. citizen was the ultimate dream, for it implied that one had lived in this country for at least five years. And in our circumstances, to survive that long seemed impossible. If only I could look into the crystal ball and see where we were going to be five years from now. . . .

While Anya and several other Russian women were setting up the table, I talked to Ghen, who was as usual chockfull of daring plans for his future.

"Actually, I'd prefer to live in Europe. You know, old boy, it's so pleasant there, and everything is so close at hand. Come Saturday, you hop in your car and a couple of hundred kilometers later there's another country, another kind of people, a different culture. A far cry from America where all states, all motels, all restaurants are governed by a single standard. You can walk blindfolded into any American motel and unfailingly find the light switch, the lamp, the bed, or the table—all in their assigned places."

I listened to him in astonishment. I thought that America was a varied and interesting country. Only a few years before, he had lived in Russia and had not so much as dreamed of ever going abroad. And here he was criticizing America with the nonchalance of a native. Unquestionably, he was an experienced man, and yet there was an unmistakable element of unreality in his dream, for where else did the immigrants have it so good as in America? Nowhere. He himself was proof of that. Meanwhile, he was spinning his fantasy.

"You know, from time to time I seriously think of getting the hell out of this place and becoming an optometrist. Good work, excellent pay. Just imagine—an office on a nice street, all you do is check people's vision. What could be better?"

"Do you know how to do it? Have you any training?"

"That's the rub. I haven't. If only I could get ahold of a license somehow. . . . On the other hand, hey, why don't we write a book together?"

"What kind of book?"

"Let's say, about Russian health care. You know the subject, while I can contribute my journalistic experience and a few connections in the right places."

"To tell the truth, a book of just that sort has been an obsession with me," I replied. "But I'm not all that sure my material will interest American readers. The book must be good if it's to have a chance."

"Who says it must be good?" he objected. "Americans will gladly swallow any kind of crap."

I looked at him in surprise, but he went on: "You're a novice here, and besides you don't speak English, while I've lived in this country for three years and read a lot. So you'd better listen to me. You can't imagine how many books are published here—hundreds of thousands of titles every year. Drop by any bookstore and you'll be sure to find books on any imaginable subject. Do you suppose all of them are good?"

"But surely there are people who read all those books," I said uncertainly.

"Exactly—all those books are bought and read. To give you an example: Anya's husband, who had never been a writer in Russia, wrote a lousy book about the sex life of famous Russian movie and sports stars. And not only was the book published, but he even earned a bundle. You would think that no one here would be interested, particularly insofar as America is so much more sophisticated than Moscow as regards all those sexual perversions. But no, the book was published."

"Well, maybe you're right," I said dubiously. "But I won't write a purposely bad book."

"Baloney," he interrupted. "The trick is to wangle some money in advance out of the publisher, and then you don't have to write anything at all. Nobody is going to ask for the money back. But even if they do, you can always con them by insisting that you're still working on the book."

Our talk was interrupted by Anya who invited us to the room next door where the treat had been prepared—a large bottle of vodka and Russian-style cold plates: vegetable salad, smaltz herring cut into pieces, black bread. The first toast was raised to the new U.S. citizen.

"May you become a millionairess, Anya!" one of the girls shouted.

"May your husband buy you a mink coat!" shouted another.

"May you ride around in Cadillacs and Mercedeses all your life!"

"No, no. May she ride around in Rolls-Royces!"

Anya had drunk two glasses of vodka; she was red in the face and laughed all the time.

"And what will you wish me, Doctor?" she asked me.

"To give birth to a beauty like yourself. Or a mighty Hercules if it's a boy. Or maybe both."

"A mighty Hercules? Like my husband?" she asked amid peals of laughter.

"Well, if he's a Hercules . . ." I said hesitantly.

"Doctor, what do you know? My husband is old, he is twenty-five years my senior. And he's short and ugly."

"Why don't you give birth to two beautiful girls then?"

"No, I want to give birth to a Hercules," she said, getting more and more drunk by the minute. "And I know a way to do it."

"What's the secret, Anya, tell us?" the others roared.

"No, no, it's my own secret," she said. "I'll only tell it to the doctor, when we are alone. . . ."

I observed with professional detachment that she had become drunk too fast and that her hands shook a little when she carried a glass of vodka to her lips.

"Will you see me home, Doctor?" she asked me. "I live nearby, on Third Avenue."

She swayed noticeably, and I had to hold her tightly by the arm. On the way I bought her a large rose from a flower girl on the corner.

"You're nice," she said, snuggling up to me. "You know, I like you very, very much!"

"I like you too, Anya."

"You should know I have a very jealous husband."

"I appreciate his concern; with so beautiful a wife one would be hard pressed not to be jealous."

"Ordinarily I don't give him grounds, but sometimes . . ." She burst out laughing. "I got married when I was just nineteen. I was a very silly little girl. He was an engineer and a rich man, a marvelous dancer and unbeatable at cards. I fell in love with him. And two years later, we left for America. Like I said, I was a silly young girl. And when we came here I started longing for my mother, for home, and wept all the time. And so, Doctor . . . Hey, we're home."

"Will you be able to get to your apartment alone?"

"There is a doorman. He'll help me. He will certainly help me."

"You're lucky, Anya, to become a citizen. A full-fledged American!"

"Lucky?" she drawled. "Lucky, you say? Why, sometimes I curse the day and hour when I got here. At other times I feel okay, though. Ah, it's so difficult to tell the whole story. Even if you are a doctor," she again laughed tipsily. I was disagreeably shocked. But business was foremost in my mind.

"Listen, Anya, I plan to write a book about Russian health care. What do you think, will your husband be willing to help me find a publisher?"

Suddenly she stopped laughing and looked at me meditatively.

"I would think he can help you," she said, and added sadly, "but . . ."

"But what?"

"No, nothing," she shook her head. "You'd better talk to him yourself, I never meddle in his business affairs—unless he asks me to, that is."

And she staggered into the doorway.

21

That night I came home later than usual, showing the effect of the libation. Irina looked at me disgustedly but said nothing. It was past midnight, and we were falling asleep when the telephone rang. Irina lifted the receiver; I saw her baffled expression.

"It's for you," she said and passed me the receiver, a look of alarm coming into her eyes.

"Hello," I said.

A hoarse male voice said in Russian:

"Stop writing those fucking articles in the Russian newspaper!"

It was so unexpected that I was taken aback. Other voices and the noise of drunken revelry were faintly audible in the background. I racked my brain trying to place the mysterious caller's voice; it sounded familiar. It could belong to an immigrant physician I had once met at NYANA.

"What don't you like about my articles?" I asked.

"What I don't like is that you are a son of a bitch," the voice wheezed.

Yes, it was he, beyond doubt. I hung up.

"Who was that?" Irina said.

"I don't know. But his voice rings a bell. I think he's one of the immigrant physicians."

The telephone rang again. Again, Irina lifted the receiver, listened for a few seconds, and slammed it back angrily.

"Him again?" I asked.

"He said, 'If you don't stop writing that crap, son of a bitch, we'll shut your mouth for you.' "

We waited at the telephone. Irina's eyes were misted by tears of fear.

"What will we do?" she said. "You've had it coming, haven't you? I told you not to write for that paper, but you wouldn't listen. And here we are, your life is threatened. Who is that man?"

"Don't worry," I said, trying to be calm. "First of all, he was drunk, and I could hear other drunken voices. His threats aren't serious."

"How can you be sure?"

"Elementary. If anyone planned to hurt me, he certainly wouldn't give me a warning. I think it was a doctor I once met in NYANA."

"What makes you think so?"

"He had a very distinctive voice."

"What are we going to do now?"

"Let's call the FBI tomorrow and tell them what happened tonight."

We could not fall asleep till dawn. All night long we thought our separate thoughts.

The next morning, Irina called the FBI and told about the night call. That same night, while I was still out, two young Americans came to our apartment. They rang the doorbell and flashed their badges. Naturally enough, Irina let them in with a good deal of apprehension.

The visitors were polite and businesslike. When I returned they had already learned the whole story from Irina. But the most important point, the identity of the caller, was still in doubt.

"Do you have any suspects?" the FBI agents asked me.

I shared my suspicions with them. With Irina translating, I explained what it took to be an administrator at a Russian health-care institution and that most of them were so heavily involved in politics that direct links with the KGB were certainly not implausible. In which case there was all the more reason to suspect that the call was more than innocuous horseplay.

The FBI men thanked us for our cooperation.

"We know that there are at least two-hundred spies among the new Russian immigrants. We try to keep an eye on all suspects. As for you, you'd be well advised to keep your distance from all of them."

The admonition was right on target. Still, to make doubly sure, Irina called FBI headquarters the next day to ascertain that our visitors had indeed been real American agents, not KGB operatives in disguise.

And a while later, the Soviet *Literaturnaya Gazeta (Literary Gazette)* published in Moscow, carried an article "exposing" me as a traitor and accusing me of assorted grisly crimes. I got word about that article from cautious between-the-lines hints in a friend's letter from Moscow. I am almost sure there must have been some sort of connection between the threatening night call and the slanderous article in the Soviet paper. But I had not read it and had no intention of doing so. I lived in America now and whatever they did in Russia was no concern of mine.

22

$\mathbb{M}$y father became ill and was placed in St. Luke's Hospital. I visited him often and helped my mother to communicate with the doctors and nurses at the hospital, debuting in the unfamiliar function of interpreter. Also for the first time, I was able to watch the routine of an American hospital. I had not worked for six months and desperately yearned for a return to the world of medicine. When would I be able to don a doctor's white gown and start my rounds?

Much was totally unfamiliar, particularly the equipment at the intensive care unit. Furthermore, the atmosphere around the patient, the rhythm and bustle of the therapeutic process, was far more active than anything I had seen in Russia. So far as I could tell, neither the physicians nor the nurses ever gave up any patient, no matter how critical. In Russian hospitals, particularly in the provinces, critical patients often die for lack of aggressive treatment. As often as not, there is nothing to treat them with, but in many cases they are simply "allowed to die."

Oh yes, it would be so much more interesting and challenging to work in this country. God, how I yearned to start practicing my profession again!

My father recovered. As a matter of fact he was for all practical purposes snatched from the jaws of death. When Mother and I were taking him home from the hospital, we gave the nurses a big box of chocolates. How else could we express our gratitude? I took Father to the apartment on West

Ninety-second Street where he and Mother rented a room temporarily. They were not settled yet, and I tormented myself on that account.

Several days later, Medicaid mailed my father a copy of his paid hospital bill for $14,000. My parents were at first frightened at the thought that they would be required to pay themselves. But when I read the bill and explained to them that everything had been taken care of, Mother wept out of gratitude while Father was astonished. How could it be that his bill had been paid for him?

"Why? I haven't done a thing for America," he kept saying in disbelief. "I haven't worked a single day here. . . ."

I completed the fourth level at Cambridge School in August and started cramming for the Educational Council for Foreign Medical Graduates (ECFMG) exam, mandatory for all foreign medical school graduates, at the Stanley H. Kaplan Education Center on Madison Avenue. I figured conservatively that it would take me at least a year of studies to get ready for the exam. Tuition was expensive, but Russian immigrants were offered a discount.

The American education system was a complete novelty to me. Russian education has stood on a solidly conservative foundation for over two centuries and not even the 1917 Revolution succeeded in shaking it off its moorings. Its chief feature is orientation toward the young—up to the age of twenty-five or at most thirty. Courses for most adults are unknown. Physicians and teachers are supposed to take advanced training courses from time to time, but nobody treats them seriously. One hundred fifty years ago Alexander Pushkin wrote: "Since we pick up our education/In bits and pieces here and there." His astute observation still holds true. Unquestionably, in some areas Russia has made great strides, but in adult education the gap between the West and Russia is as wide as ever.

So when I turned up on the second floor of an old building on the corner of East Fifty-fourth Street (it has since been razed, and now a new skyscraper looms in its place), my notion of the way the learning process would be conducted was dim at best. I expected to see an auditorium and braced myself for a college-type lecture. Instead, I saw a multitude of students, each with earphones, sitting at individual tape recorders and listening to lectures of their choice. To meet the practical examination requirements, each lecture consisted of answers to the most frequently asked questions. Along with the tapes, the students received question-and-answer booklets constructed on the multiple-choice principle.

I had never seen anything like it before.

A pretty girl behind the secretary's desk gave me a cassette and a booklet, smiled, and thanked me.

"What am I supposed to do with this?" I asked in surprise.

"Take a seat and start listening, like the others."

"But where and how can I do that?"

She escorted me to a small room studded with desks equipped with tape recorders, made me sit down at a vacant desk, turned on the tape recorder, and handed me the earphones.

"That's it?" I asked again.

"That's it. When you are through with this cassette, come for the next one."

"Thanks."

I put on the earphones, expecting to hear distinct and slow speech that I would be able to understand. Instead, the lecturer talked so fast that I could not grasp literally a single word during the first few minutes of listening. I made a superhuman effort to concentrate . . . still nothing. Baffled, I looked around to see how my fellow students were coping with the taped mumbo jumbo. Most of them were relaxed, reclining on the backs of their chairs, some even with their feet hoisted on the desk, all listening with the air of classical music buffs in a concert hall.

But a few students, mostly women past their prime, frequently took off the earphones and leafed nervously through their dictionaries. I had no trouble identifying them as fellow Russians by the many telltale signs: the way they looked and dressed; the tense listening posture; the look of sad anxiety in their eyes.

I stood up and went out into the corridor, where a group of men, most of them about thirty years old, were smoking and conversing in Russian. I lit a cigarette and joined them.

The conversation by and large revolved around the poor performance of Russian physicians at the ECFMG exams.

"Our countrymen are at the very bottom of the standings," one man commented.

"Well, not exactly in last place, but pretty close to it," another one concurred.

"Anyway, no one passes the exam at the first try."

"Oh yes, a few doctors have done just that," a third man protested.

"What's a few isolated cases when we're talking of several hundred physicians?"

"On average, it takes three tries," a fourth man interjected.

"I personally know several Russian doctors who have failed five or six times and have yet to pass the exam."

"At least we're not the only ones with problems."

"Who else?"

"A woman from the Dominican Republic has failed seven times."

"A black woman?"

"Of course."

"So what else do you expect from her?"

"Come on, there are black doctors who pass right at the first try."

"Sure, and why not, considering they've studied American textbooks and are at home with English."

"Yeah, that's right, English is our main problem."

"If only I could understand those darned tapes!"

"Some people study at home using textbooks and manage to pass."

"I know a surefire way: Get hold of copies of all the questions."

"But where does one get them?"

"On Brighton Beach in Brooklyn. You can buy a complete set of all questions for the last five years for a hundred and fifty dollars."

"A hundred and fifty dollars! Who has that kind of money?"

"People pool their resources and buy one set for five or six."

The conversation did nothing to lift my spirits. I returned to my desk, turned on the tape recorder, and attempted to listen from the very beginning. I heard the same portion of the lecture three times in a row but ended up none the wiser. The lecturer spoke too fast and his articulation was too strange for my ear. I got tired from the strain and again left the room. In the corridor, another group of Russians congregated, this time those women who were addicted to their dictionaries.

They were discussing the difficulties of learning. A woman of about sixty was saying irritably: "What the hell do I need that damned exam for? I have been retired after thirty years of working as a psychiatrist at one and the same clinic. And here I am, a veritable deaf and dumb idiot! I do wish the man who thought up this exam dropped dead!"

"Then why have you decided to take the exam?" asked another woman. "At your age!"

"Because I must work, that's why! I have a divorced daughter and a small granddaughter; we have nobody to support us."

"Maybe you would have been better off going to Israel instead?"

"We've been there," the psychiatrist exclaimed irascibly. "I would have been better off never leaving Russia, that's for sure! As a matter of fact, I didn't want to go, but I allowed my daughter to talk me into leaving, the fool! So we went to Israel. At first everything was fine: I got a job at a hospital; my daughter got married and gave birth to a marvelous girl. And then, like a thunderbolt out of the blue, my daughter divorces her husband and wants to get out of Israel at any cost. Ah, if only you knew what we had to go through to get here. It took us a full two years to obtain permission for entry, and we are still without permanent residence permits and aren't settled yet. My daughter is a musician, an accomplished pianist, but who needs her here? Americans have their brains topsy-turvy; for them a pianist must be a Horowitz, at the very least. So the upshot is that in my old age I have to pass this exam, and then another one, the Visa Qualification Exam, just to get the right to live and work in this country. And all these troubles after three decades of work and an unblemished record! You call it justice?"

The story, emotionally related by the old woman, was typical of many of us. But what could Russian physicians count on in this country without knowledge of English, without professional training to local standards? Particularly women well advanced in years!

We had been conditioned by socialized medical care, where nobody vies for popularity among the patients, where everybody is paid equally low salaries on a seniority scale. But most important, we all started our careers at a young age, that is, precisely when careers should be started. While here we would have to make a fresh start well past the normal age—at forty plus, or even fifty plus. The private system of health care is based entirely on personal competition for patients. To be sufficiently successful in private practice, an American physician must work three times as hard as we were accustomed to working. Such a crushing load can only be handled by younger people.

23

e anxiously waited for a repeat of that obnoxious telephone call. Irina was especially nervous. Out of fright, she took to carrying a large hypodermic syringe with a thick needle in her pocketbook.

"Just let them attack me, the bastards will get this needle," she hissed vengefully.

I gently mocked her, "Before you have the time to take out the syringe and unsheath the needle, your pocketbook will have long been snatched."

"I'm serious. If I have the time, I'll stick this needle in whichever part of his body is nearest. Good thing I've learned to administer shots; I'll need the skill for self-defense."

Her fear was transmitted in part to Junior, who grew increasingly sulky and talked to us, particularly me, more and more reluctantly.

I continued my struggle with cassette tapes at the Kaplan Center, listening to them endlessly. My determination started to pay off. A week later I could already distinguish separate words and was getting used to the lecturer's articulation. But it was not until two weeks later that I began to grasp the meaning of sentences—and not all of them for that matter.

At my age it's a lot easier to be a professor than a student!

Every night, leaving the Center as the last straggler at 10:00 P.M., I passed the hub of the city—Madison Avenue in the Fifties, Fifth Avenue, Fifty-ninth Street at the southern edge of Central Park. I felt totally exhausted after a day's hard work with the tapes. The streets were brightly lit, luxury cars streamed past me, well-dressed people strolled by.

But I had nothing to do with that world. I teetered on the brink of despair. As I walked I obstinately kept repeating in my mind a memorized English phrase: "I'll make it. I'll reach my goal, whatever it takes."

At home, I tried to present a more relaxed and confident front to hide my true feelings from Irina.

One day, when I entered our apartment with a forced smile on my lips, I found Irina dejected herself. She sat hunched staring at the floor, her face a study in profound, meditative gloom.

"What's the matter?"

Without looking up, she said after a pause, "I was fired."

The blow was so unexpected that it took a few seconds for the meaning of her words to sink in. I sat down next to her and put my arm around her shoulders.

"Tell me what happened."

"Nothing," she said. "Nothing really happened. The doctor simply told me, 'Thank you for your contribution. I am extremely satisfied with the work you've been doing, but I believe that with your background and skills you'll have no trouble finding a more suitable job. Here is a check for two weeks' pay in advance.' And that was that."

It was easy enough to guess what my poor Irina had pondered on her way home and while waiting for me. Her take-home pay had been almost $700 a month; and there was no way we could survive without her salary. Getting a new job was not easy and took time. What were we to do? Naturally enough, she succumbed to panic.

First of all, it was imperative for me to find a way to comfort her.

"Don't despair," I said, putting as much affection in my words as I could. "We'll think of something. What happened, happened, and the best thing to do is to leave it behind."

"I wish I could," she said tearfully. "But apart from all else, it hurts me that he treated me so shabbily. I worked like crazy, to the limit of my endurance and beyond. I did everything he told me to do. I speak English well enough and gave him no reason for being mad at me. Why then did he do it?"

"To hell with him," I said cheerfully. "My mother has a very wise saying: Whatever God does always turns out for the better. There's no doubt you'll be able to find a better job. Really, can you honestly say your job was that interesting or challenging? Of course not! You're tired and need some rest. We still have some money left, enough to last us several months. In the meantime you're sure to find something, maybe a job in your line, at a research lab."

I gave her many words of endearment. I kept her in my arms all night long. She slept fitfully on my shoulder, waking up from time to time with a shudder. Then I would start soothing her; I kissed and kissed her tear-streaked face. The next day, I skipped my studies and took her for a walk in Central Park. The day after that, we went to Fort Tryon Park, strolled in the alleys, toured The Cloisters. We discussed all options open to us but took pains to avoid mentioning Irina's setback, trying to put it out of our minds.

I had to step up my campaign for publishing a book. My volunteer helper translated several of my stories and mailed me copies. I tried to read them but, of course, given my limited command of English, there was no way I could evaluate his job. He had sent the originals to a magazine and was waiting for the verdict. At the radio station, my buddy Ghen was still busy spinning outlandish dreams, one more improbable than another, but I no longer believed in him. As I saw it, the only promising opening was to approach Anya's husband. After all, he had managed to get a book of his in print and had to know people of consequence in the publishing business.

Once, when we were alone in the studio, Anya asked me sadly, "Tell me, Doctor, why is it that sometimes I crave death so?"

"Stop this nonsense, Anya, it's ridiculous to talk that way," I said reassuringly, thinking: Aha, my beauty, something is definitely wrong.

"My husband will come to pick me up any time now," she said. "Do you still want to talk to him?"

Yuri, Anya's husband, was a highly improbable mate for the beauty queen. He was exceedingly plain in all respects: small of stature, looking older than his fifty years, rather ugly, indifferently dressed, with a morbidly sour expression carved into his face. We talked in the corridor.

"I regularly read your articles in the Russian paper and I like them," he told me. "As a matter of fact, I've long planned to consult you in your professional capacity. You see," he lowered his voice and looked guardedly around, "I need to be treated for impotence. I've learned to cope with my chronic hypertension and diabetes, but lately my sexual appetite has been waning."

"But I'm an orthopedic surgeon. I've never dealt with this kind of disturbance," I told him.

He brushed aside my explanation impatiently. "You surely appreciate my problem, Doctor. I have a young wife, and besides, there are lots of other women around. Can you find out anything for me? You move in medical circles, don't you?"

"I'll try," I promised. It was strange to hear such intimate confessions from a person I had not known just a few minutes previously, particularly considering that I was associated professionally with his wife. But there is a type of man who treats others merely as tools to achieve his own ends, especially when he is dealing with physicians. I know it only too well from my personal experience, as I've been accosted hundreds of times with wrong requests in wrong circumstances.

His beautiful wife came over, smiling. He gave her a perfunctory kiss.

"I'd like to ask you for a favor," I began, "could you advise me on how to go about publishing a book on Russian health care?"

He replied eagerly, "I know very reputable publishers who will be able to get your book off the press in no time at all—a mere couple of months. But let me warn you right off—I charge seventy-five percent commission."

I tried not to show my astonishment, but I noticed that his wife glanced searchingly at me. I continued walking beside them, trying to figure out an appropriate way of saying good-bye. Meanwhile Yuri and Anya exchanged observations on the many prostitutes who plied their trade on the street corners.

"Do you see this one?" he pointed out the girl to his wife. "She's just resumed working after a two months' absence. And look at that one. Boy, what a powerhouse."

The world of hookers obviously held special fascination for him. Cutting himself short, he pointed a finger at a magnificent blue Cadillac parked at the curb.

"That's my car. I have to go to Kennedy Airport to meet a couple of businessmen from California. Are you coming, Anya?"

She wilted, even her mouth sagged, while he waited in menacing silence.

"I'm so sick of your lunches and dinners," she said coyly. "All your business discussions and high-rolling parties are such a bore. . . ."

I jumped at the opening and said I'd better be on my way, too.

"Think of my offer, Doctor. It's a sure bet," Yuri said.

I turned the corner and heaved a sigh of relief.

At home, Irina handed me another letter from one of the magazines I had approached with an offer to write about Russian health care. We had grown so accustomed to rejections that Irina did not even bother to open the envelope. I unfolded the letter and started reading: " 'Dear Dr. Golyakhovsky: We will be happy if you agree to grant an interview to our correspondent . . . who will arrive at your premises on . . . We are willing to pay you $400 for the interview. . . . Sincerely yours . . .' "

"At last!" I exclaimed triumphantly. "The timing couldn't be more perfect. If they print the interview, it might interest a publisher or another magazine. Besides, who knows, those translations may also be accepted. Then we'll have the inside track for a book contract. Just give me a little time. Someday we'll have it as good as that hooker who's writing about her trysts with the diplomat. Maybe we'll even move to the East Side."

25

September came and Junior became a full-time student at Hunter College. He had to quit his job, so we were left without income save for the pittance I earned at the Russian newspaper and at Radio Liberty. Back in Russia, Junior had been an indifferent student and his grades reflected his attitude. Irina and I wondered whether he would rise to the superior American requirements. His English was better than mine, but still not good enough to understand lectures. I could plainly see how difficult it was for him as he came up against a barrier all too familiar to me: inability to decipher different shades of articulation. I bought him a small tape-recorder so he could tape all his lectures. At home, he would lock himself in his room and listen to the tapes again and again, sometimes into the small hours of the morning, till the message became clear. In fact, he was pushing the same stones I was trying to move at the Kaplan Center. He never unburdened himself to us, but we could see how thorny his path was.

Among the myriad new and unfathomable pieces of the American puzzle, the education system was the toughest to crack. It was as different from the Russian system as the huge American supermarkets were from the tiny and scantily supplied Russian food stores; the purpose of both seemed to be the same but what a gap in capabilities! And the chief difference in favor of the American system was its practically unlimited range of choices.

All of us were ignorant of the registration procedure at the college. We began the learning process by paying out $1,000 as an admission fee. It was a stupendous sum to put together, but there was no debate on the issue: Education was worth the last cent.

It was not till later that Junior found out that as a New York City resident he was entitled to free tuition at that same city-run college. But to qualify for free tuition, he had to earn twelve credits per semester, with a different time frame for registration for each subject. For that reason he rushed from one department to another.

How could he earn twelve credits? He took English as a major, and it alone was more than enough to fill all his available time. Yet he had to take other subjects as well. To his surprise, he found out there was a course on Ukrainian folk dances. Even though harried and surly, he laughed when telling us about that line of academic pursuit. Irina and I also had a hearty laugh (which happened to us with decreasing frequency). Junior refused to go into Ukrainian folk dances and decided to take judo instead, as he had been a student of judo back in Russia. He figured that would give him an advantage. However, the very first lesson brought the realization that he needed a special uniform that cost sixty dollars. Hoping to avoid the extra expense, he attempted to switch to another subject, but it was too late. We had to buy him a judo *gi*. Among other subjects, he also took tennis—another familiar sport that he had learned in Russia. Besides, he thought that tennis would involve no additional expenses, for he had brought his racket from Russia. Again, a miscalculation: he was required to write a composition that could not be done without a special book—another twelve dollars.

To his and our chagrin, education involved endless expenses. But Junior found out that there were special aid advisers at college whose job it was to help students with problems of course selection. Nothing of the kind existed in Russia—nor, for that matter, was there any choice. He started to use the services of those counselors and learned a lot. He even managed to have the initial $1,000 fee refunded to us.

From unrelenting pressure, chronic lack of sleep, and the crushing load of new impressions and information Junior developed a mild case of depression. I wanted badly to help him, to talk to him, but he gloomily avoided my company. Once we did manage a conversation.

"What's wrong?" I asked him.

"A strange question. Why do you suppose I should be happy?"

"You're already in training."

"Aha, that's the trouble," he snapped, "not medical training, just premed. Do you want to know how many years of my life I stand to lose—provided I'm able to make medical school?"

"Of course, I do," I said. "Had we stayed in Russia, you'd be at the medical school now, with three more years to go. Here you face at least eight years of study—four years of college and another four years of medical school. So your net loss is four years."

"Then why shouldn't I be depressed?"

I looked at him and sighed sadly. He was waiting for my reply.

"Do you care to know how many years I stand to lose?" I asked him. *"Thirty!* That's right, thirty years! A whole lifetime. I used to be a full professor, a chairman, a director. And here I have to take a medical school equivalency exam—like a youngster fresh out of school—and that's not all—afterward I'll have to go through the full course of residency training."

Junior kept silent. Having unburdened myself, I also shut my mouth. Then he said: "You won't be able to understand me anyway because of the generation gap. You have your problems, I have mine."

How true! Indeed, youth has its own problems, and that is why it is always so egotistical. Besides, he pined for his girlfriend in Moscow, the first in his life, also named Irina.

26

$\mathcal{S}$till jobless, my Irina had a bad case of nerves. I tried to distract her as best I could, anxiously watching her erratic behavior and deteriorating psychic condition.

Yet, to my own surprise, I still believed in our eventual success; not once did I feel genuine despair. My optimism was inexplicable except through my poetic nature. Only that and nothing more.

I was walking down Broadway to take another installment of my series to the Russian newspaper. After that I planned to drop by Radio Liberty to discuss our book project with Ghen, and then on to the Kaplan Center—to study till 10:00 P.M. I had twenty-five cents in my pocket and my briefcase contained manuscripts, an English-Russian dictionary, and a slim sandwich. And I was thinking: I wonder if of all the thousands of faces on Broadway a single person is as destitute as I am or faces as bleak or uncertain prospects. Yes, that's the way it is at the moment. And yet, for some inexplicable reason I feel happy. And I know that the day will come when I'll walk down this street, among these same people, as one of the well-to-do, that once again I'll belong to the genuine intellectual and spiritual elite of society. Come what may, I'll make it, dammit!

I tried to think in English.

My single most serious deficiency was lack of information. I could not yet read newspapers or magazines, while fresh information was paramount if I was to see my plans to completion. That was why I found it interesting and useful to converse with Ghen, who had that advantage over me. At his advice, I put together statistics on the state of the Russian health-care system, although to do that I had to sacrifice much time at the expense of my studies. In turn, he promised to talk to his American friends who were to put him in touch with important people in the publishing business. I could not do it alone. I knew no one, and even if an opportunity presented itself, my poor English would have precluded any possibility of negotiation.

When I plunked down my statistical tables on his desk, Ghen told me, "You know what, old boy? I've changed my mind. Why don't you write the book on your own; I have other things in mind. Besides the book seems an uncertain proposition, so the best of luck to you."

I was sorry to hear he'd changed his mind, but who knows? Maybe it was all for the best; maybe I would cope without his help.

Be that as it may, once he'd bowed out of the book venture, I was left to my own devices again. Deep in thought, I walked along nearly deserted West Fifty-sixth Street and did not notice a young man who appeared out of nowhere, near the stage entrance of Carnegie Hall.

"Hey, man, can you spare a quarter?" Even before I could respond, he added ominously, "I've just come out of jail."

That did it. I took my sole quarter out of my pocket and handed it to him. At that instant we approached the corner of

Seventh Avenue, and I leaped away from him; it's better to be safe than sorry.

Thus, with an empty pocket, but with not a scratch, I came home. Of course, I refrained from telling Irina what had happened. This time, though, she had news to tell. She had been offered a chance to enroll in a three-month bookkeeping and typing course paying a weekly stipend of $80. The number of vacancies was limited and she was to respond the next day.

Irina let me decide whether or not to take the offer. She had previously refused point-blank even to contemplate a career in bookkeeping or typing; on the other hand, she had no other options in view. I had never given serious thought to the possibility of my little Irina becoming an accountant or secretary; nor could I imagine her as one now. But the best therapy for her frayed nerves was to find something for her to do—and fast.

"That sounds great," I told her cheerfully. "You'll be around people all day long and have an opportunity to practice your English."

Irina gave me a pitiful look and clung to me like a defenseless pet.

"Well, how about that? Now all three of us are students."

Come to think of it, we could do a lot worse than that.

27

A journalist came from Chicago to interview me for his magazine *American Medical News.* Irina skipped her studies to serve as my translator. This time she lent me her services without her usual reluctance; after all, it was a concrete and promising piece of business, and I was even paid for my effort. The journalist initially planned to finish the interview within one day. As it happened, he spent two full days with us, asking questions, taping my answers, taking notes, photographing us, perusing my old documents.

I tried to conduct the interview in English, straining enormously to select proper words and construct sentences grammatically. He was sympathetic toward my struggle, but his expression was mute testimony to the difficulty he had in deciphering my babble. If it hadn't been for Irina's help, we would never have been able to complete the job.

"Frankly, I didn't count on such interesting and exciting new material," the journalist told me. "Much of what you've said will be an eye-opener to Americans. They believe that health care in Russia is really free and universally available. Don't be surprised if, after the interview has been printed, strangers start calling. It's commonplace in this country."

That was exactly what I was seeking: useful business contacts who would be instrumental in helping me find a job and having my book published. I waited impatiently for the interview to appear in print. In the meantime, all three of us went on with our studies.

I made enough progress to understand taped lectures, only to discover another glaring impediment: my dearth of knowledge in many of the basic sciences, such as biochemistry, genetics, and microbiology. I had forgotten what little I had learned as a medical school student three decades previously. Besides, in the intervening years so many major discoveries had been made that the sciences had changed beyond recognition. For instance, the DNA structure was described by Francis Crick, James Watson, and M. H. F. Wilkins in 1953, after I had graduated from medical school. At that time, all new scientific publications in the West were treated in Russia with animosity, as manifestations of "bourgeois ideology," and I never had an opportunity to study that great discovery. What practicing physician would delve into matters outside his field? There is neither the time for it nor any discernible utility. So now I was required to learn the details of the structure and functions of that double helix! It meant that I had to backtrack even further. I sighed, grieved, cursed my fate, but there was no alternative.

I realized that I should approach Americans on all matters relating to my studies. There were, of course, almost no native Americans among my fellow students, but to me anyone with a good command of English qualified as a native. I found two friends. One of them, a man of my age, a Jew from Venezuela, was a second-generation Russian immigrant. He did not speak Russian but was exceedingly friendly toward me. He told me I could find the information I needed in the seven-volume *CIBA Collection of Medical Illustrations.* It was full of information, but it cost $300. I could not possibly afford it, but at the same time I needed it badly. What was to be done?

My second friend was a woman of about thirty with an extremely nice smile, gentle and pleasant. She smiled at me for the first time when we bumped into each other at the entrance door of the Kaplan Center. Her smile stuck in my memory. I saw her every day at the same desk. She listened to tapes without visible effort, her hand shielding her eyes like a visor. An American? No, something in her manner suggested a foreigner. Her demeanor was more discreet and devoid of the brash energy and drive typical of American women; she did not put her feet on the table or sit on the floor or chew gum. And she was always elegantly dressed. I planned to introduce myself to her for a long time, but something held me back, even though she smiled at me more pleasantly with every passing day. At last I overcame my timidity and came up to her in the corridor.

"What country are you from?"

"Spain. And you, are you from Russia?"

"Yes, from Moscow. What's your native city?"

"Seville. Have you heard of it?"

"Who hasn't?" I exclaimed. "Figaro here, Figaro there . . ." I sang two measures from *The Barber of Seville.* We both laughed.

After that we spent a lot of time together, all three new Americans: the Spanish lady, the Venezuelan, and the Russian.

And when she found out that I needed the *CIBA Collection of Medical Illustrations,* she provided it.

"You can have it for as long as you want," she told me. "I'm already through with it."

It was a royal gesture indeed—to entrust me with such a wonderful and expensive book! I brought the *Collection* home and began to read it at leisure. The beautifully illustrated book, by Frank Netter, M.D., helped me catch up on the knowledge that I had missed owing to age and circumstances. And the smiling face of the Sevillian looked at me from each page.

The Venezuelan brought a copy of the magazine with my interview titled "A Happy Russian Immigrant." I had not seen it myself and did not even know that it had at last been printed.

"Congratulations! A marvelous interview," he said. "There is so much interesting material about you, and your Russian photographs are very good. You're a celebrity now!"

Choking with emotion, I took the magazine. It had a large photograph of me on the cover, along with an announcement about the interview. But no sooner had I opened the magazine than the Sevillian deftly snatched it and fled to her desk. I experienced a pleasant thrill—now she would be able to find out what I could not tell her about myself in person. She took a long time reading. It even seemed to me that she reread, for I saw her leaf back and forth through the pages. Then she came over to my desk to return the magazine and put her hand on my shoulder—a tender touch!

"What an interesting man you are—a professor, a writer, and an inventor," she whispered softly into my ear. "You are truly a remarkable person."

"Oh no, I am just an ordinary man," I protested in embarrassment, also in a whisper. But I was flattered that she thought that of me.

Her wide-open eyes looked at me intently as if she was making up her mind about something. I could feel an electric impulse through her hand on my shoulder. And unobtrusively, for it was happening in a packed study room, for an instant I pressed my cheek against her hand.

28

That night I barged home earlier than usual, brandishing the magazine. Irina and Junior read the article with a great deal of excitement. I asked them to translate because I failed to understand parts of the interview. They interrupted each other, uttered loud exclamations, laughed, marveled—it was a reaction of pure joy. Then Irina and I went to see my parents, and there she again translated the whole article, from the very beginning to the very end, for their benefit. Mother gazed at me adoringly while Father, still weak after his bout with illness, examined the photographs with tears in his eyes.

In a few days, people from all over the country started calling and writing. One of my former students turned up; he had outstripped me, passing the exam and entering a residency program in Alabama. An old friend of mine also surfaced; he had not passed the exam yet but was working as a surgeon's assistant in Houston. A physician from Las Vegas invited me for a visit. A doctor from California wanted to discuss with me ways of treating ballet dancers' injuries. A retired physician in Manhattan volunteered to tutor me in conversational English.

One telephone call was strictly business: an orthopedist from the Hospital for Joint Diseases in Harlem invited me to talk about a possible job opportunity. I rushed to Harlem without delay. Dr. Lapidus, who had issued the invitation, was past eighty and retired. In his youth, he had been among Russia's trailblazing military aviators. But after the 1917 Revolution, he fled Russia, came to America, became an orthopedic surgeon, and settled down in New York City where he had lived for the past sixty years. He had read my interview and wanted to help. A two-day scientific orthopedic conference was being held at the Harlem hospital. Dr. Lapidus personally handed out copies of the magazine to several of the most influential participants, hoping to boost my reputation among his colleagues. He was sure that one of them would offer me a job. I shouted my gratitude into his ear, for he was almost completely deaf.

He led me to the director's office where I saw a copy of the magazine on the desk. The director told me he had nothing to offer me. Then Dr. Lapidus took me to see the former director, a renowned practicing surgeon, who promised to try to do something for me and suggested I call his secretary. In this way I followed my benefactor from one influential orthopedic surgeon to another. Everybody knew Dr. Lapidus, but apparently he did not pull enough weight with his colleagues, for I was not offered a job.

The next week I attended a conference at the New York Academy of Medicine. Irina accompanied me in case her translation services were needed for a business contact. I liked the papers presented at the conference, but the audience of orthopedic surgeons impressed me even more. Most of them were young, robust men with strong, energetic features. They exuded decisiveness and drive, in dramatic contrast with their Russian counterparts. I was happy that fate propelled me to the other pole of my profession in the United States and that I had the privilege to be in the midst of those mighty warriors of medicine. But God, how desperately I yearned to belong to their community as an equal!

My colleagues ignored me and Irina was spared the opportunity to polish her translation skills. Somewhat distressed, we came out of the academy into one of the first cold nights of early fall.

As we walked down Fifth Avenue, I told Irina, "Don't worry, sooner or later I'll make it, and they'll treat me as a true equal!"

Amazed at my incorrigible optimism, Irina laughed.

We spent the next few weeks calling the doctors' secretaries. This time, I felt nothing of my previous ebullience. Of all the orthopedic surgeons I had approached, only one, an influential Jewish doctor, gave me an appointment for an interview. At the appointed time, I came to Beth Israel Hospital and called from the lobby. The secretary told me the doctor would be with me in a minute. I was about to protest that the doctor shouldn't bother as I was perfectly capable of finding his office on my own, when it occurred to me that maybe he planned to accord me special honor and wanted to personally escort me to his office. Well, if that's what he wished, who was I to object?

Numerous visitors milled about, hospital workers walked to and fro, patients were carted in wheelchairs. It was noisy and crowded. After some time the doctor appeared and, with a surge of joyful anticipation, I went to meet him.

"Good day, thanks for the invitation."

"Oh, hi, how are you? Okay?"

"Okay! I'd like to have a talk with you."

"Sure, let's find a secluded spot somewhere here," he said.

We stepped aside from the intense stream of humanity.

"Well, what is it you wanted to discuss with me?" he asked.

Somewhat nonplussed by the unbusinesslike surroundings, I told him that I wanted a job. While I talked, he listened distractedly, smiling at his colleagues who passed by, exchanging greetings and shaking hands with them. From time to time he turned back to me to say, "Yes, yes, go on."

"I'd like to find an assistant's position until such time as I pass the exam," I wound up my presentation.

"Sounds fine, wish you the best of luck," he said. "Maybe we'll have dinner together one of these days, what do you say?"

On my way home I thought bitterly, Well, okay, when Dr. S. refused to help me, that was just an isolated case. But I've been turned down more and more times now. Why? All I'm seeking is any job as an assistant. Suppose an American counterpart had come to Russia as an immigrant and approached me with a similar request. I'd certainly have done my damnedest to help him. And even if I had failed, I would have treated him with respect. Why don't they treat me in a like manner?

But the answer eluded me.

Irina flew into a rage at all Americans.

"Indifferent, arrogant, stupid brutes!" she screamed. "No sensitivity or compassion, no manners!"

She was in the midst of her diatribe when a general surgeon who had read my interview called on the phone. Politely and warmly he invited us to meet him the next Saturday and offered to pick us up in the morning.

Dr. T. was an Italian immigrant who had come penniless to New York from Naples a quarter of a century earlier. Driving us in his luxury Cadillac to his Long Island home, he told us that my interview vividly reminded him of the hardships he had endured during his first few years in America. Like me, he had spoken almost no English and had had to forge ahead on his own.

"And now I'd like to show you what I achieved over the years," he said, and he took us to his office in Queens—my first visit to a private doctor's office. Dr. T. had a veritable clinic: a large, expensively furnished waiting room with rugs on the floor and paintings on the walls; a room for his two secretaries; an office-cum-library (with rugs and paintings); a procedures room; an operating room; and a convalescence room. And everywhere the latest in electronic equipment, a multitude of expensive devices and instruments. A real medical magic castle if ever I saw one! I had never imagined that such a concentration of the best equipment could be owned by a single physician. I literally went dumb with delight. Later, we were given a warm and friendly welcome by Dr. T.'s family in his mansion. They even thoughtfully invited two Jewish neighbors with their families so we could feel at home among "our own people." Both were rich descendants of Russian immigrants. One of them asked innocently, "Well, how do you like it in America?"

"We don't see anything to like here," Irina replied tartly.

To dilute the poison of Irina's remark, I hastened to add,

"All we've seen so far has been New York City, and everybody says that New York is not really America. So our reaction is by and large to the city, not to the country."

He proceeded to try to talk me into going to Israel.

"Believe me, you'll find life far less hectic there. You'll be able to find an excellent position the day you step on Israeli soil. They'll make you a full professor from the start."

"You know, I've seen Dr. T.'s office. It's a palace. And he told me himself that he started from scratch," I said. "I also hope to be a success in America."

"You've got a point there," he concluded. "No one gets lost here."

When we were leaving, that kindly Jew tried to shove a twenty-dollar bill into my pocket. Why would he do that? Did he feel that sorry for me? Surprised beyond measure, I declined his gesture. An embarrassing scene ensued.

"All right, give the money to your son," he said finally.

Together with Dr. T., he took us home in his Mercedes. Shaking hands, Dr. T. told me, "Don't worry, Vladimir, you'll regain everything you've lost and then some. But try not to leave your European humanitarian legacy by the wayside."

It was a very timely comment in light of my latest experiences. When we came home, Irina observed, "Americans can learn a lot from Europeans, yes, sir! I wish they saw the warm welcome an Italian accorded us in his home!"

It was indeed puzzling: in a country with a reputation for compassion, I encountered precious little. But it was a fleeting thought, because all I could think about was Dr. T.'s office. He had worked in this country for twenty-five years, exactly as long as I had in Russia, but what a difference in accomplishments! And he, too, started out on his own. How could it happen?

"You know," I told Irina, "I don't think that lack of concern for me on the part of Americans I've met so far is evidence of their callousness. The truth must be different. Just being an immigrant is no big deal in this country where everyone is a descendant of immigrants and knows how hard it is to start life anew. Yet, all of them survive and achieve their goals. Yes, that's the way America is!"

Dr. T. tried to help me in job hunting and put me in touch with a popular orthopedic surgeon—with no success. I finally came to the conclusion that all my attempts to find a shortcut would fail.

But life went on. We were gradually getting used to the increasingly familiar surroundings. We became adept at following weekly sales in the many supermarkets in the vicinity. Nothing of the kind existed in Russia, but here we managed to save from ten to fifteen dollars per week through the deft use of sales coupons, particularly if double coupons were available. Bit by bit, we were getting accustomed to the incredible variety of foodstuffs on supermarket shelves, most of which were initially unknown to us. We got used to reading labels. In Russia, the consumer is never told anything about the product he buys, while in America, the label spells out the vitamin and mineral content, the caloric value, and the ingredients. Thus we learned to buy judiciously.

Every day brought something new; we never ceased wondering and marveling. We were not yet up to reading newspapers. The language seemed too abstruse for us and besides we could not afford them on a regular basis.

But New York City is an excellent teacher. Quite often we witnessed the following typical scene: A neatly dressed man, looking like a medium-level office worker, walks down the street; all of a sudden, he dives head first into a garbage can on the corner, fishes a discarded newspaper out of it, and starts reading it there and then (or tucks it under his arm to read it later). Watching this for the first time, we were amazed. People in Moscow never do that. However, the skinny Russian papers—all of four pages—are so short on news and so cheap (seven cents) that it is preposterous to expect anyone to rummage in the garbage for them. After the umpteenth time we came to realize that picking up discarded papers was an accepted norm of behavior in New York City.

I started to pick up discarded newspapers at the Kaplan Center. Irina brought home newspapers she found in subway cars. Junior, too, picked them up wherever he saw them. Thus, gradually, we came to rely increasingly on them. We were astonished at the tremendous amount of information in the papers: a dozen pages covered all imaginable subjects. However, we entertained a typically Russian, deeply ingrained mistrust of the printed word. Almost all news in Soviet newspapers is either false or tardy. We always knew that if the papers reported the opening of a new store, it was either a lie timed to coincide with the next Communist celebration, or the store had been opened two months previously and all its stock had long been sold out.

Once Junior found a notice in *The New York Times* that a new medical school was opening on the island of Dominica. Those who wished to enroll were invited to Boston for interviews. At first he paid no notice to the ad, but it ran for several days and finally got to him. One day he showed it to us.

"Here," he said, "I'm going to study in Dominica."

Irina and I stared at the paper with apprehension. What kind of scam was it?

"Where is Dominica?" I asked.

All three of us started searching for it on the map. The tiny, barely visible speck of land in the Caribbean, between Martinique and Guadeloupe, did not seem trustworthy.

"What kind of medical school would such a tiny island be able to accommodate?" Irina asked.

"Listen," I told my son, "as a former professor at a medical school I know only too well that an institute of medical learning must be based on a system of hospitals extensive enough to train the students. But how will this—what's its name?—Dominica provide the requisite numbers of patients displaying the wide range of pathologies required for training would-be physicians? I strongly doubt it can do that."

"I couldn't care less about the kind of hospitals Dominica has," Junior said. "So long as this medical school is advertised in the paper means it's there. All I need is to gain admission."

"Still you ought to find out something about it before making this jump," I insisted.

But he was already consumed by the youthful itch of impatience.

"I'll find out at the interview," he said resolutely.

Irina took his side. "If Americans are admitted by that school, it implies they do enroll there. Why shouldn't he give it a try?"

Junior placed a call to Boston and soon went for an interview. He returned to New York that same night, rushed home like a gale of joy, and yelled from the doorstep, "I've been admitted! I've been admitted! All we have to do is pay one thousand dollars without delay, and I can start in January."

Irina and I exchanged glances, not knowing whether to rejoice or moan. What bothered me was the ease with which Junior had been admitted.

Meanwhile he was holding forth excitedly. "This medical school is a regular business venture financed by a guy who sells grain to Russia. Tuition is five thousand dollars per semester, but life is cheap on that island. Yes, and we'll have to pay an additional five hundred for the air fare. The first two years, students have to stay on the island, but the faculty is all American. And during the junior and senior years, each student is supposed to find a hospital anywhere in America, including New York, willing to take him for training. But best of all, I've been given a yearly credit for my past studies in Russia. I'll have to stay on Dominica just one year, after which time I'll be back home again."

It sounded improbably simple except for one thing: Where were we to get so much money?

All night long, Irina and I discussed the new project. Finally we came to the conclusion that insofar as everything was being done officially and many Americans were eager to go to Dominica, it should be legitimate. We did not have the money, but our son's future was at stake. Accordingly, it was agreed that we would pay the first thousand and then think of a way to get the rest.

"Maybe we should wait and see before paying?" Irina asked.

"Personally, I'd prefer to wait and find out as much as I can about that school," I replied with a sigh. "But once Junior gets an idea into his head, he'll hound us until we enroll him. Besides, suppose we turn him down and he loses a golden opportunity?"

The next morning, Junior started prodding me impatiently to get that money order. When the bank opened, we were first at the counter. Then Junior raced to the post office and sent out the money order by registered mail. He was in the best of spirits; suddenly life had presented him with a pleasant surprise.

After that, Junior went to consult his college adviser who tried to dissuade him from going to Dominica. The adviser found out that the school had not yet been accredited by the American Medical Association. However, his arguments failed to sway Junior or persuade us. So what if it's not accredited, we thought. Sooner or later it will get accreditation. But pretty soon it was obvious that not a single bank was willing to lend money for tuition at the Dominica medical school. That did it; we did not have enough money for just one semester, let alone several years of schooling.

Junior took the blow hard.

"Boy, what a wonderful opportunity missed!" he lamented. "Particularly since there's a question whether I'll even be able to get into an American medical school. Maybe I should stop dreaming of a medical career and start looking elsewhere?"

Irina and I shared his anguish. Quite possibly it was all for the better that he had not left for Dominica. But we were afraid our son could not compete with native Americans, handicapped as he was by his poor English and fragile immigrant psyche. I was also tormented by my inability to provide financial backing for his studies.

So, one more setback. And, to our horror, we could not get back that thousand dollars; for all our effort, only half the sum was refunded.

"I told you we shouldn't have paid the money blindfolded!" Irina rebuked Junior and myself. As always, of the three of us she was hit hardest.

"Hello, Doctor, how are you? Long time no see," my old acquaintance welcomed me at the synagogue.

"I've been too busy. Cramming for the board exam takes all my time," I replied.

"Oh, I see." He resumed rocking violently, his beard whipping back and forth. From time to time, though, he would glance at me askance and mumble, rocking all the while. "This exam—is it difficult?"

"Very."

"Oh, I see." And he would immerse himself in praying. Then another question: "Listen, why do you have to take that exam?"

"Why? To be able to start working as a physician."

"In that case I can arrange it so you'll pass without any preparation. I can do anything, you know."

"How?" I asked in astonishment.

"It's my own business," he observed without interrupting his rocking. "All you have to do is pay ten thousand dollars and wait for your certificate. How about it?"

I was struck speechless while he went on:

"You don't even have to pay the whole sum up front; two installments will be just fine. Here is what we'll do: We'll go to your bank and you deposit five thousand in a neutral party's account. The money will be safe in the bank and no one will be the wiser. At the exam, you duly go through all the required motions, but the result needn't bother you—you'll be assured of passing. I can give you an ironclad guarantee. When your certificate comes, we go to the bank one more time, and you deposit another five thousand in the same account, whereupon the third party withdraws the money while you start looking for a job as a doctor. What do you say?"

I was stunned at the mere thought that the exam could be treated so casually as an object of commerce. And where?—at a synagogue, during a prayer session! But I still found it hard to believe that he was serious.

What could I tell this old and respectable man? Certainly I could remind him of the physician's code of ethics, of criminal liability for faking official documents, of my personal moral standard. But I knew that swindlers found it hard to believe that some people might be honest. What was the point explaining to him that never, under no circumstances, would I agree to buy the exam—even if I had millions to spare!

"No, I don't have the money for that," I told him and turned to leave.

31

The next Saturday, I went in the morning to Temple Emanu-El on Fifth Avenue, which I chose for the simple reason that it was halfway between my home and the Kaplan Center. Besides, I did not know anyone there nor did anyone in the temple notice my existence. It was a plus, for I was still in a state of shock following that prayer-time business proposition.

Temple Emanu-El is a Reform synagogue. The magnificent architecture and the splendid marble trimming disposed one to solemn meditation. The service, masterfully conducted by a rabbi, reminded me of a classical stage play. A stupendous soloist sang to the accompaniment of a superb choir. The organ rumbled majestically. As usual, I did not pray, just meditated, the beautiful music creating a congenial atmosphere for serious thinking. I took out a piece of paper and started composing the outline of a book. That morning I mapped out thirty-seven chapters. Could it be the Lord blessed me to start writing in his temple?

In uplifted spirits, I left the synagogue and went to the Kaplan Center. I couldn't wait to share the impressions of that morning with my Sevillian. She was at her desk listening to a tape, as usual shielding her eyes and forehead with her palm. I sat down nearby and put on the earphones. But I found it hard to concentrate and spent more time watching her than listening to the lecture. Did she see me? I wished she would remove her palm and smile at me as she always did. My wish was granted, filling me with jubilation. We went out into the corridor and talked, trying to disguise the intimate nature of our conversation. I told her about the music at the temple, about the office of the Italian immigrant physician, about my mood. How did she suffer my tortured English, poor thing? As a matter of fact, she must have understood less than half of what I tried to say, but she felt everything I strove to convey. I could see proof of that in her eyes, now widening with admiration, now narrowing to echo my disdain, now clearing, now misting. What a dazzling display of empathy it was!

"And it was there," I concluded, "in that beautiful synagogue, to the accompaniment of marvelous music, that I began writing my book."

Her eyes widened with surprise. "Really? You've never told me about it. What kind of book?"

"A book about Russian health care, and some of my celebrity patients."

She squinted quizzically. "But what about yourself? You must write about yourself."

"Do you think that my life story would interest American readers?"

Her eyes grew moist with tenderness. "Of course, for you are such an extraordinary person! You know what? We ought to celebrate this day. I'm sure you'll write a great book! Let's go some place."

Talking and laughing, we reached St. Patrick's Cathedral. Suddenly she grew stern. "I too want to pray. Would you mind accompanying me inside?"

"Of course. I'll follow you anywhere."

The cathedral was even more majestic than Temple Emanu-El, and here, too, an organ was playing. She prayed while I watched her.

Later, I found myself with her in a Mexican restaurant in Greenwich Village. That was my first visit to the artistic area of the city, my first visit to a Mexican restaurant, and . . . the first time in my life I could not pick up the tab for a lady.

But she forestalled me. "I've invited you so I am buying. Please!"

Somewhat embarrassed, I could only say, "Thank you. I hope the time will come, and soon, when I'll be able to be your host."

"Don't have any doubts, it will certainly come," she said. "I prayed for that."

I drew her hand across the small table and kissed her palm, while she stroked my cheek.

There was no way I could have been host that day even if I could have afforded it. I did not know how to order, could not make head or tail of the menu, had no idea of the wines. She had to guide me. We chatted and laughed. I was in top form, the first time in a long while that I was really jolly. Gathering linguistic courage, I improvised a fairy tale about us, where I was the donkey and she a bird. The donkey fell in love with the bird and she reciprocated his feelings. My imagination ranged boldly, while she dissolved in laughter.

ow I was constantly dreaming about my Sevillian whom I called *Ptitsa* (bird). Much stood in the way of my passion: I was fifteen years older and too poor for such a fashionable woman; I was deep in my studies and writing; I felt deep obligations to my family. But I couldn't help myself; a hidden struggle between reality and dream raged in my soul.

I wonder if Irina noticed anything. Engrossed in endless worries about our future, she was in a constant state of panic. Her weekly stipend of eighty dollars was the mainstay of our budget, but she could not cope with her distaste for typing and bookkeeping and finally refused to attend bookkeeping lessons, whereupon her stipend was promptly cut in half—down to $40. Desperately, she looked for a job. Every day we collected discarded newspapers, brought them home, and pored over the help-wanted section. There were plenty of job offers, but, ironically, almost all of them were in bookkeeping or typing, which only served further to dampen Irina's spirits.

I still believed that she should start looking for a job at a research laboratory, but she responded to my admonitions by yelling, with tears in her eyes, "Forget about research! There are no jobs like that for me in this country, no jobs, not for me!"

I refused to believe it. There are all kinds of jobs in America, but one must know how to look for them. From my little contact with the Russian immigrant community I knew that it survived largely through self-help. Almost all the immigrants helped one another to find jobs, mostly as hairdressers, sales clerks, or manicurists. But research scientists?

The first one I approached, a radiologist past forty, told me caustically, "They [that is, Americans] don't let our people near any research job. I tried once—no dice. Without a push, forget it, and who of them will give one of us a push? The good and untroubled life has turned their brains topsy-turvy. They are all egoists and swindlers. What rotten luck—to escape from a country of fools only to get to a country of frauds!"

Another physician was a forty-five-year-old surgeon, Dr. Kap. He and his wife were employed in research positions. I told him about Irina's circumstances, and he invited us over to brief Irina on the employment situation in her field.

"Major research centers are in constant need of workers in your line," they told Irina. "Why don't you scout, say, personnel departments? Tell them about your experience, describe your circumstances, and, most important, leave your curriculum vitae with them. Maybe something will come out of it."

The advice was simplicity itself, but for some strange reason it had never occurred to us that such a straightforward approach was possible. Irina did scout the personnel department of Columbia Presbyterian Medical Center. But since it could not be predicted how long she would have to wait for an opening and what kind of job she was likely to be offered, she did not stop going over newspaper ads. One day she came across the following: "The Institute of Aeronautics and Astronautics has an opening for a person fluent in Russian, German, and French; with some research experience; comfortable with specialized astronomical terminology, and capable of passing examination in . . ."—a long list of unfamiliar disciplines followed.

What stood out in the ad was the Russian-language requirement. Irina also spoke German and had a very rudimentary knowledge of French. Apparently the institute was looking for a Leonardo da Vinci, for who else could fit such a description?

It was desperation that drove Irina to overcome her anxiety and go to take that exam. In the luxurious building of the institute on Park Avenue, where everything stood out in such stark contrast to our habitual surroundings, she was issued three incomprehensible booklets with technical terms in a variety of languages. In helpless frustration, Irina closed the booklets and all but gave up. Still, necessity proved the stronger stimulus. How desperately she yearned for that job! And—she passed the exam!

Concurrently, fate smiled on me as well: Through the advice of an editor of a Russian daily, I found a literary agent, a woman in her fifties, an immigrant from Romania. However, she did not speak Russian, while the few chapters of my book were still in the hands of my translator. My material was read and translated for the benefit of the agent by her friend, a former Russian army officer.

"Well and good," she said. "But how do you propose to link all those medical stories?"

"My personal life story will be the common thread," I said. "I am going to write the life story of a Russian doctor."

My explanation failed to dispel her doubts, but she consented to send the manuscript to the Russian-language reviewer of a major publishing house. Now the future of my book hung on his good will. Time dragged slowly as I waited, trying to keep my nerves in check.

Meanwhile I wrote prodigiously, skipping a week of studies at the Kaplan Center. Once, when I was alone at home, the telephone rang. It was my Sevillian.

"Vladimir, where have you been? I miss you terribly," she said in a voice suffused with affection. Again I felt a powerful urge to see her.

"The Donkey will surely come to his Bird," I joked.

"When?"

"When he sprouts wings . . ."

I was torn assunder by conflicting emotions: Empathy with Irina at such a crucial point clashed with yearning for Ptitsa. But surely I could not parade my vacillation in front of a woman I liked. So I won a reprieve with another fairy-tale metaphor.

"The Donkey is dying to see his Bird, but they haven't yet developed a common language."

"Why?"

"Because the Donkey hasn't yet learned to sing like a bird . . ."

When the telephone rang another time, I lifted the receiver expecting to hear the Sevillian's voice. Instead, I heard: "This is Personnel at the Columbia Presbyterian Medical Center. Your wife is invited for an interview about a research position at a scientific laboratory."

I could hardly wait for Irina to come home from school (she still attended the course so as not to lose the weekly stipend).

"You've been summoned to a research lab for an interview," I told her playfully.

"Really?" She beamed with delight.

Early next morning, she flew to the interview, while I tensely waited at home for the outcome.

Irina rushed home like a happy whirlwind.

"I've got a job, I've got a job!" she shouted, delirious with joy. "From now on I'm a research associate at the Columbia Presbyterian Eye Institute immunology lab. It's a dream come true! Just think of it—it's exactly my professional line, the subject I have worked on for fifteen years. To hell with aeronautics and astronautics!"

"Do you see now how wrong you were doubting your future?" I said, embracing her.

Still agog with excitement, Irina proceeded to tell me in detail about the interview at the director's office: What questions he had asked, how she had answered them, how he had talked to Personnel in her presence—everything except for the salary, she was too shy to ask about her pay.

"The most important thing is that you like the job," I said, but the face of my Ptitsa loomed in my mind, and her melodious deep voice rang in my ears: "Vladimir, I miss you. . . ."

33

I was in excellent spirits. Fully trusting that my literary agent would succeed in her search for a publisher, I avidly wrote one episode after another. Of course, Irina's stroke of luck added to my festive mood.

I was glad that everything came out exactly the way I planned and that I had contributed, if only indirectly, to her success. I hoped that now Irina would calm down and peace would reign in my home. But there was yet another reason for my exuberant mood: I was in love. Perhaps that was the most important ingredient; perhaps that was the real basis of my inspiration.

I was already forty-nine years old, and yet here I was in

love, like a teenager! I daydreamed; I was restless; I lost my
head. And I could see the same thing happening to her, to my
Ptitsa. At the study center, we constantly exchanged glances
while pretending to listen to the tapes. If one of us left the
room, the other would inevitably turn up in the corridor. We
were irresistibly drawn to each other. And when the day was
done, we invariably took a stroll through the streets before
saying good-bye—till the next day.

I forgot when I had last wandered through the streets as
an infatuated kid; it must have been at least a quarter of a
century. But now I was reliving the experience of my remote
youth. I kissed Ptitsa for the first time under the Christmas
tree at Rockefeller Plaza—and I did it as timidly as I had kissed
my first girlfriend ages ago. Thereafter, we were constantly on
the lookout for secluded "kissing" spots.

I came to love the business section of mid-Manhattan,
which we thoroughly explored in our night wanderings. But
sometimes it seemed unreal that it was I who was wandering
and kissing in the streets like a love-crazed adolescent. And
the greatest miracle of all was that it was happening in the
streets of New York. Is it really me? Where am I, I kept asking myself, and could not believe it was true.

Irina apparently took no notice of the changes in me. Now
she was totally engrossed in her new job and came home exhausted every night. Having secured a research position paying
$11,700 a year, she dreaded losing it. She was still consumed
by all kinds of fears: that the grant money would run out and
her position would be eliminated; that her supervisor was dis-
satisfied with her work; the dangers emanating from the subway crowds twice every day. And, as usual, she was worried
about the future of our son and my own prospects. She was
still dubious about my chances in the literary field and believed that I was wasting valuable time on writing. Our moods
differed sharply.

To make matters worse, the long-awaited opinion finally
arrived from the Russian-language reviewer. The review was
devastating: "Golyakhovsky is no Chekhov or Veresayev" (the

two Russian writers who also were medical doctors). I was taken aback by its vicious tone, but my agent told me to relax.

"All Russian-language reviewers in publishing houses are old immigrants and fervent Russian patriots. They get mad when their beloved Russia comes in for criticism. You really have no reason to be discouraged."

"All right, I won't be discouraged, but what do we do next?"

The Rumanian said that she was going to find someone to translate fifty pages, whereupon she would again submit the manuscript to a reviewer, but this time an unbiased, American one.

"I don't have the money to pay for the translation," I said.

"I'll pay for one out of my own pocket, I'll take a risk," she said. However, she did not. Then I found a translator myself. He agreed to translate ten pages of the manuscript and to give an idea of the concept and texture of the would-be book. He charged me eighty dollars. It was torture for me to part with that sum, but I was determined to persevere.

Irina resented the extra expense. Again she complained, and we had frequent fights.

While Ptitsa kept asking me in her tender, dulcet voice, "Vladimir, when is your book going to appear in bookstores? When are you going to sign copies for your fans? I can't wait to see the day!"

The disarming naïveté of her question and the love-laden look that accompanied it were in total contrast to Irina's behavior. One woman dismissed my undertaking as a lost cause and a piece of nonsense; the other was a firm believer in my eventual success. Protecting my author's self-respect, I was gradually drifting away from Irina and moving even closer to Ptitsa. And if earlier I had been torn by doubt as to the wisdom of that romance, all I could dream of now was to possess my beautiful bird. "I am so deeply in love. If not now, when?" I kept asking myself.

I had never had an affair with a foreigner, although I had long yearned to find out what those vaunted Western women were like. From translations of modern novels and from the few foreign movies available, I believed that they must be different from their Russian counterparts.

Lack of inner freedom, so characteristic of the Russians, has a restraining impact on the relationship between the sexes as well. The hypocritical moral code of Communism condemns any kind of free relationship. Intimacy between men and women is a frequent target of persecution. However, human nature is immutable, and people in Russia do everything that men and women do elsewhere. But they constantly look over their shoulders. This is probably the reason why Russian women are generally passive in love—from the very first kiss to sexual intercourse.

But Ptitsa hailed from Spain, a country of sultry love, and her birthplace was Seville, the city of Carmen, of hot romantic blood. Once, on the eve of the first anniversary of my departure from Russia, she told me, "Vladimir, I'd like to give you a gift. . . ."

My heart missed a beat.

The golden anniversary of my parents, February 21, 1979, was nearing. Slightly more than two weeks was left, and I wanted very much to give them a celebration. Father was obviously withering away. An old man of seventy-eight, he found it hard to stand up to the hardships of immigration. No immigrant is immune to what I call "transplantation disease." Much like a tree transplanted to a different soil has to go through an adaptation process, sometimes quite painful, an immigrant has to adapt to being removed from one environment and placed in another. But while a young tree recovers fast and puts down new roots, transplantation is much tougher on an old tree.

Father sometimes repeated with mild rebuke, "You brought me here to die. . . ."

I yearned to bring him some joy, possibly his last. All his life he had loved people, enjoyed company. I wanted to provide him with one more chance to feel at the hub of a circle of friends. My parents were still without an apartment of their own, while I did not have enough furniture or tableware to hold a party at my apartment. Besides, Irina, always on the verge of exhaustion, could do without additional trouble. Logic dictated a party at a restaurant because we decided to invite fourteen guests, but such a proposition was too expensive.

Then Aunt Lyuba came to the rescue.

"Yuli [my father] is the only one of us, four sisters and four brothers, who has lived to see his golden anniversary," she told me. "I want you to give your parents a real bash, and I'll pay for half of it."

As always, she was the dearest and kindest of all! What with her generous offer, it was far easier for me to scrape together my share from our meager reserves. Now then, what was the best place for a feast? I approached Ptitsa for advice. She was delighted.

"How wonderful! I'm so glad for your parents! Of course, you should give them an unforgettable celebration! I know a marvelous restaurant, and I'll go with you to reserve a table."

The next morning I went to the bank and withdrew $200 in cash to pay the deposit for the reservation. Before meeting Ptitsa, I dropped by Radio Liberty to record my regular program. Ghen welcomed me with a sly smile.

"I've managed to get a reference testifying to my experience as an engineer with a major company."

"Congratulations! How did you do it?" I asked in surprise.

"Ah, anything can be arranged in this country," he

shrugged. "I've already been hired, the pay is almost twice what I make here, and the future looks much better."

"It means good-bye, doesn't it? Well, best of luck!"

"Wait. I decided to start there during my vacation—to get my bearings in the new place. Maybe I won't like it, then I'll come back and nobody will be the wiser. Remember, I haven't told anyone here about my plans, so please don't discuss it. Particularly with Anya."

"Why would I tell Anya, of all people?"

"You know how it happens—by accident."

The beautiful Anya greeted me at the recording studio.

"Ghen is leaving us," she announced.

"You don't say! Where is he going?" I faked surprise.

"It's a secret," she put her fingers on her lips. "He has somehow obtained a bogus engineering reference, found a plum job, and will make five times his present salary. But please don't let it slip that you learned it from me."

She nervously lit one cigarette from another; her hands shook; her eyes were swollen and restless. "My husband asked about you, Doctor. Why have you vanished?"

"I haven't. I have to study a lot, cramming for my board exam."

Nervously, she rummaged in her handbag. "Do you have any money with you? I'll write out a check and you can cash it at your bank later. I need money badly right away."

"How much do you need?"

"Let's say a hundred," she looked at me expectantly.

"As a matter of fact, I do have cash, but I need it myself today."

"Please, Doctor, dear, please help me out! I need the money right now, this minute!"

"All right, I'll give you fifty."

I figured that $150 should be enough for a deposit. Anya snatched the bills out of my hand, signed the check, nervously and hurriedly, and was gone.

I had to waste more than an hour waiting for her to return and do the recording. I was angry and jumpy, afraid to be late for the rendezvous with Ptitsa. I cursed myself for having admitted to having ready cash. When Anya reappeared, she was a new person, moving sluggishly, talking slowly, and slurring her words. I was surprised. She was followed by another female engineer who immediately led Anya to the ladies' room and returned to record my program instead of her.

Finally the recording session was over. I raced down Fifth Avenue to the 53rd Street subway station where I was to meet Ptitsa. When I arrived she was already there, and we embraced passionately. Then we walked, chatting and laughing. It was a wonderful wintry day, patches of snow glistened in the rays of the cold sun—a carbon copy of the weather from a year previously, when we had been leaving Moscow.

She took me to the Plaza Hotel, one of the most fashionable in the city. I knew little about New York restaurants, but I realized that this one must be very expensive. Somewhat taken aback by my discovery, I complained to her, but she protested.

"So what? After all, the occasion is the golden anniversary of your parents. They deserve the very best. Besides, other restaurants will charge only slightly less, but the service will be vastly inferior."

I had never been good at bargaining. So I did the logical thing and put my trust in her judgment. As we discussed the menu, she discussed each course with the passion of a true daughter of Spain. All she lacked was a fan to look the epitome of a classic Spanish lady—so hotly did her eyes burn and so cunningly did she glance at me now and then.

"Let's go upstairs," she said after we discussed a menu and reserved a place for my parents. "I'd like to show you something."

We were already riding in the elevator when it dawned on me that in all likelihood she was going to present me with the promised gift. Silently she unlocked a door and stepped into a room with natural lithe elegance, head held high and hips swaying.

All I could see at first was her eyes—burning like embers, eager, impatient. They grew larger and larger until I could see nothing else. We were kissing passionately. Finally, I took a breath and began discerning what the room with the closed curtains contained: a table laden with food next to the bed; a bottle of expensive Cognac; a box of chocolates. Ptitsa pointed to the bottle. "That's for you."

Then she pointed to the table. "That's for you too."

I looked at the bed, but she was silent. "And that?" I asked.

"That's for both of us. . . ."

I pointed a finger at her. "And that?"

She laughed. "That's for you alone!"

I poked a finger at my chest. "And how about that?"

Ptitsa flung herself at me. "That's for me alone! For me! For me alone!"

She was everything I hoped to find in a Western woman. Caressing Ptitsa, just as I had imagined in my wildest dreams, she kept repeating, "Sí, sí, sí. How wonderful!"

And she talked and talked in her beautiful, dulcet native tongue.

Totally drained, we lay side by side, sipping Cognac. "Vladimir, what's the real reason why you left Russia?" she asked.

"To meet you," I replied.

I tried hard not to feel guilty toward Irina because I had long been angry with her. But neither was I going to brandish my infidelity before her. It seemed to me I would be able to hide my affair from her—somehow.

With Ptitsa there were no problems; she was divorced, with not a worry in the world.

Since that first time when I had come home past midnight and quietly slipped into bed, trying not to wake up Irina, Ptitsa and I met more and more often. Irina was glumly silent and never asked what had kept me so late. What kept me, of course, was my Sevillian. We were madly in love. I behaved like Romeo, although, considering our age difference, I could easily qualify as his grandfather. And I kept a love diary—where I described our trysts in transparent allegories. Irina had never read my diaries before, so I did not bother to take any precautions. Taking my cue from Boccaccio, I depicted in colorful, Decameron-inspired detail how the Donkey made love to the Bird.

As time went on, a gnawing thought started preying on my mind: It was time to stop, enough of the euphoric debauchery. I felt enormous gratitude to Ptitsa for the powerful emotional outburst she had let loose in me. Also I was grateful to her for getting my English "unstuck"; I was still unable to speak correctly but was no longer ashamed of making mistakes. And that was an important step forward. Lord Byron was absolutely right when he said that the best way to master a foreign language was to learn it from the lips of a beautiful woman. And of course, I was supremely grateful to her for the marvelous generosity of a Western woman's soul she had thrown open to me—both in love and in all its attributes. For all my gratitude, though, I never lost sight of the fact that my real place was with my family.

The trouble was that I did not know how to loosen the knots of our affair gradually so as to spare Ptitsa as much anguish as possible. I started telling her increasingly often that I had to devote more time to serious study, that I had to write my book, that I was tired. She would respond to all my laments with a dutiful "Sí, sí," and then follow up in her spellbinding voice, "Tomorrow?"

Finally I got to calling her "Bird of Prey"—only half in jest. I composed a story about how the loving Bird sprouted eagle talons and beak and how she carried the poor Donkey to her aerie on top of a tall cliff. Listening to the fairy tale, Ptitsa laughed: "Sí, sí, sí."

But I went on, "Wait a minute, it's too early to laugh. When the Bird of Prey brought the limp Donkey to her aerie, he could not live among the clouds and died."

"No!" she exclaimed. "It can't be! Why did he die?"

"Because the next morning, after a happy night of love, he left the nest to graze as was his habit. But there was no meadow high up in the cliffs, no grass to graze. He lost his balance and fell into the precipice. . . ."

She was on the verge of tears. "No," she said. "It's not true that the Bird caused his death."

"How do you know?"

"Because she loved him."

"Yes, it's true. But sometimes love, too, kills."

I did not tell her that it was I who was perishing because of her love.

Meanwhile, the atmosphere at home was heating up. Irina all but stopped talking to me, eyed me sullenly, and was constantly deep in gloomy thought. Finally the gathering storm erupted and everything bottled up in her gushed forth.

Early in the morning, I woke up because I sensed Irina at my bedside. I opened my eyes and saw her looming over me, my diary in her hands.

"What is it?" she asked.

I had no trouble realizing what it was but, to gain time, pretended that I was still sleepy.

"This? It's my diary."

"Don't you play games with me," she hissed. "I've been reading this thing all night long and I'm asking you now: What is it?"

"It's, well . . . ah, a . . . fairy tale . . ."

"A fairy tale? Who is that Donkey, who is that Bird?"

"Nobody, just what they are—a donkey and a bird."

"Like hell they are! I realized everything long ago. Don't think I'm a fool."

"What did you realize?"

"I realized that you've betrayed me and Junior. At a difficult time like this you've decided to abandon us, just like a coward. You are having an affair with a rich bitch, amusing her with fairy tales and caresses. Yes, yes, I know it! I found her real name and her telephone number in our telephone book."

I sat up in bed and reached for her. "Come on. This is nonsense."

"Don't you dare touch me! Go to your Bird and act like the ass you've so aptly described yourself. Do you think I couldn't recognize you in the description? I can even compliment you on the literary merits of your characterizations. But I don't need you as that ass."

"Come on, Irina, don't take it all that seriously."

"And how do you suppose I should take it? As a purely literary endeavor? Oh, now! I'm sick of your literary pretensions! You've been deceiving me for a year now with your dreams of providing for us with your writing. Where's the East Side apartment you promised? 'We'll live on the East Side,' she mocked me. 'We'll live better than the whore who is writing memoirs about the Soviet diplomat.' Like hell we will!"

"And what exactly do you mean by that?" I flew into a rage in my turn.

"What I mean is that, for all your promises, you've turned into a jackass."

"I still believe that my book will be a success."

"You can believe anything you want, but I no longer believe you. As a matter of fact, I've lost all faith in you. I don't know about your philandering in Moscow, it's all in the past now. But if only I had known that something like this would happen here, during the most trying period in our lives, I would never have left Russia. Here I am, working like mad, pinching every penny, racking my brain over how to earn a little extra—while you're having fun with a bitch who's bought you with her wealth!" Irina started crying.

"There, there . . . take it easy, will you? It's not the way you imagine. What's all this nonsense about betraying or abandoning you?"

"I hate this country, I hate everybody here." She went on, choking on her sobs, "We used to be the elite, but look at us now—lepers, beggars, scum! Has anyone helped us here? And now you've decided to follow their lead. It's all your fault. They've changed you."

"What are you talking about? What does this country or its people have to do with it?"

"They have changed you for the worse. Never would I have believed you could betray us! I wish we hadn't come here. Yes, yes, I am sorry we did! What kind of future awaits us here?"

"You're wrong! I haven't changed one bit, and there's nothing to be afraid of in our future. Take it easy, will you!"

"God, my God!" she moaned. "Left alone! Alone! All alone!"

Her words were a wail of agony, ringing in my ears. I felt so acutely sorry for her that tears welled up in my eyes. I embraced her, overcoming her resistance, and tried to kiss her tear-streaked face. She pulled away.

"Go away, go away. I don't need your kisses, I don't want anything from you. I've made up my mind to divorce you."

"Divorce me? You can't be serious," I exclaimed in despair.

"Oh, yes, I am. I've even found out from our American neighbor all the pertinent legal stuff."

"Irina, you must understand that all this thing, I mean everything that has happened, it's not serious. Please understand and try to forgive me. It's all over, believe me."

"I can't believe you now. If you could be unfaithful at such a time . . ."

"Again that nonsense. Yes, I was infatuated with that woman. Yes, I was . . . unfaithful to you. . . . But it has never occurred to me to betray or leave you. Don't you realize that such things do happen, that people do cheat . . . ? But how can you understand? You, who don't know the taste of unfaithfulness?"

"What do you mean I can't understand? Of course, I do. I was unfaithful to you once, but I stopped just in time because I could clearly see the danger to my family," she said calmly.

What? My Irina was unfaithful to me? How was I supposed to take this news? Taken aback, I kept silent. Having been caught myself, it was stupid to hurl accusations at her. But I had to react somehow.

Meanwhile she went on, "The only reason I've told you is to make things easier for you. It's not my intention to cause you any more pain than I have to, but my decision is final: I am going to divorce you and leave for Israel. I'll work on a kibbutz and, God willing, maybe with time I'll find peace."

Mercy, Lord, now this! She had taken a long time to think it through in her solitude. But what about our son? How much did he know? As if reading my mind, Irina said, "Junior knows everything. He's on my side."

I tried to say something, but she cut me short and in great agitation set about getting ready to leave for work. I could hear from the bedroom how she got dressed, jerkily and sloppily, how she paced the room, sighing loudly and crying softly. Several times I came to the door, but she turned away. She had unburdened herself of what she had long kept bottled up, and now was not the time to try changing her mind; she had to calm down a bit before I could do anything. I heard her slam the door, leaving. Unable to decide what to do and worrying about her—who knows what she would do alone—I rushed into the hall, bent down, and peeked through the keyhole. She was waiting for the elevator, weeping. She was swaying and had to lean against the wall. All of a sudden, as if cut at the knees with a scythe, she began to fall. Quickly I was at her side, picked up her limp body, and carried her inside. She was almost unconscious—a psychogenic fit.

I put her on the bed, kneeled down, unbuttoned her coat, and gave her a drink of water. Gradually she revived and looked at me as if studying. I timidly kissed her on the cheek. She did not turn away. I kissed her again.

"Please forgive me, please. . . ." I whispered, kissing her on the lips. And suddenly I felt her lips move in response. In spite of all she still loved me.

36

That morning, though weak, Irina somehow went to work. I insisted on walking her at least as far as the subway station and later called her at the office to make sure she had reached it. Myself, I stayed at home to collect my thoughts. How was I going to put our lives together again?

The first thing I did was to tear to pieces and throw away my diary with the incriminating fairy tale. "To hell with all those diaries, fairy tales, allegories," I thought. "Who am I— Jean-Jacques Rousseau?—to take the world into my confidence about my intimate life?"

Having disposed of the diary, I felt better. But the notes, of course, were but the last and least significant link in the complicated chain of events that had inexorably led to the blowup. My paramount concern was to prevent Irina from rashly filing for a divorce and leaving for Israel. If I managed to stop her, sooner or later I would be able to resurrect our relationship, of that I had no doubt. Even at the height of amorous bliss with Ptitsa not for an instant had I lost my deep affection for Irina. These were loves on different planes.

My mind raced, feverishly sorting out recollections of all our years together. So, I am not the only black sheep in the family; Irina, too, has eaten of the fruit of sin. No matter how much people all over the world talk and think about the problem, few learn the truth about their spouses. If my infidelity had not been brought to light so flagrantly, I would never have found out about Irina's either. Many years ago, while still a very young man, soon after our wedding, I had silently pondered that grave question: How would I react if I found Irina cheating on me? And even then I had come to a firm decision: I would not reproach or punish her. If she sinned, it would remain her own, profoundly personal business, while I loved her too much to be a stern judge.

No, I must do my damnedest to prevent a divorce, it's the only way to preserve the relationship with my son—if only for later! To imagine that I won't be able to see them again! Or that I will see them only occasionally, as a stranger. But Irina and I simply cannot live without each other. Her desperate cry "Alone! All alone . . . !" was still ringing in my ears. How could she think that way? Never, never will I let her stay alone, away from me. As long as I am alive, she won't be alone! And she also loves me or why else did she kiss me after all that happened?

Why, why have we edged to the brink of separation? The question kept turning in my mind. Irina blamed our new environment, but she was wrong. Her diatribe was merely a hysterical lunge at an imaginary enemy. The real cause of trouble was of a different nature. Both of us were victims of an acute social and cultural shock. Both of us were strained beyond the limit of our endurance to withstand the onslaught of change. But while I fared much better, what with my intrinsically strong nervous system and a shell born of past hardships, Irina succumbed to the immigrant's syndrome. All her life protected by me from reality, she was particularly vulnerable. The cumulative stresses surfaced as mutual dislike. But no dislike can be as acute as that between husband and wife, particularly in harsh circumstances. And our circumstances were as difficult as could be. Our personal drama embodied a long period of upheavals extraordinary in scope and depth, and it erupted like an explosion set off by a chance spark.

My heart ached. Something must be done to prevent a tragedy. I had to talk to Ptitsa, to explain everything to her. Everything what? What and how shall I say to her, "Sorry but my wife takes exception to our affair"? Will that do? Or, "Circumstances triumph over love"? I mercilessly mocked myself, anticipating that any explanation would make me very small, whatever excuse I managed to come up with. Ah, the unavoidable talk—I cringed at the mere thought.

She was at her regular desk at the Kaplan Center. But she was looking expectantly at the door instead of listening to the tapes with her hand over her eyes like a visor. When I entered, she rose to meet me. We went out into the corridor.

"Vladimir, what happened?" she asked anxiously.

"Ah, my poor Ptitsa, the unavoidable happened . . ."

"I know," she interjected. "Your wife called me on the phone."

"She did?" I asked in surprise. "When? What did she say?"

I was shocked to learn that I had maneuvered Irina into such an unpalatable undertaking. How she must have suffered, talking to my mistress!

"Let's get out of here so we could talk," Ptitsa said. I trailed behind—like a true donkey.

"Okay, how did it happen?" she asked again once we were outside.

"She found my diary."

"Was there any mention of me?"

"I wrote down the fairy tale, 'The Donkey's Bird,' but she understood."

"What a stupid slip on your part," she exclaimed. "Why didn't you hide your diary and by what right did she snoop in your personal notes?"

"What does it matter now?" I replied. "Besides, the diary was actually the last straw. She knew the truth anyway. What did she tell you?"

"She was furious."

"I am sorry, Ptitsa, but you must understand. . . ."

"Of course I did. I would be angry too if I were she."

"What did she say?"

"Too much. But what really struck me was her conviction that I 'bought' you. Vladimir, I'm not rich, not at all. But I felt I could afford anything for the sake of our love."

"I know. What else did she say?"

"She told me never, never ever, to so much as talk to you."

"It's jealousy," I said.

"What's your decision, Vladimir?" She looked at me expectantly.

"I will certainly talk to you, but . . ." I faltered.

"But what?"

"She's my wife. . . ."

"You don't love me anymore?"

"Love never ends abruptly; it slowly peters out."

"Are you willing to extinguish your love for me?"

"Ah, my Ptitsa . . ."

"Ptitsa, Ptitsa," she mocked me, pouting.

"So many things are on my mind," I said. "You know how much I have to do. Your love was like a gift of Providence to me. I could never imagine that I was destined for such a blissful experience. It was a reward for all my suffering."

"Was? Did you say 'was'?" She hung her head and tears gushed out of her eyes.

"I will always remember you, Ptitsa, your place in my heart is secure as a beautiful memory, but I . . ."

She gave me such a piercing look that I stopped against my will. Her eyes, looking at me through a veil of tears, expressed myriad emotions: misery, longing, passion, and contempt.

"You're an old man, Vladimir," she said and turned away.

No, that Sevillian was not about to make a scene. She simply poured out her scorn and was on her way. I watched her walk—proudly, head held high, torso inclined backward, hips swaying, exactly as she had once led me into the room she rented at the Plaza. I watched, feeling that her departure indeed left me older. Well, that was only natural; we never overcome our vices; they leave us. I was returning to my rightful place in life, beside my Irina.

37

rina avoided talking to me, particularly if our son was present. But they conversed behind my back, and I saw them counting the money we had—down to the last cent. In the kitchen Irina hung a slogan with a single word, *Survival!* I took my bedding to the small sofa in the dining room. Turning sleeplessly on my makeshift bed, I strained my ears, listening to what Irina was doing in the bedroom. Every night she paced the room, sighed, coughed, apparently cried, and also read sorrowful poems by Sergei Yesenin, a lyrical Russian poet unsurpassed in his ability to express the innermost emotions (a one-time husband of Isadora Duncan).

However, she no longer mentioned divorce or departure to Israel. It was a good sign. I was prepared to endure any kind of punishment except that. I took pains not to remind her, even obliquely, of that old episode of her infidelity. Now that I had mulled things over, I felt profound guilt toward Irina. With the benefit of hindsight I came to see that no matter how angry I was at her, I had no right to deal such a severe and rude blow to her pride. Having realized that, I made up my mind to suffer the bitter aftermath with utter humility.

Irina told everything to my parents and Aunt Lyuba. Each reacted differently.

Lyuba, an earthy and intelligent woman, observed, "Things like that happen to many men pushing fifty. It is a typical midlife crisis. It will pass."

My mother tried to console me, "Irina won't divorce you.

She just wants to give you a scare. But you have no reason to be so despondent, she still loves you."

Father sided with me out of male solidarity. "She's the one who is entirely to blame. With her nasty temper, she had it coming to her all along."

Father had become much weaker since his golden anniversary. His features were getting sharper; he was a very sick man. In the middle of April he was hospitalized and put in the intensive-care unit. I went to the Kaplan Center every day but was no longer able to concentrate on the lectures. Try as I might, I was constantly preoccupied by my desperate plight.

Now I saw Ptitsa only from afar. She did not talk to me; her eyes avoided me. I felt bitter that her love was so abruptly supplanted by disdain. Nor could I write—my feverish brain refused to obey me and produce cogent sentences. Then my agent called with still more bad news—all her attempts to get publishing houses interested ended in failure. In order not to give Irina any further pretext to be angry with me, I cleaned my desk, put all my rough notes away, and even stopped thinking about the book.

When our son was not home, Irina yelled at me, "What have you done! Oh, what have you done!"

I tried to humor her—all in vain. She would erupt again and again. Sometimes I felt I was losing my mind.

On April 29, Mother, Junior, and I went to visit Father. Almost all the time we stayed in his room he lay with his eyes closed, breathing heavily, all but oblivious to our presence. It was an extremely acute case of cardiac-pulmonary weakness. Before leaving, I kissed him.

He opened his eyes and said, "Take care of Mama."

Late that night, the hospital called to notify me that my father had passed away. I picked up Mother and we all went to pay our last respects. His body was still warm.

Father's death brought us somewhat closer together, but the atmosphere at home was still heavy. Mother stayed with us for a few days, but I could see that she was uncomfortable being with us in her grief.

Everything I did at that period was marked by listlessness.

I was crushed and destroyed. One gloomy, endless night I entered the bedroom and lay down next to Irina. She pretended to sleep. I started kissing her, she did not hold back. I pressed myself against her and made a timid attempt at a caress—she responded. And it all happened as if we were making love for the very first time.

She whispered in my ear, "How much we still love each other!"

Well, finally we were through the cleansing flames. In the words of Shakespeare's sonnet:

> No want of conscience hold it that I call
> Her "love" for whose dear love I rise and fall.

My drama stamped me with indifference toward everything I had craved a few short months previously. I stopped writing the book; stopped believing that a publisher would come along; stopped thinking that literature would provide me with a living, no matter how modest. I even stopped publishing my stories in the Russian newspaper. I did devote myself to my studies. But for a long time, all my efforts were in vain. I listened to the tapes distractedly; the words again reverted to mumbo-jumbo; my language proficiency diminished. Everything had to be done from the very beginning again. Against my inner resistance, I imposed a spartan regimen on myself: I rose at 4:30 A.M. and half an hour later I was already at my desk, recapitulating the material from the previous day. At 8:00 A.M. I left for the Kaplan Center, carrying a sandwich for lunch. I was the first to enter the study center and the last to leave it—at 10:00 P.M. I walked both ways so that, in spite of fifteen hours of daily studies, I still managed to cover about five miles on foot. At 11:00 P.M. I went to bed for five to five and a half hours of uneasy sleep.

And my hard work bore fruit, albeit slowly. Unfortunately, the time to take the exam was nearing at a very fast clip. This exam was absolutely necessary for all foreign graduate doctors.

In the face of my self-denial and perseverance, Irina tried to spare me additional aggravation. She was still nervous, but far less irascible and angry. We saw little of each other, and talked rarely. And I saw even less of Junior, who stuck to his own arduous routine. It was peaceful and gloomy in our home.

From time to time, I still went to Radio Liberty to record fragments from my would-be book. Each program brought me a fee of a hundred dollars, which I could little afford to give up. When I went to the radio station for the first time after a month's hiatus, the first person I saw at the station was none other than Ghen, manning his old desk.

"Hello, old boy, glad you dropped by," he said casually.

"I didn't think to see you here again," I said in astonishment.

Ghen shut the door, lowered his voice, and launched into an explanation. "You know, old boy, I worked for two weeks with that company but then decided to return. Here one doesn't have to break one's back, everything is familiar, just like a good old Soviet office. In the private sector they all work like crazy! We started at seven-thirty and toiled without letup till eight P.M. True, I racked up a lot of overtime pay, and career prospects were also good, but . . . too much work! I value my personal freedom above all else. Here I can go out anytime I wish—to take a walk, get a breath of fresh air, relax. While at that company, I did not have a minute to *think* of rest, much less take it. No, sir, Americans have no taste for living; all they can do is work. Strange people, or maybe they have their brains topsy-turvy?"

I did not have a single day's experience of working in the company of Americans so I could not form an opinion as to whether or not they had their heads screwed on topsy-turvy or straight.

"Well, and what about you?" Ghen asked. "Have you signed a contract for your book? How much have you wangled out of the publisher as advance payment?"

I told him my story as my only friend.

"Take it easy, old boy," was all he could say.

But at least he had listened; I needed to unburden myself.

The beautiful Anya was in her studio, as usual absent-minded and nervously chain-smoking. I could not help admiring her looks. But I had to tell her that her check had bounced. It was not a pleasant subject for a conversation, but I wanted my money back.

"Anya, my bank refused to cash your check for fifty dollars," I began, but I could not finish the sentence.

She blushed and jumped up in agitation. "Please forgive me, Doctor dear! I didn't know. It's all my husband's fault. He transferred all my money into his account without telling me."

"Don't take it so hard, no harm was done."

"I feel so bad about it! I can imagine what you thought about me!"

"Believe me, I had other things on my mind."

"All the same, I'm so ashamed. I'll return the money. When do you need it back?"

"Preferably right now."

"I don't have any cash on me. I'm so sorry. Wait, let me try to borrow it from someone."

She grabbed her handbag and rushed out, enormously agitated. I waited and waited, but she did not come back.

Ghen looked in and asked, "You aren't done yet?"

"I am waiting for Anya. Where the hell is she?"

"I saw her leave the building."

"You mean she is gone for the day?"

"Looks like it. Didn't she record your program?"

"No. Why else would I be here?"

Another woman engineer was summoned to do the recording. Anya did not reappear that day.

Some time later she did pay back her debt.

"Please, Doctor, don't be mad at me," she said with a pathetic smile, and added softly, her lips quivering, "I have trouble with my husband. If only you could understand!"

That I certainly could.

But she went on, "I'll take you into my confidence because you are a doctor. My husband has long been totally impotent. To quell my sexual appetite, he got me hooked on liquor and drugs. At first I resisted, but now I can't do without the stimulants. And recently he's been down on his luck. Do you want to know what he does for a living? He plays cards at airports, finding suckers and fleecing them. Have you seen his Cadillac? He uses it as a cab, taking passengers—though not just anybody. They've got a regular gang there. They even deal in narcotics, buying them on the spot from South American couriers. When he lost a lot of money, he decided to go into a new business—pimping. He makes me go with him to the airports more and more frequently, but now he no longer introduces me as his wife. Do you know what I think?" She hesitated and sobbed softly. "I think he plans to turn me into a prostitute. I'm scared of him! Please, Doctor, don't tell anyone. I beg you. I'll be okay, don't worry. I've made up my mind to leave him . . . soon."

I was at a loss for what to say and how to react to her story. That she behaved erratically had been obvious to everybody, but I did not expect to hear this. However, I could not dwell on her misery too long; the day of the ECFMG exam was at hand.

㉙

The exam was held in the huge ballroom of the Statler Hilton Hotel. Registration began at 8:00 A.M. I came half an hour early and found a rapidly swelling crowd of young doctors. The nearly 1,300 men and women generated as much noise and prattle as a good-sized bird market. It was immediately apparent that nearly half of them were Indians and Pakistanis. Indian faces dominated the crowd; some of the women wore saris, some men turbans. Another large group was made up of Orientals: Filipinos, Thais, Chinese, Indonesians. There were people from Latin America and the Caribbean: Puerto Rico, Haiti, Jamaica, the Dominican Republic, Grenada. Europeans were few, mostly Russians, Poles, Romanians, Italians, Spaniards, Greeks. By contrast, there were quite a few Americans, graduates of foreign medical schools in Italy, Spain, Mexico, the Philippines, and Caribbean islands. And almost everybody was young—not yet thirty.

I was stunned by the numbers and ethnic diversity of the examinees. It was an invasion: thousands of physicians from underdeveloped countries, where the educational system was far inferior to that in America, rushed to fill the gaps in the U.S. health-care structure. I could never imagine that my colleagues in more than half the world had it so bad!

And other questions kept dogging me: Did America really need so many foreign doctors? Was a country with such rich educational resources really incapable of meeting its need with its own citizens? Why did so many native Americans go to study at subpar medical schools abroad to bring their inferior standards back home?

People representing different cultures, religions, languages, political leanings, traditions, and professional backgrounds got together in the grand ballroom of the old New York hotel. Under the watchful eye of proctors, all examinees were to answer 500 multiple-choice questions—some a single line, some half a page long—in eight hours.

I could hardly imagine how the whole affair could be organized to avoid confusion and violations. It was clear that many of the examinees had developed highly sophisticated methods of cheating and exchanging information. There was much talk on the subject in the waiting crowd. Some of them knew the answers beforehand and shared them with their own friends. Thus, for instance, a rumor made the rounds that some of those who had taken the exam in the Far East—Indonesia, the Philippines, or India—several hours previously (due to the time difference) had already dictated the questions and answers to their compatriots in New York over long-distance telephone. Others made arrangements to sit one behind another so as to be able to swap information. There were quite a few married couples, no doubt each with its own system. Finally, I recalled the offer to buy the exam. I would not in the least be surprised to learn that some of the physicians had already paid for the "guaranteed success."

The Russian group was readily indentifiable by a telltale sign: It alone was dominated by women, most of them in their forties and older. I also saw the Communist doctor who was my prime suspect in connection with that mysterious night call. I listened intently to his hoarse voice and concluded that my suspicions were well-founded.

Many of them were plotting to use the various tricks I could recall from my student past.

"So remember, if the right answer is marked *A,* you show me one finger; if it is *B,* two fingers; *C,* three fingers; *D,* four; and *E,* five. Clear? I'll also use this code to signal you. And don't forget to keep your hand on your knee to my side of the aisle, out of the proctor's line of sight."

"My sister will be in the lobby while the exam is on. She has a textbook in her handbag, and as soon as I go to the ladies room, she will follow me, pretending we are total strangers. Naturally, she'll have the handbag with her. In the ladies room, I'll look up whatever I need in the textbook, whereupon we'll leave separately."

As a former professor, I felt it would be embarrassing to be part of such schemes. Accordingly, I kept aloof.

It took the organizers about an hour and a half to set up all the examinees, brief them on the rules, and distribute tests. Along with everybody else, I was issued a numbered, sealed booklet. On command, we all opened our booklets and proceeded to answer the questions. Silence set in, broken only by the rustling of turning pages. The first three questions were familiar to me from the Kaplan course, and I had no trouble finding the right answers, but the next ten or so baffled me and I lost a lot of time pondering them. But there was no time for thinking. Either one knew the answer or one didn't, in which case the best thing to do was to go on to the next question without delay. Unfortunately, I did not possess the know-how of handling an exam of this sort. Besides, I experienced considerable difficulty in grasping the meaning of some of the longer questions. I had to read them over and over again, losing still more valuable time. So it came as no surprise when an hour later I found myself far behind schedule, for my immediate neighbors were deep in the booklet while I was still stuck on the first page. I grew edgy and hurried up. Within the three hours prior to the first break, 180 questions were to be answered, and it was better to give any randomly selected answer than none.

The strain of reading and agitation took their toll. A buzzing started in my head. Without interruption, I swallowed an aspirin pill I had the foresight to keep at hand. Gradually the buzzing died down, but then all my muscles started to ache as a result of my constrained posture. From time to time I watched my young American neighbors out of the corner of my eye. They read the questions and marked the answers rapidly. It was clear that they knew everything and cracked the questions like nuts. Many of the Indians also worked fast. Quite a few of the examinees began handing in their answer sheets an hour before the deadline, while I still faced a lot of unread questions. When break was called, I still had about twenty unanswered questions. At the very last instant I marked the same answer, C, on all of them; some of the Cs conceivably could be right.

During the first break the crowd was even noisier. The examinees feverishly compared answers and argued about their merits. The Russians bombarded Americans and Indians with questions, and the latter answered readily—why not, it was too late to make changes.

Listening to all the talk around me, I soon found out that I had made several mistakes, particularly in relation to basic sciences. And the exam was by no means over. How many more mistakes was I going to make? Again I attacked the hundreds of questions, almost half of which were only vaguely comprehensible to me. The medical portion of the exam was followed by an English test, which if anything was even tougher: grammar, language structure, and conversational English with the text recorded on tape.

A woman who had been running to the ladies room almost every hour left once more and did not reappear. During the next break I saw her weeping in a circle of sympathetic friends.

". . . so the fourth time I was followed into the ladies room by a woman. . . . How was I supposed to know who she was? And she turned out to be a proctor . . . Oy! . . . And the instant I opened the textbook she pounced on me . . . and dragged me to the chief. . . . Initially they intended to kick me out but then relented and allowed me to continue . . . but with a warning that my only chance to pass would be to score at least ten points above the average. Ten points! I'll never be able to score that high. Mother dear, what are they doing to me-e-e-e!"

To my surprise, she was the only one caught cheating, although scores of proctors kept an eye on us at all times.

The exam ended at 8:00 P.M. I was completely drained.

Young doctors lingered at the hotel discussing the answers, but I hurried home.

Irina was waiting for me with dinner on the table. She watched compassionately as I listlessly munched my first meal of the day. And I talked and talked, sharing with her my impression of the exam. It really made a powerful impact on me. Although I had taught medical students and young doctors for seventeen years, I could not imagine a test of knowledge in all areas of medicine could be that serious and thoroughgoing. Really, this exam was as different from the ones we had conducted in Russia's medical schools as American supermarkets were from Russian food stores.

I was impressed by the carefully thought-out organization and the precision of execution. As for the failure of the organizers to detect the cheating, it couldn't be helped. A crowd so motley and large was bound to contain its share of cheats— people coming from all over the world were bearers of deeply embedded traditions and habits born of their ethnic characteristics and cultures. Honesty is a problem of ethics; dishonesty is a matter of traditions.

Already plunging into slumber, I told Irina, "You know, to pass right off the bat I would have had to come to this country twenty years ago, and even then it would have been iffy. But don't you worry, I'll pass that darned exam!"

Irina heaved a deep sigh. She felt sorry for me.

40

The very next day I was again at my desk at the Kaplan Center working hard. I was sure there was no way I could have passed the exam. To make the task of memorizing the abstract formulas of scientific fundamentals somewhat easier, I started drawing illustrations of the mechanisms of all cell and tissue processes. Visual memory helped fix the information in my aging brain.

Long and tedious weeks and months of arduous work dragged by. My only source of pleasure was American medical textbooks. I was happy with the progress in my reading ability, although I still had to consult the dictionary hundreds of times a day. Besides, I really liked the way the textbooks were composed.

During my life in Russia I had read hundreds of textbooks and also collaborated on a few textbooks of my own. But in Russian textbooks, the material was always littered with obligatory references to the political works of the founders of Marxism-Leninism, as well as quotations from medical authorities recommended by the Party. Special medical censorship saw to it that the rule was complied with. The state-owned medical publishing house, Meditsina, the only one of its kind in the whole country, laid down the rules: Most references were to be to Russian authors, with foreign sources accounting for not more than a third of the total—and the fewer the better. Straightforward and clear-cut presentation was a rare exception. Editors manhandled the textbooks so badly that the products of their labors were hardly readable at all. The printing quality was poor, the execrable illustrations were few and far between.

But even those inferior textbooks were in short supply—along with all other necessities. It took special luck to buy one in a bookstore, and medical school libraries were so poorly stocked that as often as not one book had to be shared by two students.

The first thing that struck me about American medical textbooks was their exceptional printing quality. But I was even more impressed by the manner in which material was presented: terseness of thought, clarity and precision of language, strict selection of quotations and references, free of flotsam. And of course, an incomparably richer bibliography, although I found American authors referred to their Russian counterparts even more scantily than the other way around. Russian medical science is all but unknown in this country.

Finally, paralleling the general abundance of America, textbooks are also plentiful. Any subject is covered in dozens of widely available books, one better than the next one, so that choice is a serious matter.

It is good to be able to open one's eyes a little wider even at the age of fifty—better late than never. The more I learned, the more I liked it. For the second time in my life I studied medicine, and again the world of knowledge, which I had missed or forgotten, opened up before me. Thoroughly hooked now, I studied some areas in considerable depth. Other students besieged me with questions, and I read them microlectures on the structure and functions of DNA or RNA, for example, using my own drawings as illustrations.

At last, I received my results. Barely controlling my hands, I tore the envelope open and quickly found the score: 67 for the medical exam (eight points below the passing score) and Unsatisfactory on the English test. I spent the rest of the day in gloomy meditation. When Irina came home from work, we went for a stroll along Central Park West. I talked and talked, arguing with myself what changes should be made in my training to be successful the next time. Irina kept sympathetic silence. She again felt sorry for me.

She was gradually calming down; her nerves were getting steadier. Our relationship had entered a new phase. Earlier, each new hardship had only driven the wedge between us deeper, whereas now travails bound us ever closer.

I was not overly discouraged by my failure, for I knew that to expect otherwise would have been unrealistic. However, my spirits were getting more and more dejected. The plight of my mother, alone and still homeless, dampened my mood even further.

"You know, sometimes I wander through the streets thinking, how could it happen?" she told me. "There was my husband, a wonderful man, a marvelous physician who had done so much good for so many people. All of a sudden he dies and—nothing, not a trace of him. There was our life, which we had built together for half a century, and again nothing, nothing left. . . ."

I felt acutely sorry for her. But is there a way to help a widow, even if she is one's mother? No such remedy exists. Her woe is intensely personal and private.

Soon Mother was given a one-bedroom apartment in a city-subsidized building on our street. But her joy was poisoned.

"Just to think that Father died a bare few months before he could see this apartment! What a source of joy it would have been to him. He wanted so desperately to have his own apartment in this country. In Russia, it took us three decades to get an apartment of our own, while here I've had to wait merely twelve months. But it has come too late."

All of a sudden, my beloved Aunt Lyuba, who had done so much for all of us in this country, passed away. It was her visits to Moscow in the 1960s that had planted the seeds of my desire to see America. I felt bitterly sorry to have achieved nothing while she was still alive. How much joy and pride she would have derived from the knowledge that we were getting off to a good start in our second life!

Ironically, the day she died I received news that *Medical Economics* had accepted my article for publication. I had long forgotten about the material translated by my friend Mike from Washington, D.C.

The journal serialized my article in two issues. I received $1,000 in royalties and another $1,000 as an award for the best article of the year. The money could not have been more timely, for we still eked out a living on Irina's salary alone. And just at that time the grant under which Irina worked ran out, and she had to look for another job. This time around, however, she knew what to do. Without fear or panic she went to Personnel and soon landed a job at the same university, at the cardiac physiology laboratory under Dr. Michael Rosen. This job was even more to her liking than the old one, and the salary was higher—$14,000.

At the end of 1979, an international event occurred with enormous implications for Russian Jews. The Soviet armed forces invaded Afghanistan. The U.S. government banned grain sales to Russia; the Soviets retaliated by halting Jewish emigration. So emigration ended as it had begun—abruptly. That was exactly what I had feared so much while waiting for permission to leave. Thank God we had left just in time and now were safely in America.

"Every morning I thank God that we are here, not there," my mother said. "As I wake up in the morning my first thought is that I am in America! I went to St. Vladimir's Church to thank the Lord."

I decided to go to the synagogue, which I had not visited for a long time, to sit and think, which was my way of praying.

41

Soon the day came when we were again assembled in the grand ballroom of the Statler Hilton. The crowd of examinees was equally large and again dominated by Indians and Orientals, although the faces were new to me. Only the Russian group was basically a carryover from the previous exam; there were several newcomers, but the old-timers were almost at full strength. This time I felt more confident, though not nearly enough to be a sure success. From the very start I felt how much easier it was for me to answer the questions. They were not repeats from the previous exam, but there was a lot of symmetry.

Practically all questions contained a hidden catch, and only thorough knowledge of the subject could lead unfailingly to the correct answer. Lacking knowledge of many theoretical subjects, I had not noticed this subtlety the previous time. But now I could guess the most likely answer even as I read the question, and then quickly running down the choice of answers I could put my finger on the one I had already deduced. Thus the second exam was a creative process for me. But what a price in toil and sweat I had had to pay to attain such a level!

This time I was comparatively calm after the exam. Waiting for the result, I continued my studies and made new drawings for my own sake. I even decided to resume my program at Radio Liberty, which had moved to a new location on Broadway in the meantime.

When I called Ghen, he said, "Have you heard the bad news, old boy? Anya is dead."

"Dead? Why? How?"

"It happened last week, like a bolt from the blue. She was taking a bath at home and drowned by accident."

I was crushed. The beautiful Anya, the tragic belle of the immigrant community, had perished! And under singularly strange circumstances, too. Suspicious, I made up my mind to find out as much as I could about her death. When I came to the radio station, Ghen told me some of the details and Anya's closest girlfriend supplied some more. What struck me most was that Anya had been taking the fatal bath in her dressing gown.

It became immediately clear to me that the beautiful girl had committed suicide.

"You think so, old boy?" Ghen asked naïvely.

"It couldn't be anything else. Believe me, I've seen a lot of suicides over my long career in medicine."

"No, it can't be true."

"But who would ever take a bath in a gown?"

"Maybe you're right," Ghen concluded. "But it's still hard to believe. Rumor has it that the autopsy showed she was drunk at the time of her death and even had some narcotics in her body. The last few days she had behaved strangely—nervous, restless, absent-minded."

"She was steeling herself for suicide," I said. "She was thinking of death all those days. That accounts for her strange behavior. When she stepped into the bath, she knew she would be found dead, and did not want to be seen naked by strangers. That's why she put on her gown."

"Perhaps you're right," Ghen said grudgingly.

"It's all her husband's fault." Anya's friend joined the conversation. "She'd complained to me about him for a long time. He's a creep!"

"Where was he at the time?" I asked.

"He wasn't at home when she died. The police interrogated him and even kept him under suspicion for a few days, but they couldn't find anything implicating him in her death.

Still, I'm telling you, it's all his fault," the lady insisted. "If only you knew the horrible things she'd told me about him. I don't want to stir up that filth so as not to offend the memory of my poor dead friend."

I, for one, knew well enough what she meant. As I remembered my conversations with Anya, everything led to the inevitable conclusion that her death was an escape from the fate to which he had condemned her.

Sometime later I read in the paper about the "mysterious death of a Russian immigrant." It was reported that the husband of the late Anya, Yuri B., was found shot to death in his apartment. The police ruled out the robbery motive in Yuri's murder because $10,000 in cash was found in the apartment and there were no traces of a struggle. It looked like a typical gangland-style execution. Yuri's murder also provided a possible clue to Anya's suicide—she might have decided to kill herself before being killed by the Mafia.

I felt sad remembering the beautiful girl. Mysterious are the ways of immigrants' providence. . . .

I received a letter from Dr. Irving Cooper, an internationally renowned brain surgeon. He wrote that he had read my articles in *Medical Economics,* that he liked them, and that they had inspired him to organize an international symposium to discuss problems of socialized medical care. He invited me to speak on the subject of Russia's public health-care system. The symposium was to be held in Florida; I would be paid a fee of $1,000 and full travel expenses. For starters, he invited me for preliminary discussions to Valhalla, where he headed the Institute of Neurosurgery of the New York College of Medicine.

On a hot summer day, Irina and I went to Valhalla by train and then took a bus. Irina accompanied me as an interpreter, for I was unsure of my ability to maintain a business conversation. My poor fluency in English still dogged me. I also had another problem, a torn-off sole on one of the shoes of my only summer pair. It hobbled me, and when I sat down, I tried to tuck my feet deep under the chair. The need to focus on my feet all the time was unnerving.

The institute was a model of a classic academic establishment. The secretary escorted us to the waiting room decorated with his diplomas from all over the world. I counted sixty of them and sat down. Soon we were invited to see Dr. Cooper. A typical American, tall and gray-haired, he met us at the door of his office, put us in armchairs, and proceeded to explain how glad he was to see Irina and me and how happy he was to know that a distinguished specialist of my caliber had elected to live and work in America. Meanwhile the distinguished specialist was busy tucking his feet as far out of sight as he could. I told our host that, true, I did live in America now, but I did not work yet, faced as I was with the need to pass the exam and undergo residency training first. He assured me with courteous confidence that my training program might be shortened in deference to my considerable experience.

Then we discussed the forthcoming symposium, and he extended an invitation to Irina as well, apparently realizing that I could not cope without her linguistic help. Finally Dr. Cooper took us on a tour of his hospital. He wanted to hear my opinion on a few of his recent operations. Trying not to lift my feet lest the torn-off sole thump, I slid behind him down the corridors, aided in no small measure by the freshly polished floor. As I moved in this curious fashion, I could easily pass for a speed skater in training or for a madman. And when we approached a patient, I would immediately press my knees to the bed, hiding my feet under it.

A tactful and polite gentleman, Dr. Cooper never mentioned my gyrations. When we were taking our leave, he told us that one of his two homes, in Naples, Florida, where the symposium was to be held, would be at our disposal. I thanked him and made a mental vow to buy a new pair of shoes for the symposium—particularly in view of the forthcoming fee.

In general, poverty did not distress me. Hectic studies, which occupied all my day from early morning till late at night, left me little time to worry about our finances. I recalled how Aaron Burr, a famous figure in American history, lived in European exile in abject poverty after a stint as vice president of the United States and never complained about his circumstances either.

But sometimes poverty did intrude, when contrasted with somebody else's affluence. Once I was walking on Central Park West in exceptionally foul weather, when a Buick Regal squealed to a stop beside me. The driver stuck his head out and called to me in Russian, "Want a lift, Doctor?"

It took me a few seconds to recognize the watchmaker who had been my fellow guest at the hotel early in the immigration period. Then he had been sour to everything he saw and never stopped cursing. Now, driving me in his shining Buick, he no longer found fault with America and concentrated on his successes instead.

"I have a small business of my own, with two employees—fellow Russian immigrants. I've set up a connection with sailors who shuttle between Russia and Latin America. They bring Russian watch movements that I buy at bargain prices through agents. We insert those movements in the cases of famous Swiss watches and sell them to the public as genuine articles—cash only, please, and forget about the sales tax. Naturally, people snap up my goodies. But let me give you a friendly piece of advice: Don't buy my merchandise. You'd be better off buying a genuine brand-name watch. It'll cost you about three hundred bucks, but you'll get the real thing!"

Sitting in his Buick, nothing could be further from my mind than the idea of buying an expensive watch. I was thinking that for two decades I had owned cars in Moscow. I had been a real automobile buff and had loved to drive, but now there was no knowing when I would be able to get behind the wheel of my own car. That Regal was one hell of a set of wheels, but not for me.

Like a natural disaster, immigration broke down everybody and everything. It was impossible to predict who would perish and who would survive; who would sink to the bottom and who would prosper. One thing was clear though: One had to fight for a place in this new life.

The time was approaching when the exam results were due. Breathing hard with anxious anticipation, I grabbed the envelope from the mailbox—what did it have in store for me?

I failed by just one point, failed again! It was almost a full year since I had begun cramming, and yet it was not enough. What a disappointment—to miss by a hair! Fate conspired to put a limit to my dreams; the unlucky streak was still on. My spirits sank to a new low.

When Irina came home from work, no explanations were needed. She found me brooding in silence over the medical drawings I had made, my hands tucked between my knees. Irina sat down beside me and put her arms around me. Thus we sat for a few minutes, gloomily pondering the same dismal prospects.

Then I said with savage impotence, "If all my efforts to pass the exam fail, I'll get a job as a barker for a brothel. I can see it now—me standing on the street corner, pressing dirty pictures into the hands of passersby. A pretty future, ain't it?"

In response, Irina showed me *The New York Times* she had picked up in a subway car.

"Look," she said. "There is a help-wanted ad here."

I glanced casually at the ad she underlined. A hospital in Manhattan needed a paramedic. I didn't care one way or the other.

"Okay," I said indifferently. "Let's send them my résumé."

43

One morning, my mother came to us all aflutter. Pointing to an issue of the Russian daily newspaper, she blurted out excitedly, "It says here that Leo Golyakhovsky, a former Czarist military officer, passed away. Don't you see, he was my cousin! Here—the patronymic is the same. The obit contains a telephone number. Let's call, maybe some of my relatives are still alive!" (When I was seven, my parents had given me my mother's Russian family name because I was taunted by my classmates for having my Jewish father's name—Zak.)

It was a big surprise indeed. Several of my mother's relatives, all of them high-ranking officers of the Russian Imperial Army, had left Russia with their families in 1918, in the wake of the Bolshevik Revolution. For sixty-two years Mother had not had word of them and did not even know if any of them had survived the hasty flight from the Communists.

I dialed the number. Just as we thought, several members of the family had survived and lived in Yugoslavia till the end of World War II, whereupon they again had to flee Communist persecution, this time to America. Two of Mother's female cousins and the recently deceased cousin had safely made it to the New World. There was also a niece, Lyudmilla, an M.D. The second and third generations were already in evidence.

Mother went to attend the funeral and to see her relatives after a separation of sixty-two years. It was a moment of sobs and laughter, exclamations and silence. Her relatives lived in New Jersey and in Chicago. They vied with one another inviting us to visit. Irina and I were too busy to travel, but Mother met with her newly found kin on many occasions.

Also, Mother began to study English—at seventy-eight! She steadfastly attacked the language, studied several hours every day, attended a language school for immigrants, and, bit by bit, learned to speak a little. But of course, given her age and the stressful life of an immigrant, she could not hope to acquire a good command of English. Even what little she did pick up was a startling achievement, considering the odds.

Oh yes, indeed, the stresses of immigrant existence were too high for all of us. Even I, with my indomitable optimism, found the burden all but unbearable. For all my effort, the fight for a second life had so far yielded fruit so scanty as to be barely discernible. The prospects for success were inexorably receding like the horizon—the further you go, the farther away it moves. An enormous concentration of effort was needed, while my stamina was all but depleted. I could feel my health was deteriorating rapidly.

Something strange happened to my left leg. Suddenly such an acute pain developed in my thigh that I could hardly walk at all. I had not fallen or bumped my leg, but the day the pain first arrived I had walked about a hundred blocks at a fast clip, hurrying to my studies. On the way back I could barely limp to the bus stop. What could it be? For several days I hid my condition from Irina, trying not to show my limp. But my winces and bent posture did not escape her notice.

"What's wrong with you?" she asked.

"Nothing serious. It'll go away." I tried to sound as nonchalant as I could.

"But what's the matter?! You're in pain," she insisted.

"My thigh hurts. I don't have the foggiest notion why."

"Maybe you should have it X-rayed?"

"Let's wait. I hope it will go away by itself."

However, the pain persisted, driving Irina wild with anxiety. I did my best to dispel her fears, but she grew increasingly distraught.

"I'm scared for you," she said. "You've changed enormously, particularly since you developed this thigh condition. Maybe I'm to blame for it."

"You?" I asked in surprise. "How on earth can it be your fault?"

"You know, when we were in the midst of that time, I was really mad at you, mad as hell. So once I went to the chapel in Presbyterian Hospital and beseeched God to punish you: 'Dear Lord, if you exist, please make him suffer.' "

"Why, it's nonsense," I said, putting my arms around her.

"But I am afraid he had heard my prayer," Irina went on. "When your leg started to hurt, I went to the chapel once more and again prayed: 'Please, Lord, relent. I didn't ask you to cripple him!' "

She pressed herself sheepishly against me. I felt like crying and laughing at the same time; I did not believe in miracles, but I could see how hurt she must have been to implore the Almighty to visit revenge upon her husband.

Irina kept insisting that I go to the doctor and have my thigh X-rayed. I stubbornly refused, primarily because I felt I could not spare any time from my studies. Besides, we could not afford a visit to the doctor or the costly X rays. I decided to wait awhile; maybe the affliction would loosen its grip by itself.

Sometimes, when I was on my way to or from the learning center, the pain would become so intolerable that I could not take a single step. Then I would go plop down on the curb, right where the attack caught me, swallow a Tylenol pill, bend over, and start rocking back and forth to alleviate the pain. At such moments, I must have seemed a strange figure, but in the streets of New York City one can slowly bleed to death without attracting anybody's attention. Not once did a single passerby volunteer help.

Once, however, when I was in my rocking mode, a tiny fuzzy dog ran up to me, sniffed me, then lifted his hind leg and urinated right at my side. The dog was on a long leash, the other end of which was held by his owner, a massive man with a thick beard. Thus forced to stop, he proceeded to inspect me from his impressive height with some surprise.

"Excuse me, but are you Jewish?" he asked suddenly.

With equal surprise I glanced up at him. "My leg hurts, that's all. But your guess is right, I'm Jewish."

"And what country are you from? Judging by your accent, you must be French."

"N-n-n-o," I mumbled through clenched teeth, fighting a fresh stab of pain.

"From Scandinavia then?"

"N-n-n-o."

"Poland?"

Damn him, what does he want from me? Even his dog was pulling away, straining at the leash, but he still towered over me, pressing on.

"I'm from Russia."

"I thought so!" he said unexpectedly. "Are you an immigrant?"

"Yes."

"Do you plan to go back to Russia?"

"I've told you I'm an immigrant."

"Yes, of course. Do you like it here?"

"You mean here on the pavement?"

But my bolt of wit was lost on him.

"No, I mean in general—do you like it in America?"

"Yes, I do, especially when my leg doesn't hurt."

"And what's wrong with your leg?"

"Who knows?"

"You should consult a doctor, he'll tell you."

"I'm a doctor myself."

"You? A doctor? Hey, it's great! Do you practice medicine here?"

"No. I'm still training for the board exam."

"Tell me, is it true that medical care is free in Russia?"

I stood up and limped away, but he followed, peppering me with questions, all of a rather primitive variety. Finally I lost patience and told him, "I've written a book that answers all your questions."

"What's the title? Who's the publisher? Can I get it at the library?"

"Unfortunately, the book has not been published yet. Maybe never."

"Why?"

"I can't get a publisher."

"Have you written your book in English?" he asked.

"No. My English isn't good enough for that. I wrote it in Russian, but I have a translator."

"What you need is an American co-author!" he exclaimed.

"I've thought about such an option. But I don't know anyone."

"I can help you!" he shouted in great excitement, his small eyes squinting at me. "I'm a free-lance journalist and co-author of two books. I think I could work on your manuscript with you. I personally know the editors-in-chief of all magazines and publishing houses. I could talk to some of them and get them interested in your book. They trust me," he added boastfully.

His perseverance gave me an uneasy feeling.

I did not like him. But then it was merely my first impression. If he was telling the truth, his offer sounded tempting. After all, he had written two books! We exchanged telephone numbers.

44

My condition failed to improve. Clinical self-examination by palpation and checking the freedom of movement and sensitivity indicated that the pain spread along the femoral nerve. But why had it flared up with such intensity? I might have suffered a hemorrhage in the nerve trunk followed by inflammation, in professional terms—neuronopraxis, a rather rare disease. By the same token, the pain might have been a symptom of some other pathology, say a tumor. What kind of tumor? There was no saying without an X ray. I made up my mind to go to the emergency room of a hospital because there treatment was provided for everybody. I knew that the emergency room physician would be relatively inexperienced, a resident or a house officer certainly far less competent in such matters than I was myself. But it was paramount for me to see the X ray with my own eyes. If it proved to be a tumor, then maybe I would have to consult an experienced specialist and pay for the consultation. But who knows whether there would be any point in that? The tumor might turn out to be a variety that would defy any human effort to defeat it. This particular site usually hosted a deadly sarcoma, in which case the outcome was a foregone conclusion.

I did not share my reflections with Irina. There was no point in scaring her with unconfirmed speculations. One day we both went by subway to Presbyterian Hospital, where she worked at a research lab. We came to the Emergency Room.

It was my first visit to an emergency room in America and the first ever as a patient. However tense I was because of the pain, I could not suppress my curiosity and avidly watched the American system of medical care in action. The environment was a world apart from what I was used to in Russia. But the atmosphere—the fuss and bustle, the throngs of patients, the harried staff—was a carbon copy.

We had to wait for a long time. All the doctors were busy tending to patients with really urgent problems: hemorrhage, loss of consciousness, acute chest or stomach pain. Poor people having no medical insurance, myself included, were huddled in a large waiting room. Irina sat at my side, trying to alleviate my physical and mental anguish. I had not shared my worst apprehensions with her, but I could see in her face that hers were hardly more optimistic than mine.

Her doctor's gown and the ID card of a medical center employee were instrumental in slightly accelerating my progress in being seen.

As expected, the physician who examined me was a man younger than my son. On learning that I was an orthopedic surgeon, that doctor, actually a first-year intern, was abashed and told me frankly that I would be better off consulting somebody else. But I informed him that all I needed was a look at the X ray of my thigh.

While the X ray was being developed, Irina went for a short while to her lab. I rested on a cot, alone in the small examination room, thinking, It's a good thing she's gone, because very shortly the youngster will bring my X ray and one look at his face will tell me right off that I am in trouble. Or maybe he won't be able to read the X ray, but I will—at a glance. I've seen thousands of X rays of malignant tumors and knew their contours. But it's one thing to see a tumor in somebody else's X ray, and another thing altogether to be confronted with it in one's own. If worse comes to worst, what then? If what I fear comes true and I have just a few months to live, I must complete my book. It will be something to remember me by and maybe a source of some material comfort to my dear ones.

The doctor entered wearing a confused expression on his face.

"You know, there's something there," he said hesitantly.

"What is it?" I asked with a lump in my throat.

"I think just age-related changes. But you'd better have a look for yourself."

He put the film in the X-ray film viewer, and I fixed my eyes on the picture, raising myself on the cot by the elbows, and feeling beads of sweat breaking out on my forehead. Inch by inch I carefully explored the X ray, trying not to miss a single detail. No, there were no signs of bone degeneration. My worst premonition was not borne out. I fell back on the pillow, a feeling of enormous fatigue flooding my body. At that instant, Irina came into the room and her anxious glance brushed the doctor's face, then mine, then the film in the viewer.

"Thank God, nothing bad," I told her.

Irina smiled weakly, not daring to believe the good news. The doctor scratched his head. "Still, you'd be well advised to consult a real specialist," he said.

"Of course, the doctor is right, you should see a good specialist," Irina agreed eagerly. "Who's the best orthopedist in our hospital, Doctor?"

"In the whole of New York City you won't find anyone more competent that Dr. Stinfeld, our professor and former chief."

"In that case that's who we'll consult," Irina said firmly.

I did not resist; let her have her way. The tense wait for the verdict left me drained. But I also felt a surge of jubilation; there was a future after all, and I could plan for it again.

When we were leaving the hospital, I asked Irina to show me the chapel.

She led me to a small, quiet, semidark interdenominational chapel in the passageway between two hospital buildings. We sat there in silence for a few minutes, holding hands. And I pledged to God that come what may, I would finish my book.

45

Whether due to the salutary effect of time or because I knew now that I did not have cancer, my pain abated. I was still sure that no doctor would be able to help me but decided to yield to Irina's insistence—mostly to assuage her worries. She got me an appointment with Dr. Stinfeld who, sight unseen, prescribed a battery of tests and a dozen additional X rays as a preliminary to the examination. Although I had to pay for all those analyses, the depth and thoroughness of his approach impressed me. In Russia, we never did so many tests, mainly for lack of technical capability. Here everything was complete within one day—incredible speed; a Russian hospital would take from five to seven days to do fewer tests.

Dr. Stinfeld had a stupendous office: several rooms stocked with equipment I never imagined existed and the facilities stunned me. In spite of my poor condition, I could not help thinking, What a pleasure it must be to work in such an environment, with such equipment!

Dr. Stinfeld himself, his manner and the thoroughness with which he examined me, made a marvelous impression. Still, he failed to arrive at an unequivocal conclusion.

"To be on the safe side," he said, "let me refer you to an experienced neurological surgeon. Let's hear what he says."

The neurosurgeon had an even more imposing and splendidly equipped office and was even more famous than the orthopedist. However, he could not diagnose my affliction either.

Then I told him my assumption that I had had an inflammation of the femoral nerve and even drew a picture to illustrate where and how the pain reaction had occurred in my view. After a long discussion he agreed with my theory.

It was two years since I had last approached a patient. Now fate made me my own patient, with a very difficult diagnosis to boot. For all its sad ramifications, the experience suggested that I had not lost my diagnostic touch. The question was, however, whether or not I was destined to ever treat patients besides myself. Having seen at first hand the exceptional professional conditions and technical capabilities of American physicians made me miss my calling still more acutely. How long would I have to endure this abstinence?

When I finally began to recover, Irina's health gave out. She found it even harder to withstand the stresses of our life than I did, and the trials of recent years left her on the verge of total collapse. She needed rest badly, but we had no money for a vacation. We discussed what limited options were available to us, seeking possibilities of inexpensive rest. Finally, we calculated that the most affordable way of spending a vacation would be to rent a subcompact car and stay a couple of weeks in upstate New York. But we did not even have a credit card. Ghen came to the rescue. He rented a car in his own name, indicated in the form that I would be his driver, I paid him back in cash.

"Who knows what tomorrow may bring?" Irina and I mused. "So let's live like there is no tomorrow."

For the first time in more than two years, I sat behind the wheel of a car, driving home in a blue Chevy Citation and experiencing pleasant and all-but-forgotten sensations. Irina and Junior were waiting at the curb when I proudly pulled over. During the previous quarter of a century, I had owned six cars. Driving a car gave me a long-forgotten feeling of well-being. Irina was happy as well. She always liked to ride with me although she could not drive. (Very few Russian women can drive; a woman driver is a rare sight indeed in that country.)

The next day, we set out for the Adirondacks by way of Albany. I got repeatedly confused about the road signs and lost my way more than once. Russia has no expressways, with their systems of exit and entrance ramps and hundreds of signs. All they have there are narrow highways with level crossings and traffic lights.

Everything we saw on the way seemed to spring straight out of the few American movies we had seen: gas stations, motels, McDonald's and Howard Johnson's restaurants, farms in the distance. It was our maiden American road trip and for the first time we felt like true Americans—no different from everybody around.

"How strange, we are driving in America, our America!" we kept saying.

We checked into a small, old motel on the shore of Blue Lake. The landscape was beautiful, the air clear and mountain crisp. It was a wonderful place for hiking. But Irina was so weak that she could barely manage a few steps at a time. Now it was my turn to play the nursemaid, never leaving her side.

When Irina regained some of her strength, we set out on a tour of upstate New York resorts: the Thousand Islands, Finger Lakes, the northern Catskills. We had never seen so much beauty, so many varied natural wonders concentrated within a relatively limited area. Comparing it with the fairly uniform and dull Russian landscape, I felt, again and again, an upswelling of joy at the thought that this was now my country, that I had left Russia behind for good. Man does not depend solely on social conditions and laws of society; he is a child of nature as well. Love for the nature of his country is man's filial feeling. Irina and I fell in love with our beautiful new land. We were in a constant state of enthusiastic euphoria.

It had been a long time since we shared such a strong feeling of joy and contentment. The mutual reveling in America's beauty brought peace to our tired souls and helped nurture our newly resurgent love. Thus American nature paid us back for our affection—in kind.

On the way back we drove to Boston, with a view to spending a day on Cape Cod. The crazy traffic of the metropolis squeezed me into multitiered crisscrossing expressways. With my lack of experience, I was so nonplussed by the seeming chaos that I rolled along in the motor avalanche without the remotest idea of the direction. It was impossible and even dangerous to stop—streams of cars were hurtling along like whirlwinds on both sides. Somehow or other we passed through Boston and turned south, still in a daze from the unnerving experience. All of a sudden, we saw an ancient ship and old buildings to our left. What could they be? We read the name on the plaque: Plymouth Rock. Aha, some dim recollection told me it was a site of historical significance. We decided to stop for a short while . . . and ended up spending the whole day in the beautiful museum.

The story of the Pilgrims coming ashore in December 1620, of the hardships that befell the first 102 American pioneers, the deaths of most of the settlers during the first year, the suffering, hunger, and helplessness, gave us a powerful jolt. And the monument to the American Indian who was the Pilgrims' friend and protector, who taught them how to farm their new land, was a symbol of friendship in adversity.

Isn't it the sublime example of the cost one must pay to become free, I thought. And here we are, 360 years later, fighting for our right to be free, fighting for our future. Of course, there can be no comparison between our difficulties and the hell they had to go through. But one truth holds today as firmly as it did centuries ago: It takes determination and courage to earn the right to be an American.

e returned home well rested and invigorated. With my determination to fight for my future thus replenished, I resumed my studies for yet another round of the examination ordeal. This time I felt that my stock of knowledge and ability to walk through the maze of intricate questions were sufficient to pass the medical exam. As for its language portion, the complicated exam in grammar, syntax, and vocabulary was still beyond my ken.

Stanley L., the journalist with whom I had talked while writhing in pain on the curb, called me.

"I've bought a house," he said. "Come to the housewarming party and bring your wife. I've already talked around about your manuscript."

It was quite a while since I had opened my manuscript or even given it any thought—so preoccupied with my studies had I been.

Besides, I knew that the dim hopes I pinned on the book made Irina angry. But somehow I got the nerve to broach the subject and nonchalantly initiated her into my dealings with Stanley.

"As a matter of fact, I have little hope of success," I finished my story. "But all of a sudden this journalist, a professional, pops up and he seems genuinely eager to help. Of course, if you think I shouldn't dredge up this whole book business, let's forget it, and I won't talk about it."

Irina knew that the book was my cherished dream and that sooner or later I would revive the idea anyway because one cannot escape from oneself. After our reconciliation and vacation her tolerance threshold was much higher than before, so she relented.

"Let's see the kind of man he is and the terms he's going to offer," she said. "Then we'll be able to make an informed decision."

Stanley was a hospitable host. He pounced on us at the doorway and proceeded to introduce us around in an expansive manner.

"This is a doctor, recently out of Russia, a future celebrity. We're cooperating on a book project. And this is his charming wife who is slated to become a millionairess when her husband strikes it rich both as a physician and a writer."

"Really? How marvelous!" the guest would exclaim. "Tell me, what is that book of yours about?"

"Medical care in Russia."

"It's gonna be a best-seller!" Stanley shouted. "You'll see, the book will be made into a movie! Millions, millions of dollars!"

Irina plainly did not like that kind of talk. Indeed, given our precarious situation, it was rather premature to predict heaps of money. With barely disguised irritation, she countered the host's irrepressible yells.

"We're not after riches. Money doesn't make happiness."

"It's sour grapes talk on your part because you don't have enough money now. Believe me, your very first million will do wonders to your outlook right away. I know the taste of success. I've written two books, both of them best-sellers," Stanley rejoiced boisterously.

"Why don't you show me your books?" I asked, to break up his skirmish with Irina and discharge the tension.

"One is titled *How to Be Your Own Electrician.* I collaborated on it with a leading expert on electrical engineering. The other one is *How to Be Your Own Mechanic.*"

Without further ado, he plunked down two volumes on the table. Taken somewhat aback, I leafed through them.

The subject matter of his books struck me disagreeably. My God, I thought, what kind of writer is he? There is not a whiff of style in all these technical instructions. How can he be my co-author? My book is a life story of a person, in fact the life stories of many people; it's a fabric woven of events, dialogues, and ideas.

But Stanley was in no way attuned to my thought process or to the feelings Irina and I shared. He belonged to a breed of thick-skinned man unendowed with either sensitivity or with wit. He was drunk, which only served to make him, if anything, even more boisterous.

"I had a talk with the editor-in-chief of R and H and I told him about you. He was very much interested in the idea. Since he knows me as a best-selling author, I think he'll agree to publish our book."

"My, my, it sure didn't take him long to think of my book as his own!" I thought, while he carried on.

"When are you going to have a translation?"

"What translation are you talking about when *we* haven't completed the manuscript yet?" I asked, stressing the cooperative pronoun *we*.

But unable to grasp my barb, Stanley bellowed, "Listen, while the book's being translated, you should tell me a couple of anecdotes. I'll use them to compose an outline of the manuscript and write a proposal. I'll send them to a few publishing houses and the highest bidder will get the job. I'm going to ask for $100,000. Well, how about it?" he asked me proudly, as if he already had the money in his pocket.

"Nobody's going to pay that much."

"Nonsense! You can't imagine the masterpiece I'll make out of the outline and proposal. The public loves them. I know the American readership. A hundred grand it will be!"

He stuck to me like a burr, his small, screwed-up eyes never leaving my face, while he proudly escorted us about his brownstone. We walked up and down the stairs, listening to his noisy explanations and taking care not to step on the small, fuzzy dog that always accompanied him.

We left late that night. The huge Stanley stood at the top of the stairway and shouted in his stentorian voice, "Walk carefully. You're now rich and famous!"

When we put some distance between ourselves and his house, Irina said, "I didn't like him one bit. What kind of idiot is he to talk of riches when he knows our present circumstances?! It's downright distasteful."

"America isn't a country of subtle personalities and refined manners," I told her. "Money reigns supreme here, and money is the chief subject of conversation. Of course, he behaved like a moron and a boor. But he assured me of his ability to find a publisher and secure a handsome advance. Even if he exaggerates, there must be something for us because he himself counts on making money on the deal."

"You'd better keep on guard with him," Irina advised. "So far as I'm concerned, he's a fake."

"Well, I haven't made any commitments, have I? Let's see what he can do. What really struck me was his books. What kind of a writer is he? I haven't the slightest idea of how we could possibly collaborate."

48

n several occasions, I visited Stanley and tried to tell him some of the stories I had written in Russian. What with my limited vocabulary, I had a hard time conveying any subtlety of meaning, and the stories in my rendering lost all merit. However, Stanley was in no way non-plussed by the job I was doing on the language. He concentrated on minute (and in my view irrelevant) detail, asking numerous questions.

Hearing a story of how I had dined with Nikita Khrushchev back in 1962, he asked, "Was the table made of wood?"

"Yes, it was a wooden table."

"What kind of wood?"

"Oh, I don't know, maybe oak."

"And what color?"

"Light."

"The whole table was light colored? Including the legs?"

"I didn't notice."

"And how many legs did it have?"

Amid such minutiae the tale lost all its import and Khrushchev's personality and behavior were forced off center stage. When I said that Khrushchev drank brandy in large glasses, bottoms up, Stanley responded with a barrage of new questions.

"What kind of brandy?"

"Armenian."

"Price?"

"About thirty rubles a fifth, I would guess, maybe more."

"How much would that be in American money?"

The question "how much did it cost" dominated the interrogation. In general, Stanley was mainly interested in journalistic detail—granted sometimes illuminating, but irrelevant to the tenor of my stories. I realized that Stanley's input in our joint venture would be to garnish the material with a mass of trifling detail of the sort described above. Needless to say, it was not the kind of co-authorship I sought. What my stories really required was editing to adapt them to the thought patterns of an average American reader. Stanley was patently unsuited for this purpose, and my initial enthusiasm rapidly receded. By contrast, his elation grew by the day, leading him to predict, increasingly frequently and ever more loudly, success and heaps of money.

We did not discuss the terms of our cooperation, except

that I once expressed the hope that he would treat me fairly. He responded immediately.

"I should get at least forty thousand dollars from the advance payment; it's my minimal yearly standard of living."

His words rankled, considering that my annual living standard was zero and he obviously didn't care whether I ate or starved.

However, I did not have enough time to devote myself to the book project. The date of the exam was nearing and I—God knows how many times!—recapitulated the material so as to be able to pinpoint the correct answers in a matter of seconds. My brain would have to work as fast as a computer. To complicate matters still further, the questions and answers were in English, which continued to give me much trouble. I would typically spend the first half of the day at home, reading textbooks and going over 300 to 400 questions from the Kaplan course and the previous exams. In late afternoon, when Irina and Junior came home, I would go to the Kaplan Center to do an almost equal amount of work. My personal best was 1,200 questions in a single day. I trained myself to such a level of proficiency that I could unfailingly answer between 80 and 85 percent of the questions—enough to get a passing grade at the exam. But what a hellish workload it was! I could not afford to be distracted by anything at all.

So when a telephone call interrupted my studies one day, it was with a good deal of reluctance that I lifted the receiver. A woman's voice called out my name, "Dr. Golyakhovsky?"

"Speaking."

"My name is Carol. I am secretary to the chief of the orthopedic surgery department of St. Louis's Hospital in Manhattan. Are you still interested in a job?"

Dragged away from intensive cerebration and caught unawares, I reacted sluggishly, "Excuse me, what did you say?"

"I said if you're still interested in a job, you are invited for an interview with Dr. Puz."

"What kind of job?" I asked again.

"Didn't you send us your résumé?"

It was not until then that I remembered. Over four months

previously, I had succumbed to Irina's prodding and sent my résumé to a hospital that advertised its need for a paramedic.

"Oh yes, yes, of course. I did!"

"Well then, are you willing to come for an interview?"

"Sure! When?"

"Will tomorrow, one P.M., be convenient to you?"

I sat stunned, unable to gather my agitated thoughts. I called Irina first.

"What's the matter? Anything happened?" she asked in a panic.

"Nothing. I just received a job offer."

"Really? What kind of job?"

"Do you remember we sent a résumé in response to a help-wanted ad?"

"Yes . . ."

"The chief's secretary called and told me to come and talk."

"When?"

"Tomorrow."

Agitation was evident in Irina's voice, "Skip school tonight, let's discuss things."

We discussed the job offer, so long-awaited yet so sudden, into the small hours of the night. What kind of job it would be; what duties it would involve; in general, what awaited me there.

Irina had grave premonitions. "I keep thinking—what if your duties call for a lot of physical effort? Will you be up to it?"

"There's no reason to worry! To the best of my knowledge, paramedics are not required to haul weights."

"But what if you're assigned to the ambulance service? Then you'll have to lug patients on stretchers, won't you?"

"Everything is mechanized in this country. I'm sure there will be some labor-saving devices."

"But it's dangerous work!" Irina said thoughtfully. "Just imagine yourself among those thugs, called to pick up a crime victim . . . all those underworld gorillas around you . . . all of them with guns."

Under the impact of Irina's worried vision, I pictured myself as an ambulance orderly, in a regulation white shirt over a bulletproof vest, hospital emblem on my shirtsleeve, girded with a belt supporting a heavy bag with all the necessary paraphernalia—hypodermic syringes, needles, solutions—working in a slum neighborhood densely populated by the criminal poor, at night, in any kind of weather. The picture brought me little solace.

Close to morning, Irina fell into a fitful sleep. Her fears moved me. Indeed, after many years of being the wife of a department chief, she had difficulty picturing her husband as a paramedic. But I was glad to have a chance to work, even if the job was hard or dangerous.

The next day, Dr. Puz welcomed me with a genuinely American beaming smile.

"I can see from your résumé that you're a physician and an orthopedic surgeon," he said. "Unfortunately, all I can offer you is an orthopedic technician's position. I'm sure you deserve more and I wish you success. In the meantime, if you agree to take the job, you'll be helping us in the hospital and clinic, applying and removing plaster casts and setting up traction devices of all sorts. Since you're an experienced physician, you'll be able to teach our young residents plaster techniques. What do you say?"

I felt a mountain being lifted off my shoulders; the job description sounded much better than what Irina and I had dreaded. I would be doing what I had done for many years, in a field where I prided myself on being somewhat of an expert. Besides, I would be working in the hospital, handling patients.

"Of course, I agree!" I tried to reciprocate his smile.

"Splendid. Let's go to Personnel then, I'll introduce you around, and you'll discuss all the pertinent details with them. You know, I liked you at first sight, the instant you stepped into my office. I'm certain you will be an asset to this hospital."

"And I liked you the instant you smiled," I responded. "I'll do my best, you can count on that."

From the beginning I was amazed at the warm attention

everybody I came in contact with lavished on me. I saw only smiles around me, the explanations were patient and polite, everybody was eager to help. Over my quarter-of-a-century-long career in Russia I had changed quite a few jobs but in spite of my far more exalted positions, never had I felt as welcome as I was feeling here.

Naturally salary was the burning question, but I did not feel it was proper to ask it at the very beginning. I made some mental calculations and arrived at the conclusion that I would be paid at least $10,000 to $11,000. Together with Irina's $12,000, it would add up to $22,000 to $23,000. Well, not bad, not bad at all, provided my guess is right.

"You'll be paid at an hourly rate of eight dollars, which translates to an annual salary of fourteen thousand three hundred dollars," the personnel chief said. "And every six months, you'll get a three-percent raise."

Over fourteen thousand dollars!

"Excuse me, but may I ask you a question?"

"Sure."

"May I take my ECFMG exam in two weeks? You see, I hope to pass and enter residency training . . ."

"Really? How wonderful!" the personnel director exclaimed jubilantly, as if she had spent a lifetime waiting for me to pass the exam. "Of course, by all means take the exam and then come to work. Best of luck!"

From the pay phone on the nearest corner I called Irina.

"Well?" she asked in a voice dripping with foreboding.

I poured out all the news at once: the kind of job, the salary, the wonderful way everybody at the hospital treated me.

"Thank God!" she said jubilantly.

That night, our family, including Junior and my mother, got together in an atmosphere of contentment that we had not experienced for a long time.

Still in high spirits, two weeks later I sat down at the exam together with hundreds of foreign doctors. Again fuss, bustle, worries, and talk about cheating raged around me. Some examinees managed to learn the forthcoming questions in advance. They even boasted how cheaply they had paid for the exact intelligence, a mere $1,000. But oblivious to all mundane concerns, I confidently answered one question after another—almost as fast as the native Americans.

The next day I reported to my new job.

I came to the hospital with an hour to spare in order to find my workplace and be able to start work exactly on schedule. It was a point of honor with me to demonstrate that I could match the Americans at their game—working efficiently, losing no time, going full blast from the first to the last. I had always believed that an American institution was the acme of organizational and managerial skills.

As it happened, however, the department chief was on vacation and in his absence nobody seemed to have any idea of where I was supposed to go and what I was supposed to do. Anyone I approached welcomed me effusively and smiled. And that was that.

I roamed about the hospital for a while and finally found myself at security, where a pretty girl photographed me and issued me an ID card indicating that I was assigned with the nursing service. I went to the basement to get my uniform—white pants and a white shirt.

The window where uniforms were issued was filled with a totally blank face of a middle-aged black woman staring stonily at a point beyond me. My attempts to attract her attention were to no avail even though I placed myself directly in front of her; she did not react in any way.

Finally, on a hunch, I flashed my ID card at her. She gave it a sideways glance and disappeared. I waited. Finally, she reappeared, as dispassionate as ever, thrust a bundle at me and froze in the same stance, her eyes fixed on a distant point in space.

The bundle contained blue pants and several blue shirts. But I was certain that I rated the white uniform befitting any person who came in contact with patients.

"Excuse me, it's not what I need. . . . Excuse me, could you give me a white uniform? You see, I'm going to work at the orthopedics department where my duties involve contact with patients."

Her face betrayed no emotion whatsoever. What was I to do? I had worn white gowns all my life; white was the color of my trade. Hell, no, I would not give it up on account of that dumb harridan! So I went up the chain of command to fight for my rights.

While I was trying to find out the identity of the proper authority, lunchtime arrived, and for nearly two hours I could not track down the person I needed. When at last I did corner him, I took a long time trying to get my request across to him. Then he called the stony female on the intercom and embarked upon a lengthy discourse trying to convince her that I was indeed worthy of a white uniform. Finally I again found myself face to her impassive face. She heard my plea, said, "Tomorrow," and banged the window shut, although she had a full hour to go before the end of her shift.

The next day, after I finally got my white uniform, a kindly woman named Peggy, deputy chief of the nursing department, personally escorted me to the basement where another woman, head of central supplies, welcomed me exuberantly.

"Welcome aboard! How wonderful!"

She had no idea what to do with me and admitted as much. I told her that the department chief offered me a job as an orthopedic technician, that I used to be an orthopedic surgeon back in Russia, and that I hoped to become a doctor again and go into residency training.

"Really? How interesting! Wonderful!" she bubbled. "And after you're through with the training, do you plan to return to Russia?"

"No. I'm an immigrant, a political refugee."

"Really? How wonderful!"

She led me to a large room chock-full of orthopedic equipment: crutches, walkers, traction splints, boxes of plaster.

"What a mess!" she said, turning to me. "I've been trying in vain to cajole the management into assigning someone to bring a semblance of order to this chaos. Will you do it for me, please?"

She dazzled me with a charming smile and vanished. I began hauling things to different corners, sorting the items by function and size. Well, work is work is work. A long time ago, while still in Moscow, I had told a friend of mine that in the early phase of immigration I would not regard any kind of job, even that of a nurse's aide, as being beneath my dignity. It had been a prophetic insight.

At home, I kept silent about my duties.

"How do you like your job?" Irina asked me eagerly.

"Very much."

"What do you have to do?"

I did not want to tell a lie. "I'm still getting my bearings."

"But you've been there for a week."

"The chief's away, so I haven't yet really started on the job."

"Then why are you so tired?"

"Because I have to speak English all day long and it's damned hard."

It was only partially a lie. The storeroom where I worked was next to the auxiliary services: the engineering department, the laundry room, supplies, and so on. Their employees constantly walked back and forth past my room and all took a lively interest in the new man, myself, busy stacking splints and crutches. They would stop and ask me questions: Where did I come from? What was I doing in this place? Who was I? Upon learning that I was a Russian, some of them asked more questions.

"Is it true that Russians want to fight America?"

"No, it's not. The common people don't want a war."

"What did you do in Russia?"

"I was a physician, an orthopedic surgeon."

"A doctor! You must have been a rich man."

"No, nobody's rich in Russia. They have Communism there, so everybody's poor."

"And what are you doing here?"

"I'm an immigrant. Here I work as an orthopedic technician and try to become a doctor again."

The younger of them jerked rhythmically and danced to the beat of invisible music.

"Are you going to open your own office?"

"Well, first I have to pass a special exam and get some training."

"And after the training, do you plan to go back to Russia?"

"Oh no, there's no returning. Once you leave it's for good."

"But why? How so? Would you be deported to Siberia?" they asked, laughing. However meager their knowledge of Russia, they did know of Siberia.

"You bet," I replied, also laughing.

"How strange. I, for instance, left Jamaica, but I come to visit my family there every year anyway," one of them said.

"And I left Venezuela but I also go visit," said another.

Those workmen, all of them black immigrants from Central and South America and the Caribbean, became my first friends at the hospital. I had never socialized with blacks before.

After I cleaned up the storeroom and put it in order, I was transferred to the third floor, where the patients were. The supplies chief was displeased. She called the management and tried to get me back.

"Vladimir is exactly the kind of man I need here!" She listened. "Damn them!" She slammed the receiver and turned to me seeking my support. I expressed sympathy with her plight but left her domain with much relief.

The third-floor matron did not know what to do with me either. "For starters, you'll be helping our postoperative patients to learn to walk again."

And I went to perform the functions of a nurse's aide.

This work was somewhat more satisfying and interesting, if only because it involved contact with patients. Most of them were old—in their seventies or even eighties—weak from age and further weakened by illness and surgery. They clutched at me, hung on to me, while I walked them about the room or along the corridor. I used the opportunity to make cautious inquiries about the operations they had undergone. I was keenly interested in observing the immediate results of surgical intervention.

I was amazed at the operative vigor of American surgeons. In Russia, hip or knee replacement surgery on old-age patients is a rare occurrence. Here the results were quite good, but many of the patients could not walk unassisted. Looking around me, I could not help wondering why those poor people had been subjected to operations that offered little if any promise, and why they had consented to being operated on.

Once the matron ordered me to cart a patient to the operating rooms. I put the patient on a wheeled stretcher and set out on my first trip to the sixth-floor operating theater. The resident took the patient over while I lingered behind to see how a knee replacement procedure was being prepared. Everything was interesting to me, particularly the many unfamiliar technical devices and machines. I had stepped to the side near the door when the operating surgeon, Dr. Walter, came in.

"Enough of your goofing off," he said. "Get scrubbed for the operation."

I did not know the meaning of the verb *scrub* and could not understand his order.

"Are you talking to me?" I asked.

"Who else? You'll assist me, if you wish. You're an orthopedic surgeon, aren't you?"

"Yes, I am."

"Fine. Let's operate together then."

I cannot adequately describe the emotions that swept over me. It was almost three years since I had so much as entered an operating room and I was happy just to breathe its air. I assisted at that operation, then at another; then a neurosurgeon turned up and asked me to assist him as well. The time was already 11:00 P.M. but I was still at work. At my request one of the scrub nurses called Irina at home and told her not to worry because I was in the operating room.

"What happened?" Irina asked in alarm. "Anything wrong?"

"Oh, no, don't worry. He's assisting at an operation, not being operated on."

It was well past 1:00 A.M. when I finally came home. Irina anxiously waited, worrying how I would make it home at such a late hour in the dreaded subway.

"I assisted at three operations!" I declared, puffing out my chest.

It is a well-known maxim that man was created by work. And if one has already been created, what does work bring him if not self-esteem and gratification? Precisely the feelings I had not experienced over the previous two years.

I brought home my first paycheck on my fifty-first birthday. Again all four of us sat at a festive dinner, and I was gratified to see grins around me, particularly the one on my son's face. It was a long time since he had smiled that way at me. I was glad to be regaining my dignity in his eyes.

Soon Junior had another occasion to appreciate my burgeoning moral authority. Here is how Irina told the story:

"I worked at my lab and was very busy when they called me to the phone. It was Junior. He told me: 'I've just got the mail. Dad has passed the exam.' Beside myself with joy, I screamed and ran around the lab yelling, 'My husband has passed the exam! My husband has passed the exam!' My colleagues shouted congratulations but none of them knew what kind of exam it was and what it was needed for. So they asked me, 'What's the significance of his passing that exam?' 'It means that he can become a doctor once again!' I replied."

Junior called me at the hospital as well and left the message with the chief's secretary. She did not understand it and passed on the message in a garbled form to a resident who informed me that my son had passed an exam. Thus, before coming home I had not an inkling of my success. But when I opened the door, Junior pounced on me, brandishing the letter and proudly pointing at my high score. I was dizzy with jubilation.

Junior was so boisterously glad that he jumped around me like a big puppy. He poked his finger at the score and, somewhat in jest, but also with childish seriousness, called me "M.D." I could see in his face that he had finally made up with me; joy and achievement bridged the gap between us. Well, it was normal; parents should earn the respect of their children.

Junior had his own academic problems. In a year's time he was to graduate from college. To be accepted by a medical school in America he needed the highest grades possible. He was also required to pass the Medical College Admission Test (MCAT)—again with the highest grades. Only then could he realistically count on success. We knew from many examples that for an immigrant to become a medical student was similar to a camel squeezing through the eye of a needle. Just two or three kids out of hundreds made it. Naturally Junior was beside himself with anxiety, and he worked hard. More and more often he felt the need to discuss his studies at home. Again I was becoming a greater authority in his eyes than his mother, whom he ignored with the mindless arrogance of youth.

"If you had to study as much as Dad and I do, you'd surely crack under the strain," he would tell her condescendingly.

He was clearly trying to form a male alliance, and while it was funny to watch him, Irina's pride was badly wounded.

"You dumb, snot-nosed punk," she yelled at him. "I was graduated from the Moscow University before you were born and got my Ph.D. degree when you couldn't even write yet!"

"I don't care. What happened a long time ago in Russia doesn't count," he replied in English, trying to affect a clipped British inflection.

My translator, Mike, finally sent over the first hundred pages. I had been waiting for over a year. I passed them to Stanley, who was delighted.

"Vladimir, why haven't you ever told me your stories are so spellbinding?" he shouted. "That story about Nikita Khrushchev is absolutely remarkable! Such an extraordinary Russian leader and such an interesting personality! Why haven't you told me?"

"I tried my best but I had difficulty expressing myself. Besides, you always barged in with questions."

"What do you mean—barged in? All my questions were very important, substantive corrections and amplifications of your stories. Americans like to be told everything—the color, the smell, the price, above all the price. Now I can put everything in order, write a proposal. Success is guaranteed. In a month or two we'll have a contract."

51

For several days I assisted Dr. Walter in the operating room, and he was happy to have qualified help. Then Dr. Puz, the chief, returned from his vacation and suggested that I help him.

I established friendly relations with the scrub nurses, particularly with a vigorous and high-spirited black man named Ezra. I already felt at home in the operating room when the matron, Ms. Fren, who had been absent for some time, returned to work. She regarded me darkly and several times sharply rebuked me for petty infractions. Even when I tried to help her in some matter, she angrily declined, "I'll do it myself if you don't mind."

Once, when I was scrubbing for yet another operation, she told me testily, "Vladimir, according to my supervisor, you have no right to scrub."

Dr. Walter and Ezra tried to explain to her that I was a highly experienced orthopedic surgeon, but she insisted, with stubborn spite, "Under the state law, he has no right so much as to approach patients as long as he doesn't have a license."

"But he has passed the exam qualifying him as a physician in this country."

"It makes no difference. Without the license, he has no right to be party to the treatment of patients."

Seething with the impotent indignation of helplessness, I had to cut short scrubbing my hands with a brush dipped in antiseptic solution. That time I spent the operation behind the surgeons' backs.

Gradually, my duties crystallized into a well-defined pattern. Three times a week I helped residents to see patients at the clinic, applying and removing plaster casts. When I was asked for the first time to apply a long leg cast, I inquired which method they would like me to use. I could do the job blindfolded, having applied casts of that kind thousands of times. But each hospital has its own technical nuances.

The attending physician, Dr. Fab, a tall and handsome young man, with a mellifluous voice and beautiful inflection, told me, "I'll do it myself."

I was embarrassed. I had no intention of having an attending physician, a big shot in the hospital hierarchy, doing my job. Nor did I want to create an impression that I did not know how to apply such a cast. Therefore I protested, "No, no, I'll do it, no problem! All I want to know is how you want me to apply the cast. Let me do it."

"Vladimir," he said, "I'm not afraid of a little work."

And he applied the cast with authority—elegantly and fast. It was not his skill that impressed me, but the way he said, "I'm not afraid of a little work"—unpretentiously and merrily. In my eyes, that was the epitome of the true American ethic. I remembered that phrase.

Every morning I still came to the operating room to help the nurses move the patients from the stretcher to the operating table. It was a difficult physical task and they were glad to have me at their side. Then I helped the anesthesiologist prepare for administering anesthesia. When one of the surgeons scrubbed the patient's skin, my duty consisted in holding aloft the arm or leg to be operated on. Sometimes it took an excruciating effort, with my arms and back going numb with strain.

After that I would tie the sterile gowns at the physicians' backs, set stools under their feet (if necessary), and station myself behind them. From my vantage point, I directed the light of the operating lamp to the wound, wiped sweat off the surgeons' brows, ran little errands for the doctors and nurses—to bring this, to pass that.

After the operation, I helped apply the plaster cast, pouring water into a pail, bringing and carrying away boxes with plaster dressings. Then I again transferred the patient from the table to the stretcher and, together with the anesthesiologist, carted him or her to the recovery room. The work was physically demanding. The muscles of my back, arms, and legs ached constantly. I was quite fit, but to do such heavy work in one's fifties was different. I never talked about my ordeal at home, but a nagging thought kept nibbling at my mind: What if my heart gives out?

Whenever I was left alone for a few minutes, I watched with keen interest the American surgeons at work, feeling much like a retired musician who goes to concerts to critique active players. I felt sad and asked myself, When, oh when, am I going to wield the scalpel again?

I had yet to pass an English exam, Test of English as a Foreign Language (TOEFL), which was particularly difficult for physicians. Only then could I claim a temporary license, putting me on an equal footing with American doctors and enabling me to seek admission to a residency training program. It was not until I enrolled in training that I could apply for a license that would give me the right to practice medicine in this country.

Our chief permitted me to sit in on conferences for residents and promised to let me assist at operations as soon as I obtained a temporary license.

I behaved as my job position dictated. At the fair of business relations, one must conform to the limitations of one's label. Everybody treated me well, and I tried to meet all requests and execute all orders with maximum dispatch and diligence. With a quarter of a century of experience behind me, I had no trouble applying plaster casts or performing other procedures. I had honed my plaster technique in Dresden, East Germany, in 1966, in Europe's premier plaster workshop, which had been operated by five successive generations of a single family. In fact, my plaster casts were superior to those applied by many young doctors, who lack necessary skill. And usually they never missed an opportunity to compliment me on my work.

Only one chief resident, Mexican Dr. Arturo, ignored my skills. A man of poor managerial ability, he kept his job by toadying to his superiors. And one other doctor, Dr. H., the scion of a Russian immigrant family, persecuted me without letup. He had a habit of engaging me in a conversation, lounging on the sofa in the doctors' room, and forcing me to stand in front of him. He always spoke in whining tones.

"Vladimir, where the hell were you this morning?" he would ask me.

"At the residents' conference."

"Why a technician would want to attend such a conference beats me," he would say, spreading his arms in a theatrical gesture, and then would go on, "What are you going to do in this country?"

"I am planning to enroll in a residency training program with an eye on subsequently becoming a practicing orthopedic surgeon."

"At your age? You must be out of your mind!"

"I am the same age as you are."

"I wouldn't even try if I were you. And in general, why did you leave Russia?"

I was reluctant to give an answer to a Jew, and the son of Russian immigrants to boot. If he had not seen the light so far, he never would.

"I wanted to come to America," I replied reluctantly.

"Really? Well it's up to you, of course. Listen, it is my duty to let you know that you are overstepping the bounds of your authority."

"How?" I asked in surprise.

"Scrub nurse Ms. Fren has informed me that you cart the patients from the operating theater to the recovery room."

"Sure, I do—together with the anesthesiologist and one of the residents."

"You have no right to do it."

"Okay, I won't from now on."

It was patently absurd even from the legalistic point of view, for I was nothing but physical force pushing the stretcher.

Needless to say, I had difficulty restraining myself. I burned with a desire to tell him to go to hell, but I kept my mouth shut. I often had to hide my wounded pride. Well, that's the way things are for an immigrant. One has to develop a very thick skin. In fact, the whole adaptation process for an immigrant can be distilled to a test of endurance.

Tying the gowns at the surgeons' backs in the operating room and then standing behind them during surgery, wiping the floor and setting stools under the surgeons' feet, I often recalled one of my teachers, Dr. Sergei Yudin, a giant of a surgeon. In 1949, that internationally renowned genius and member of many academies of sciences was arrested by the KGB and exiled on trumped-up charges of being a British spy. (Actually, he operated on the British ambassador in Moscow and saved his life.) Deported to Siberia, he worked in a tiny rural hospital as a nurse's aide, tying the surgeons' gowns and wiping the floor. In a short while Dr. Yudin had a fatal heart attack.

Sad thoughts crowded my mind, but I made a resolve, again and again, that I should and would overcome. And I also thought that whatever humiliating trials would be visited upon me, I had to safeguard my intellectual integrity and self-respect.

52

Yet despite the punishing physical load, I found my work interesting. I enjoyed the novel company of Americans going about their business. I watched with immense interest the human types, the nature of relationships. Constantly comparing my observations with Russian recollections, I came to an important conclusion: Americans at work differed from Russians as much as their country differed from Russia; freedom and professional competence were the crucial difference. While Americans were free, all Russians, whatever their positions, cowered and cringed at all times. And while Americans naturally differed from one another in terms of professionalism, on average they were far more competent than their Russian counterparts.

Only the fat woman who issued uniforms never ceased to amaze me. Once a week I presented myself before her to exchange my soiled uniform for a fresh one, and not once did the exchange come off without complications. It was not enough that on the few occasions she could be found at her post she remained totally impassive and mute. Most of the time she was either absent or late or gone for the day. I often wondered how such a "worker" managed to hold down her job.

The hospital seemed to me the epitome of extravagance. There was never a problem of a patient lacking in something. Any drug, any test, any kind of equipment was either readily available or procured without delay. The word *no* did not exist. To me it was amazing, because the word *nyet* (no) was king in Russian hospitals. Even the exclusive Kremlin Hospital in Moscow, which served only the supreme rulers and members of their families, could not compare with this hospital in the range of available drugs and equipment.

When scrub nurse Ezra laid out on the instrument table a set of scalpels for meniscectomy, I was stunned. Never in my life had I seen such a variety of instruments for that relatively minor surgical procedure.

I could not contain my excitement.

"How rich our hospital is!" I told one of the residents.

He looked at me in surprise. "You must be kidding, Vladimir. It's a poor hospital. You can't even imagine what a rich hospital looks like."

I lacked the capacity to imagine anything better. Or maybe what I really lacked was not imagination but American experience.

I found it difficult to get used to the fact that many of the devices were disposable. I could see hypodermic syringes should be thrown away, although they were of a quality I had never seen in Russia; it was a new and strange sensation to see them discarded after a single injection. But when a sophisticated and precision-made plastic device costing at least $500 was treated in a similar manner, I was upset.

My friends explained to me, "It's true that the device is expensive. But if it's to be used a second time, the preparation will cost even more than a replacement. It has to be broken down into component parts, washed, cleaned, reassembled, and wrapped. It would take several people several hours of work, and labor is very costly. So by throwing it away we actually save money."

Yes, human labor is an expensive commodity in America—unlike Russia, where work, including that of a physician, is cheap.

Amid all those reflections and concerns I received a letter from Dr. Cooper, the neurosurgeon, with tickets to the international symposium on socialized health care to be held in Naples, Florida.

Somewhat apprehensively, I approached my chief for permission to take a weeklong leave of absence, but to my surprise he readily gave his permission and wished me oratorical success and a good rest, as always dazzling me with his smile. I am sure that under similar circumstances not a single Russian director would support an undertaking of this sort, much less smile at the impertinent underling.

I gleefully sat down to write my paper, to be delivered in English. Alone, I could not cope with the task. So I wrote it in Russian, Irina translated the text into English, and then we persuaded our American friends to polish her translation. Then I started memorizing the presentation, with Irina watching my pronunciation. It was a time-consuming and tedious job.

I remembered the humiliation of having to hide my feet during our first meeting with Dr. Cooper, so I bought a new pair of shoes specifically for the forthcoming trip. We also decided to bring along a supply of instant coffee and a small electric immersion heater capable of boiling a cup or two of water. Dr. Cooper had promised that all our needs would be taken care of, but we wanted to make sure that whatever happened coffee would be available to us.

While we were preparing for the trip, Stanley called and declared that he had finished the proposal and could assert with utmost confidence that our book would be published. I came to see him on the eve of departure to pick up a copy of his proposal and of a chapter he had edited.

As always, bugles of triumph blared in his voice. "I've composed a whale of a proposal, a real beauty! Any publishing house would be sure to snap up the manuscript and pay whatever advance I demand. When you come back from Florida, the contract will be ready for your signature. Consider the book as good as published!"

I began reading the proposal. Stanley wrote that I had disported myself riding around Moscow in a Politburo limousine and that I had been just about the most important figure in Russian medicine. Then followed a list of food Khrushchev and I had consumed, in minute detail and itemized by cost. The impression one got was that having had our fill, the Soviet leader and I had put our heads together and compiled a balance sheet of the dinner. Moreover, the proposal strongly implied that Khrushchev and I had been great friends and spent a lot of time together, eating and drinking to our hearts' content at the expense of the Soviet people.

"It's not true!" I exclaimed.

"What's not true?"

"I wasn't such a big shot. I didn't ride around Moscow in a Politburo limo, and I have no idea of the cost of food on Khrushchev's table. Besides, I spent less than an hour at that table, as a small fry, an accidental guest of no consequence."

"Ah, Vladimir, poor Vladimir!" Stanley exploded like an oversize drum. "How can you be so naïve? You really amaze me! Believe me, I know the taste of the American readers better than you do. The American readers like to know the cost of everything. And I also know better than you how to sell a manuscript to a prospective publisher. Go to Florida and forget your worries. Everything will be done the best way imaginable. The important thing is to get the money. When you come back, the contract will be waiting for you. And then we'll discuss all the particulars."

All right, I decided, let him set a contract, but I'll write the book entirely on my own and check the excesses of his imagination. Even if the American reader "loves" to be bamboozled, I won't do it. I won't let Stanley get away with exaggeration.

53

The day of our departure I was at the hospital and was about to leave when a patient came to have his leg cast removed. He was a homeless derelict, dressed in dirty rags and reeking nauseatingly of sweat and some other indefinable stink. But the ultimate in horror was his cast. During the three months he had worn it, it had turned into a solid cake of foul-smelling dirt.

The nurses and receptionists at the clinic covered their noses and turned away in disgust when he happened to be near. I was assigned the job of removing his cast. I put on a paper gown, a surgeon's skullcap, a face mask, and rubber gloves and led the patient to a room slated for subsequent cleaning. We were left face to face. I cut the cast apart with a vibrating knife and removed it. Then I had to wash off the layers of dirt that formed a solid shield over his skin. Myriads of lice crawled under the cast.

While I was thus engaged, we talked. The bum turned out to be quite intelligent and even cultivated, but completely gone to seed. Having completed my work, I washed my hands in a hurry and rushed home where Irina was impatiently waiting. I grabbed the suitcase and we ran to the subway station, to take the Train to the Plane, to Kennedy Airport. There was precious little time until takeoff.

It was fascinating to fly over the eastern seaboard of the United States, the captain reciting the states and cities. My seat was at the window and I could get a good view of most of the sights he pointed out. I was deeply moved, of course, to fly over Washington, D.C., and see a tiny Capitol, less than a matchbox in size.

In Miami, we changed to a small, twin-engine propeller plane and within forty-five minutes landed at the small airport of Naples, where a young woman met us.

"Welcome!" she exclaimed jubilantly. "My name is Jeanette. I recognized you from your photographs. But I could never have imagined that a professor of surgery of your fame would look so young."

The honorific *professor* brought a sheepish grin to my lips. It was some time since I had been treated with such diffidence.

"I'm Dr. Cooper's housekeeper," she went on. "But this coming week I'm going to live with you in the 'small' house my boss has placed at your disposal. So I'll be taking you home now, you'll take a little rest and then go to a dinner party with the doctor in the big house. Come on, we're pressed for time."

She drove us in a Cadillac to a beautiful house surrounded by a tropical garden. There were three bedrooms and five other rooms. The refrigerator was bursting with provisions, including champagne. In the kitchen we saw an espresso coffee maker.

"I've prepared these things for you," Jeanette said. "Would you like some coffee?"

Irina and I exchanged a glance and burst out laughing. There would be no need for the immersion heater we had brought along "just in case."

We unpacked in a richly appointed bedroom and had barely enough time to change clothes before Dr. Cooper personally came to fetch us in his Mercedes-Benz. He was brimming with hospitality.

"Welcome to Naples! Be my guests, enjoy your stay, feel free to do whatever you please. Jeanette will help you."

"Your hospitality is most appreciated. It's all so pleasing and unusual to us, newcomers to this country."

"Great! Let's go to my place now. I'll introduce you to my

wife and the other participants in the symposium. Everybody's dying to meet you."

The "big" house was deeply recessed in a park. In fact it could be more fairly described as a little palace. Dozens of luxury automobiles were parked in the driveway.

Dr. Cooper introduced us to his guests in a spacious, lavishly furnished living room.

"Dr. Vladimir and his charming wife, Irina, also a doctor. Let's give them a big hand. Dr. Vladimir is an internationally renowned orthopedic surgeon, recently out of Russia. It was his article that gave me the inspiration to convene this symposium."

Everybody applauded and people started to come over to shake our hands.

We drank cocktails, chatted with other guests, ate a sumptuous meal, and heard classical music performed by a small orchestra hired specially for the occasion. From time to time, Irina and I exchanged glances. I surreptitiously pointed to my new shoes that glittered as brightly as those of the other guests.

We were awakened by the twitter of birds and the shrieks of pelicans. How new and wonderful everything was! The rich furnishings of "our" house, the breakfast already cooked by Jeanette, the very fact that we were in Florida! It was early spring, the day was sunny, and our spirits were in tune with the surroundings. We went to the garden for one last rehearsal of my presentation, with Irina playing the part of the audience. My poor girl, how many times she had to contend with "Socialized Health Care in Soviet Russia!"

The symposium was attended by luminaries from all over the world—the United Kingdom, Canada, Sweden, Zimbabwe, Haiti, mainland China—all countries where health care was socialized. There were a few American physicians who came to share their impressions. It was a very interesting and useful gathering. The local paper and TV station gave it extensive coverage.

I was featured in two telecasts: a solo appearance in an

interview about Russian health care, and together with Irina in an interview about our past life in Russia. It was yet another first for us—to take part in a live TV show interrupted by commercials every few minutes. We had been apprehensive, but the TV people worked so smoothly that the actual experience proved less nerve-racking than we had feared.

On the last day of our stay, Dr. Cooper's millionaire friend and neighbor threw a party for the symposium participants. Other millionaire neighbors were also in attendance. To my surprise, quite a few of them turned out to be unprepossessing. I felt so much at home among them that I even sang a popular Russian song, "Dark Eyes," to the accompaniment of a jazz combo at the side of a huge, illuminated swimming pool. And the bright stars of southern skies twinkled and glittered above.

"Vladimir, coffee!" the chief resident, Dr. Arturo, ordered brusquely the first morning of my return.

I looked at him with surprise. From time to time, we took turns bringing coffee to the morning conference, but it was nobody's, and certainly not my, obligation. Still, I could ill afford new enemies, so I was about to comply with his order, when Dr. Ricks, a young attending physician, said, "Wait, Vladimir, let me come with you to fetch coffee for *him*."

At least the resident was embarrassed. Later on, when we were left alone, I spoke to him, "Listen, it's not in my job description. I'm not a doctor here, but at least I am an orthopedic technician. I'm supposed to be putting on plaster casts, not running your errands."

"You misunderstood me," he said. "I'm sorry."

But I could see he seethed with suppressed fury.

That day, a thirty-six-year-old woman was brought to the Emergency Room with a fracture and dislocation of the ankle. I was to assist the chief resident in examining the patient.

"I'll set the bone and put on a plaster cast," the hostile Dr. H., the attending physician, told the resident. "Then please refer her to my secretary."

"The patient has no medical insurance," the resident told him.

"No insurance? Then you take care of her and give her an appointment at the clinic."

I was prepared to give the resident a hand, but he rudely shoved me aside. Standing behind him, in my usual place, I watched his clumsy attempts to put on the cast. He administered local anesthesia poorly, and the patient screamed when he tried to set the fractured bone. The patient was discharged with the bones incorrectly positioned in the joint and a sloppy cast.

I saw the X rays and knew that he had not helped the patient. I had to do something lest the young woman acquire a permanent limp.

"Listen," I told him, "let's redo the cast together. I'll show you how it can be done easily."

"You've told me yourself you're not a doctor," the resident said. "And I am. I promised not to send you to fetch coffee, and you shouldn't interfere in matters that only licensed doctors are qualified to handle. Understood?"

I was not so much offended for myself as sorry for that poor patient. I bitterly recalled how Dr. Cooper had introduced me to his guests: "an internationally renowned orthopedic surgeon." Sure, that was me—but it was me of bygone days. But the resident did not care about my past standing, and as a result, the poor woman would limp till she died.

One night Stanley called on the phone and declared in his stentorian voice that I was to see him right away. Bursting with anticipation, I ran to his place, leaving Irina and Junior at home waiting for me to return with the contract.

"Well, how did you like it in Florida? Did they receive you well there?" Stanley boomed as soon as I appeared in his doorway.

"It was wonderful and the reception was marvelous. Dr. Cooper put us up in his luxurious house. I could never imagine a doctor could be so rich."

"Listen, Vladimir!" Stanley screamed like Joshua's trumpet, "I'll make you richer than your Dr. Cooper!"

I was used to his bragging and did not respond.

"Show me the contract," I said instead. "What's the name of the publishing house?"

"The contract is almost ready," Stanley replied. "But first we must sign our private agreement. It's been drawn up in conformity with state law, you can fully trust me. I've already signed my copy, now it's your turn. Sign here."

Suddenly, his voice became gentle and unctuous. I did not like the curious persistence with which he tried to shove the several sheets of paper into my hand.

"I'll read it at home," I said.

"Sure, sure, it's your right," Stanley cooed. "You can even consult a lawyer. Remember, though, that lawyers don't come cheap. But everything's in perfect order. You come out with the best terms imaginable."

He went to see me off, dragging his tiny pooch along.

Irina and Junior hoped to hear, at long last, of the book's publication. Instead I brought Stanley's agreement. Still, it was a business document and had to be read closely. We all perused it together. The agreement opened with a statement that Stanley would be considered the principal author although I would get top billing. I was obligated to supply him with material by telling him stories and jokes. I retained the right to supervise the text he would produce. He would get 65 percent of the profits, I the rest. I was to pay all translation expenses out of my share. All legal liability in connection with the book was also mine. Finally, I was also to give Stanley exclusive control over all my eventual publications as long as I lived.

I was discouraged, Irina was furious, and Junior openly teased.

"Well," he said, "are you going to sign or not?"

"Of course, I won't! Would you?"

"I don't care! It's entirely up to you."

"I could see from the very start that he was a crook," Irina hissed. "Like most of the people here. You shouldn't have got entangled with him at all."

"You're right as usual. But I had no choice. I still don't."

Again all my hopes were dashed. For three years I had been trying, on and off, to sell my manuscript and was ready for a compromise if that was what it took to get the book published. But any compromise could be stretched only so far. I simply could not sign my manuscript over as a gift.

Stanley called me the next night. For the first time in our relationship his voice did not blare like a trumpet, but sang like an oleaginous flute. "Did you sign the agreement?"

"No. I don't like the terms."

"What don't you like?"

"Almost everything. Why should you be the principal author?"

"It's just a turn of phrase, nothing else."

"The manuscript has already been written by me; your task is nothing more than adaptation."

"Okay, let's scratch the principal authorship clause," Stanley sang like a gentle cello. "It's just as well. Your name is going to be on top anyway."

"Sure it will. Now why should your cut be sixty-five percent?"

"Ah, Vladimir, Vladimir! You can't imagine the sky-high fees you'll command after the book is published."

"I'm not a Henry Kissinger and won't get the kind of money he's paid."

"You'll get more! Believe me, you'll be paid thousands for each appearance as a guest speaker!"

"Nonsense! Now answer me: Why are you to control my writings as long as I live?"

"Actually, I don't know why I put in that clause. It was a mistake." He sounded plaintive, like a weeping saxophone.

"And I'm going to consult a lawyer. You've told me yourself I'm within my rights to do so."

"It's going to cost you a fortune!" Stanley shouted. Then he changed the tone and sang like a gypsy violin, "I'm fond of you, Vladimir! You're like a member of my family."

"Aha, that's why you think nothing of robbing me blind!"

"Let's meet and modify the agreement the way you see fit."

"No, first I'm going to consult a lawyer."

I called my first American friend, the lawyer Allan Prince, and asked him for advice. Allan invited me for lunch.

"Tell me, have you promised him anything or signed any kind of document?" he asked after I told him my story.

"No."

"Good. Then you owe him nothing. Forget about him."

"That I'll do with pleasure. But I can't forget about my manuscript. I hoped so desperately that a publisher and a contract were within reach—and all of a sudden everything came to a crushing halt again!"

"Show me your manuscript. I know a few people with excellent connections in the publishing world. Maybe I'll be able to recommend your manuscript to them. But I'm not promising you millions," he added with a smile.

I felt better. I trusted Allan and hope again stirred in my breast.

55

The woman with a fractured ankle returned to the clinic for a control examination two weeks later.

"Hello, how are you?" the resident greeted her effusively.

"I'm in a little bit of pain and my toes are swollen. Is it the way it is supposed to be?"

"Of course. Pain and swollen toes are inevitable after a fracture. Let's take a control X ray of your foot."

"Thank you. I hope everything will be all right."

"Everything should be fine," he assured her.

But when the X ray was brought in, it was apparent that nothing was fine. Standing behind the resident's back, as befitted my lowly station in life, I could clearly see that the bones were misaligned in the joint. The patient looked on with hopeful anticipation.

"Umm, yes," the resident said. "Not bad, not bad at all. Still, we'd be better off replacing the cast."

"Again?" she exclaimed in fright.

"It happens sometimes, you know . . . rather often in fact. It's not always possible to set the bone right the first time around. We'll have to give it another try."

"Maybe we could dispense with it, Doctor?"

"Believe me, we must try. But it will be the last time, and after that everything will be just perfect."

She listened raptly, as if to an oracle. He turned to me

and snapped like a commanding officer, "Remove the cast, Vladimir, and put on a fresh one! I'll help you."

While I was cutting the cast off and preparing a new one, the patient kept up the conversation, "He was very attentive, my doctor, isn't he?"

"Oh, yes, of course," I replied, busy with the cast.

"And so intelligent!"

"Very . . ."

"How long have you been doing this sort of thing? I mean plaster casts?"

"For a long time."

"What are you—a physician's assistant?"

"No, an orthopedic technician."

"I see. . . . Would you by any chance know why it couldn't be done right the first time?"

"How should I know? It's up to the doctor," I replied cautiously lest she become suspicious.

"Oh, I see. Tell me, will the doctor be around to help you?"

"You bet."

"I do hope this time everything will be all right."

"I am sure it will."

The resident was busy with other patients, but he dropped by for a minute. He felt her foot. "Begin putting on the cast," he told me. "I'll be right back." He left again.

It is virtually impossible to set the bones right two weeks after the fracture occurs, because by that time bone fusion is already in progress and fresh tissue, albeit soft, has started to form between the fragments. However, with enough skill, the defect can be corrected almost completely. I had coped with such a difficult task several times in my past practice, and now I was doing my utmost to right the fractured foot. The patient endured the pain stoically, but she kept repeating in alarm:

"Where's my doctor? Why isn't he coming to help you?"

The resident stepped in, put on rubber gloves, and proceeded to make believe that he was helping me.

"Good, good, just one more second," he cooed. "Aha, here we are!"

After I was through with the cast, he wiped the sweat off his brow.

The patient was looking at him worshipfully.

"Thank you, thank you so much," she told him.

Then she was carted in a wheelchair to the X-ray room. Naturally I was curious to see how well I had done the job and, feigning indifference, followed suit. The X ray showed that the fragments had been set in an all but ideal alignment. Feeling as if a great load had been lifted off my chest, I rushed back to show the X ray to the resident.

Attending Dr. H. was talking to him.

"Where in hell have you been?" he asked me sourly.

"I went to fetch the X ray."

The resident took it out of my hand and showed it to the attending physician.

"Well, not bad, not bad at all," he said. Then he turned to me. "Vladimir, take the X ray back and return here immediately!"

All of my joy of a creator drained off. I went out into the corridor with the patient.

"Listen," I asked her, "why don't you have medical insurance?"

"I just forgot to get any. Why?"

"Well, you could have gone to a private doctor."

"What difference does it make where to go for treatment?" she exclaimed.

There was a lot of difference. And her story was a good case in point. Had she gone to a private office, she would have gotten a lot more attention and would have been treated by an experienced physician rather than a neophyte.

At the exit, she smiled at me, "I forgot to thank you. You, too, are a skilled technician."

56

$\mathbb{A}$ new chief resident, Dr. L., arrived under a rotation system. It was a relief to me, but others were also pleased. Dr. L. was a big, vigorous, merry, businesslike man. He epitomized the classic type of an American who excels at anything he does—be it in cowboy boots, in baseball stripes, or in doctor's white.

With his advent, things picked up in our department. He took care of everything and never looked at the clock. More importantly, he did everything well and with gusto. In a hospital, much of day-to-day life depends on how smart and efficient the chief resident is. It was a pleasure to watch him preparing the operating table, all the while shuffling his feet in a dance and crooning a popular song. I never tired of helping him and was even a bit sorry that I did not know the song and was too old to dance with him.

He called me "Dr. Vladimir" and always found an opportunity to compliment me on my work.

"Beautifully done! You are a great man, Dr. Vladimir!"

He asked me to do much of what I had not been allowed to do before and even tried to talk the scrub nurse out of her intransigent refusal to let me assist at operations. But to no avail.

I tried my luck at the English-language exam twice, but failed the grammar both times. I studied hard every day starting at 5:00 A.M., resumed studies after work, and crammed till midnight. I also tried to listen to the radio as much as possible, particularly to talk shows. It gave me an opportunity to hear different voices and get used to different speech patterns. Listening to the radio, I felt I was learning much about America.

I now bought *The New York Times* every day. I pored over that paper with its first-class news. I wonder if there is another newspaper in the world that can hold a candle to it. So far as I am concerned, reading only this paper and nothing else is enough to make one a highly educated and widely informed person.

I also bought the first book for my future library, *America,* by Alistair Cooke. I watched some of his TV shows about America. They were the first I could understand completely. The intellectual acuity of Cooke's presentations struck me and I decided to let his book be the cornerstone of my home library.

Listening, reading, and watching, I came to learn more and more about my new country. Every day I added to my stock of knowledge and understanding. However, there is only one way of gaining real understanding of a country and society: to work side by side with its people. Before taking a job at the hospital I had not known Americans. One had to see them every day from early morning till late at night, to share their interests and listen to them, in order to gain an insight into the accepted standards of life and human interaction. It is a particularly difficult task for a newcomer from Russia, a country where everything is an exact opposite to any society that can claim to be a democracy.

During one of the operations, standing behind the surgeons, I calculated that the nine persons in the operating room, including the patient, represented three races—white, black, and yellow; nine ethnic groups—a Greek, a Swede, an Italian, an Indian, a Hispanic (Panamanian), an Israeli, a Vietnamese, an Anglo, and a Russian; six religious denominations—two Roman Catholics, two Protestants, two Jews, an Orthodox Christian, a Hindu, and a Buddhist. Eight of us were first-generation immigrants and only one was a native-born American.

All of us immigrants spoke English poorly, each with his

own awful accent, so that the Americans had a hard time understanding us. All of us came to America from countries with different cultures, different social conditions, poor economies. And yet, all of us were here, working together, feeling at home among native Americans; all of us were in the process of settling down or had already put that hurdle behind us; and all of us either had achieved or hoped to achieve a better life than in our native homelands.

It was amazing how fast we all adapted to the entirely novel environment. How could it happen? I could come up with only one plausible explanation: the American model of society and economy, its working environment, suited us all. We watched Americans and tried to imitate them to the best of our abilities.

With surprise and delight I saw the motley personnel of our hospital cooperate and work as a cohesive unit. Breakdowns that could adversely affect the patients were unheard of; everything was done fast and skillfully. Bottlenecks did arise, but they were always promptly eliminated. And friction was there, but it was never allowed to burst to the surface. No one ever raised his or her voice. Each worker efficiently went about his assigned tasks and the whole engine rolled along, never jolting or stalling.

It baffled me. Russian hospitals are in a state of permanent crisis, beset with insuperable difficulties that always ultimately affect the patients in a negative way. Besides, the personnel there live in a state of permanent internecine warfare, with noisy quarrels erupting constantly, everyone pitted against everybody else, in spite of the fact that all are native-born citizens of the country, raised in the same traditions and under the same conditions. Friction is particularly pronounced among different ethnic groups, each one hating the rest of the bunch: Russians hate Moslems, Moslems hate Russians, Georgians hate Armenians, Armenians hate Georgians, and all of them are united by their hatred for Jews. It is a hard task for any manager to harness his underlings and keep them working.

Now I was discovering a new truth for myself: If a society

rests on a secure economic foundation and democratic principles, it moves forward, involving in its advance everyone who
is part of that society.

Young Dr. L. certainly had no inkling of the generalized
conclusions I derived from watching him. And I often recalled
the simple expression uttered by Dr. Fab: "I am not afraid of
a little work."

57

Stanley did not let me alone
and continued to call me at night.

"I miss you, Vladimir. Why don't you ever drop by? We
could have gotten the contract and the money long ago. All
the publishers keep asking me about the manuscript."

"All of them?"

"Well, maybe not all, but certainly most of them. Let's
rewrite our agreement."

"Sorry. I'm going to find a publisher myself."

"But without my help no publisher will touch your book."

"We'll see."

My friends Allan and Margaret Prince invited us to dinner
in their home to introduce me to Mr. Seymour P., an influential man in the world of art. He turned out to be an
exceptionally nice gentleman, attentive, affable, and efficient.
He had already read a few translated stories from my manuscript.

"I won't be so presumptuous as to assess the whole book
on the basis of a couple of stories, but what I've read is inter-

esting," he told me. "Why did you need a co-author? So far as I can see, all you need is a good editor. I'll send your manuscript to a friend of mine, one of the best literary agents in the business, and from then on you'll take over and deal with him on your own. Agreed?"

"Of course!"

And I began waiting, counting one week after another.

Junior, too, was impatient. He was waiting for the result of his Medical College Admission Test (MCAT). Finally his result was in—he scored above average, but not high enough. Junior grew surly and declared:

"That's it! It's clear no medical school will admit me."

"What makes you think so?"

"Don't you know the kind of score it takes to make it to medical school? I know people who didn't qualify with a twelve-point average, while mine is below ten."

"True, but the MCAT score is not the only thing that counts," I said.

"Why don't you consult your college adviser?" Irina added.

At my hospital, I consulted Dr. L. and other residents who had only recently been medical students themselves. The consensus was that, given his MCAT score, Junior's chances were fifty-fifty.

Several days later our son told us, "I've talked to the adviser. He believes that I have a fifty-fifty chance of success and recommends applying to many schools. But I feel it will be a waste of time and money."

"You must do as he says," I said.

"Do you have any idea how much it will cost? Each application costs at least thirty-five to fifty dollars, and some schools charge even more."

"You should do it whatever the expense. Mother and I can afford now to pay as much as it takes."

"Well, I don't care," he uttered his buzz line. "If both of you want it and are willing to pay, so be it. But I'm sure not a single school will so much as give me an interview."

He sent applications to twenty-five medical schools and grumbled for several weeks.

"Remember, you wanted it, I didn't. I've just done your bidding. And as for me, I don't care."

The applications cost us $1,500.

When one waits for something to happen and urges the time to move faster, it slows its pace as if testing one's patience. Several weeks passed before I finally heard the voice of that literary agent in the telephone receiver.

"Yes, yes, Mr. P. gave me your wonderful stories and I've read them. Excellent material! Why don't you give a call to my assistant. Her name is Mrs. H."

A few more weeks passed, and at last I was in Mrs. H.'s office. The office was more imposing than any I had seen before. Dozens of books were exhibited on shelves. I saw it as a good omen and thought, Maybe one day my book, too, will be among them.

Mrs. H. had trouble understanding my broken English. What was adequate for the hospital, where almost everybody spoke with a different accent and twisted the language out of all recognition, was patently out of place in a literary agency. However, New Yorkers never interrupt newcomers to correct their mistakes.

I told her about my literary and professional plans, while she punctuated my halting speech with excited exclamations: "Really? How wonderful! Splendid!"

I think, though, that the exuberant response reflected not so much the interest my story evoked as her excellent manners, because she barely understood half of what I tried to say. We agreed that I would call her from time to time to check on the progress of her quest for a publisher.

The day of our silver anniversary, October 4, was drawing closer. I badly wanted to give Irina a symbolic gift, a contract with a publishing house (including the advance check, naturally). For this reason I called Mrs. H. at her office almost every week to find out if she had any good news to report. Editors in several

publishing companies had already read the manuscript and responded in a positive manner, but, unsure of the book's com-
mercial prospects, had turned it down. Each time Mrs. H. tried
to cushion the blow by saying, "Don't get discouraged. The
publishing business always moves at a snail's pace. We'll find a
publisher, don't worry, but it will take time. Sometimes it takes
years."

Thus the gift to Irina did not
materialize. Instead, our son gave his mother a pleasant surprise.

"I got a call for an interview from the medical school in
Syracuse, in upstate New York," he told her. "I don't care.
I'm all but sure they won't take me, but I thought you might
welcome the news about the invitation."

Irina was delighted. The interview was no guarantee that
Junior would be accepted, but it meant that he had a chance.
After his medical school admission exam score he had been in
a depression, but now he came back to life. The first call for
an interview was followed in short order by two others—from
New York and Chicago.

"Well, how about it?" we told him. "And you thought it
was a waste of time to apply."

"I don't care. I have a feeling that nothing will come of it
anyway."

We had to find a way to instill some confidence in him. I
used any suitable occasion to instruct him how he should behave at the interview. Since my authority had lately burgeoned

in his eyes and I had been the one to compel him to apply, he listened to me fairly patiently.

"So far as I can see," I told him, "the purpose of the interview is not simply to hear your answers, because standard questions always elicit more or less standard responses, but it seems to me that the primary goal of the questioning is to assess the impression made by the interviewee."

"What should I do to sway them?"

"Just be yourself."

"That's a surefire recipe to get a kick in the seat of my pants."

He came back from the Syracuse interview glum as glum can be.

"It's finished," he declared gruffly, "I failed. There's no way they'll accept me."

"What happened?"

"I behaved like a fool. I don't even remember the answers I gave to their questions. What I do remember is I couldn't bear looking the interviewer in the eye. I just prayed for the whole thing to be over."

"That's all?"

"Well, they gave me a tour of the building and showed me the premises and equipment. I talked to a few students."

"About what?"

"I asked them about the school and they answered. . . . No, there's no hope. The only benefit is that maybe at the next interview I won't be so pathetic."

He was crushed. Irina and I felt little better. Three weeks passed. All three of us were in low spirits. I was still waiting for a potential publisher and made another try to pass the English-language exam. But the dominant theme of those days was Junior's fate.

One night I planned to attend a scientific conference of orthopedic surgeons at the New York Academy of Medicine and came home for a fast snack. I was listlessly munching my dinner when Irina returned. She thrust her head into the kitchen; there was a strange expression on her face.

"You really don't know?" she asked.

I shook my head. "What don't I know?"

"Our son has been accepted at Syracuse!"

I looked at her, stunned, the meaning of her words sinking in very slowly as if from afar—as a thunderclap rolling in.

"Yes, yes, he's been accepted." Irina beamed. I had not seen such a smile for a long time, and that was why she looked so strange to me.

"I thought you knew, because there's a letter from Syracuse on his desk that you might have read. It says in so many words, 'We are happy to inform you that you have been admitted to our medical school . . .'"

Only then did the realization come. My reaction was unexpected—all of a sudden I started crying. Irina and I embraced, laughed, kissed on and on, and could not calm down.

All our suffering and hardship had been worth it.

Two weeks later, a letter came from New York Medical School notifying Junior that there, too, he had been accepted.

"Do you agree now that there was a point in sending out all those applications?" I asked him again and again.

"And I don't care," he would reply and all three of us would burst out laughing.

Any hospital, whether in America or Russia, is a place of adventure.

Once a patient was brought to our emergency room, a man of twenty-six, who had been hurled out of a speeding car in Greenwich Village. His right leg and right arm were broken in several places and he was in very poor condition. I put his leg in traction and applied a plaster cast to the broken arm. Dr. L. gave me a hand. Then we took the patient to a large, eight-bed room and put him in the corner bed.

We were hardly done when the telephone at the nurse's station in the corridor rang. A male voice asked to talk to the physician responsible for the patient. Dr. L. was busy and asked me to respond.

"Listen, you lousy bastard," the voice said, "take good care of [the patient's name followed]. And remember, if anything happens to him, I'll waste you!"

I told Dr. L., "Somebody is threatening to kill the doctor who treats that guy. Maybe we should call the police?"

"Come on," he shrugged. "It's babble. Let's wait and see."

The next day, another resident heard similar tough talk on the phone. To my surprise the doctors casually brushed the threat aside. However, the patient's condition was improving and there was no reason for the threat to be implemented. As the patient got better, friends came in a stream to his bedside. All of them were young or middle-aged men, wearing leather jackets and tight-fitting pants or blue jeans with wide belts and tall cowboy boots. Many wore leather caps with a tiny visor.

Apparently those who had called with threats were among the visitors. I was fascinated by them and wondered who they might be. They didn't look like mobsters, but . . .

The corner where the patient's bed was located was cut off from view by drawn curtains. As I visited him I could see that with every passing day new postcards appeared on the walls; in a few days they covered all the available space. My God, those were some postcards!—naked male torsos; male genitals in all colors, sizes, and positions; shots of buttocks from all imaginable angles; and a great assortment of homosexual love scenes. If I had any lingering doubts, Dr. L. dispelled them.

"What's so mysterious about it?" he asked, laughing. "The patient is a male prostitute, very popular in this area. The visitors are his clients who can't wait until we discharge their pet."

I had never seen homosexuals at close quarters before and was totally ignorant about their ways.

"Aren't there gays in Russia?" Dr. L. asked me.

"Sure there are. But there homosexuality is a criminal offense; gays are packed off to Siberian labor camps for seven years as perpetrators of crimes against public morality. So they hide their sexuality."

"Why are they hounded?"

"Please, don't ask me. Everybody is subject to persecution; gays are no exception. The answer to your question is very simple, there's no freedom there."

"Yeah," Dr. L. said meditatively. "There you had no freedom; here we have too much of it."

The gay patient stayed in bed for several weeks because he developed necrotic complications in his broken leg. He besieged the staff with pleas to let him leave.

"You'll have to stay in bed a few more weeks, damaged nerves mend very slowly," I tried to explain to him.

"When, oh when?" he exclaimed in exasperation. "I'm losing two to three hundred bucks a day!"

His friends no longer threatened us with death, but they, too, waited impatiently. They pestered the physicians and nurses, their behavior rude and even obnoxious.

Once, passing by the corner, I had a glimpse of the goings-on behind the curtains: I could see through a narrow crack that the patient was performing oral sex on one of his visitors. Another visitor was posted outside as guard. Aha, so he still plied his trade even as a bedridden hospital patient! It was clear now why he and his clients were so eager to have him freed from all those restraining orthopedic devices.

I was less amazed by the homosexual activities than the death threats to physicians, the aggressively defiant behavior, and the unceremonious manner in which they imposed their own routine on the hospital. I was also amazed at the tolerance of the staff and physicians.

When I shared my observations with Dr. L., he laughed, "Everybody's been to the peep show. Those clients of his have even tried to dismantle the traction splint from his bed."

"In that case why hasn't anybody put a stop to it?"

"What? Do you want us to deport him to Siberia?"

"Just kick him out of the hospital and that's that."

"Then he'll sue for discharging him before full recovery."

"We could prove he was discharged for violating the regimen."

"To prove it you need facts that'll stand up in court. And if you try to collect such facts, his lawyer will charge us with unwarranted intrusion in his private life. Like I said, there's too much freedom in this country."

I sought the opinion of a nurse.

"Do you know what the patient and his visitors do behind those curtains?"

"Sure, I do," she grinned.

"And? What do you think about it?"

"It's up to them. If they're so horny . . ." She shrugged.

"In that case they should seek psychiatric help."

"I don't know. It's their own business. Personally I couldn't care less. It's a pity, though, that there are so many of them. Lots of young women can't get married because of a shortage of men."

"Don't you think we should discharge the patient?"

She shrugged and went about her duties. All nurses are busy and have no time to chat.

I had lived almost half a century in a society that allowed itself to be bullied from above, by its rulers. Now I witnessed an opposite phenomenon—a society that allowed itself to be bullied from below.

60

The hospital surgeons socialized in a small hall in front of the locker room in the operating wing. The anteroom contained an old sofa and three well-worn leather armchairs. Some surgeons liked to doze off; others preferred to tell jokes. Hospital news was relayed. But most often the talk was of treatment strategies. Senior doctors shared their experience with younger colleagues and regaled them with interesting reminiscences. Young doctors asked questions and received comprehensive answers. The atmosphere was relaxed and friendly, calling to mind a large family gathering.

Paper coffee cups in hand, the surgeons crowded at the X-ray film viewer, talking of operations, complications, methods of treatment, the happy or tragic outcomes of their cases. It was truly an "in-house academy of surgery."

Technical personnel rarely dropped by, and if they did, only on business and for a short time. For this reason I could not muster the courage to enter the anteroom, though I was dying to be part of the proceedings. Usually, if I had time, I would station myself near the doorway and try to listen. The American surgeons were generally far more knowledgeable than their Russian counterparts—testimony to their superior medical education and excellent residency training. Besides, I also liked the easygoing relationship between the old and the young, the chiefs and the subordinates, so unlike the stiff hierarchical order common to Russian hospitals. But no matter how well many of the physicians treated me, so far as they were concerned the label "orthopedic technician" was plastered all over me.

I even received an offer to join the nonmedical service workers union, District 1199 National Union of Hospital & Health Care Employees. I had no idea of what American trade unions were all about except that they were an enormous power. I was sent to talk to the local union organizer who was held in very high esteem by the union members. One of them described her in glowing terms. "She's one hell of a fire-breather, a real, out-and-out leader. You name it, she gets it."

"Where can I find her?" I asked.

"She works in the basement, Room B-51."

I went to look for her.

To my surprise, Room B-51 turned out to be the storeroom where I had once had to fight for my white uniform with that obnoxious fat woman.

"Could I see the union organizer?" I asked her.

The masklike face turned in my direction. "What do you want?"

"I'd like to talk to the union organizer about my personal affairs. Where is she?"

The mask turned away. "Shoot."

"I told you I want to talk to the union leader, not to you."

She turned still further away, heaved a huge sigh and ossified.

I waited, but she stayed in an attitude of total contempt.

"Where's the union leader?" I asked impatiently.

"I am her."

I was stunned. What kind of leader could she be? I rushed from the room, all thought of joining the union gone.

61

I acquired a new duty: to translate for Russian immigrant patients. Their numbers were swelling, and most of them were old and spoke no English. They had a lot of complaints, but nobody could understand them.

Once a resident physician named Peter asked me to translate for a Russian patient, an old man in his eighties with a suspected case of cancer. When we entered the room and I addressed him in Russian, the patient immediately launched into a litany of complaints: "What kind of hospital is this? What kind of doctors work here?" he screamed. "Nobody wants to talk to the patients in this place! American doctors pay no attention to their patients!"

"Please. Don't get upset."

"Don't be upset? I've been here for two days already, yet no one's said a word to me."

"You don't speak English, do you?"

"Of course not."

"And Americans don't speak Russian. Now with my help you'll be able to communicate with them at last. This gentleman here is your doctor. His name is Peter, in Russian—Piotr, Petya. What would you like to tell him?"

"I'd like to tell him that Americans have their heads screwed on wrong! That's what I'd like to communicate to him!" the patient said furiously.

"Why's he so angry?" Peter asked.

"He's angry because no one understands him. Why do you think Americans have their heads screwed on wrong?" I asked the patient.

"Because I've been here for two days, and they've drawn blood from my vein five times and X-rayed me three times."

"That's because you're being examined."

"I need to be treated, not examined!"

"It's impossible to treat a patient without preliminary examination," I told him gently.

"What's he saying?" Peter asked.

"He's wondering why so many tests are needed."

"Tell him we need even more tests. Otherwise we won't be able to diagnose his ailment properly."

"What's he saying?" the angry patient demanded to know.

"That they'll have to take another blood sample from you."

"I won't let them," the old man declared.

"What's he saying?" Peter asked again.

"He doesn't want to submit to another blood test."

Peter sat down on the patient's bed, put his arms around him in a gentle embrace, and told me, "Vladimir, I'm going to speak. Please translate simultaneously, okay? Sir, my grandfather also came from Russia and, were he alive today, he would have been your age. When he came to America as a young man, he spoke not a word of English. He told me about himself many years later. And he, too, found life very hard because nobody understood him . . ."

Peter's words had a magic effect; the old man calmed down and listened without trying to interrupt. I translated as fast as I could.

Peter went on, "I realize how difficult it must be for you not to be able to speak or understand English, but it's all right. The important thing is for you to get well. And all of us here, doctors and nurses alike, will treat you as we would our own grandfathers."

Listening to the translation, the old man was moved to tears.

"What a wonderful young man!" he sobbed, stroking Peter's hair. "Tell him he can take as much of my blood as he needs for his tests."

I translated for Peter's benefit.

"Please come to see me every morning," the patient asked the physician.

"Of course, I'll take care of you," Peter answered.

He kept his word and they became friends. The patient began to recover and never again got angry or upset.

But one day Peter could not come to see him; the night before, he had been assaulted with a knife near the hospital.

About 5:00 P.M., when it was still quite light, Peter left the hospital in his white physician's uniform and set out on foot toward the residents' building, a mere three blocks away. Suddenly he felt a prick in his neck and a heavy hand on his shoulder. A hoarse voice said from behind, "Give me your money or I'll slit your throat."

Fortunately Peter had a twenty-dollar bill in his pocket. Without turning his head, for he felt the tip of the knife pressed against his skin, he fished in his pocket, took out the bill and handed it to the mugger. The hood snatched the money and shoved Peter so he fell on the pavement face down. As he was falling, the knife slashed his neck. He was lucky in that no major vessel was cut open or else he might have bled to death. When Peter turned his head, the mugger had already disappeared behind the corner.

The next morning, Peter did not come to work. That night I told the patient that his favorite doctor had been taken ill himself.

"What happened?" the patient asked in surprise. "Only yesterday he was in perfectly good health."

"A minor injury . . ." To spare the old man's feelings, I did not want to tell the truth.

"I can see you're holding something back," the patient said. "You must tell me. I love Peter as my own grandson."

I told him. The old man was shocked.

"What? A doctor mugged? A doctor, in his white uniform, assaulted by a mugger? In a New York street? What does it mean?"

After a while he calmed down.

"I knew Russia's underworld pretty well because I used to be a lawyer," he told me. "The Russian thugs had their code of ethics. They never bother physicians because doctors are their potential protectors. I knew horrible individuals who would kill as a matter of course, but they never digressed from their code of ethics. America is a more civilized country, but the thugs here are worse than their Russian counterparts."

Peter recovered and reappeared, to the joy of the Russian patient. They became so close that somehow they managed to communicate without using my translation services. Needless to say, I didn't mind. At least now I had a little more spare time. I went to the anteroom of the operating rooms and called Mrs. H.

"Congratulations, Vladimir," she said jubilantly. "Mr. Mar has read the manuscript and agreed to publish the book. He wants to meet you. How about December twenty-first, six P.M.?"

Naturally I called Irina without delay. She was busy.

"Hi," she said impatiently. "Calling for lack of anything better to do?"

"This time you're wrong. I have something to tell you."

"Really? What?"

"I've got a publisher," I said proudly.

62

$\mathcal{D}$ecember 21 is the shortest day of the year. But it seemed to me it would never end. The hours dragged by interminably. Though I kept very busy and did not even have time to eat lunch, I thought I would never live till 6:00 P.M. But finally the torture was over and I was sitting at a table in an English pub on Sixth Avenue.

Mr. Mar asked me what I wanted to drink. Not knowing the names of the various cocktails, I simply doubled Mrs. H.'s order—a Bloody Mary. What it was I did not dare to ask. But when it transpired that Bloody Mary was vodka-based and that we were not going to eat anything, I wished I had made a more prudent choice. I was hungry and the very first sip went to my head, with the result that my fluency dropped precipitously. However, I did not order food, letting the publisher be the master of ceremonies. In the meantime I did my best to concentrate on what he was saying.

"I liked your stories. But in their current form there is little to hold them together. I'd like you to write more about yourself rather than about other people. The book must deal with yourself, with your own story. It must be your personal memoir."

"I avoided writing much about myself for fear the American reader would not care about my personal life."

"Americans like life stories," he told me. "The autobiography of a Russian doctor is likely to touch a chord in them. Write about yourself in as much detail as you can, describing your emotions. Unfamiliar with Russia, the reader must 'feel' the text and sense the 'smell' of the things described."

His idea certainly suited me. He went on asking questions and recommending what I should include in the book. I showed him my Russian photographs and he told me they would be printed in the book as well. It was all I could hope for and more. But I did not get the courage to ask about the advance payment, and neither the publisher nor my agent mentioned the money.

The next day, I sat down to modify the manuscript in keeping with the publisher's wishes, adding descriptions of events and intimate moments and emotions. For some time now, I had been a regular reader of American books and had a pretty clear idea of how to present my story in a way acceptable to the American reader. Words flowed effortlessly.

Meanwhile, my agent was negotiating the contract. The publisher initially offered me $7,500, and even that paltry sum he proposed to pay piecemeal. By that time I owed almost as much to my translator. Besides, I was to pay the agent and the lawyer, so there would be almost nothing left for myself. I did not dare to bargain, but apparently the agent heard such disappointment in my voice that she managed to get $11,000 out of the publisher. It was still no great sum, for much of the material had yet to be translated. Nevertheless, I basked in the knowledge that my book would be published.

Again Stanley called. "Vladimir, when are you going to see me? We could have pocketed the money long ago."

I replied triumphantly, "I've found a publisher myself and any time soon will sign the contract. On my own, without any co-author."

"How much will you get?"

"Anything I'll get will be mine and mine alone."

"Well, well," he said in a voice ringing with the cold metallic tones of a trombone. "Just you wait, Vladimir! Don't forget that you've learned to write from me!" and hung up. It sounded like a threat.

I was sick and tired of Stanley and did not pay any attention to his noise this time.

A few days later, when I was busy in the operating room, the chief's secretary called and left a message for me to get in touch with her. What does she want from me, I thought in disgust and decided that there was no reason why I should be in a hurry. Still, I finally called her.

"Your son called and asked me to tell you that you passed the English exam," she said.

"What? Say it again!"

"You've passed the English exam."

No, it was not a dream. She said it twice.

"Do you have any idea what it means to me?" I asked her.

"How should I know?"

"It means that I've become an American doctor! Thanks a million. I'm coming to the office. Is the chief there? Yes? I'm coming."

Beside myself with joy, I ran to the liquor store across the street and bought a bottle of Moët champagne. Bottle in hand, I arrived at the chief's office and prevailed on him and his secretary to drink to my success. We clinked glasses.

"To your success, Doctor Vladimir!" the chief said.

His words rang like music in my ears. But I had to exploit my success.

"When you hired me, remember you said that you believed in my future?"

"Of course."

"May I take the liberty of asking you to change my status, so I could legitimately assist in the operating room?"

"I'm going to make you a fellow," he vowed.

I was overjoyed; at last I was going to become a physician, no longer a technician!

At home, a beaming Irina was waiting for me. She flung herself in my arms. We kissed, laughed, gamboled. Only now were the opportunities of the new life, of which we had been dreaming for more than three years, opening up before us. What a joy it was to realize that the worst was finally behind us! How happy I was that she, my wife, my friend, my faithful assistant, the only true love of my life, had been by my side.

We had to celebrate the good news. We invited our friends,

Allan and Margaret Prince and Seymour P. with his wife, to the Russian Tea Room. The restaurant was still beyond our means, but the events we were going to celebrate merited a special occasion. Irina was elegantly dressed and highly animated. Sitting in the restaurant with our friends, Irina and I thought in unison that that night was a kind of symbolic return to our former social status, to the traditions of our bygone life.

Finally, after a monthlong wait, my ECFMG certificate arrived in the mail. I came home to find it on my desk next to a note from my son: "Congratulations to an American doctor!" In the course of my professional life I had been awarded nearly two dozen diplomas and certificates, but none of them was as dear to me as this one.

The next morning I took a copy of the certificate to my chief.

"You promised to change my circumstances as soon as I got my physician's certificate. Here it is."

I took pleasure in showing the certificate to my friends among the physicians and harvesting their unanimous congratulations.

Even scrub nurse Ms. Fren told me resentfully, "I heard you've passed the doctor's exam. Congratulations."

But my circumstances did not change. The chief did nothing for me.

My colleagues kept asking me, "Well, Vladimir, when are you going to get permission to assist us at operations?"

"The choice isn't mine," I shrugged helplessly. "I'd be glad to oblige."

Dr. Walter, the one who had asked me to assist him at the very start of my career with the hospital, was particularly impatient.

"Did you talk to the chief?"

"Yes."

"What did he say?"

"Nothing definite."

"Are you allowed to assist me or not?"

"I can't. Nothing has changed."

"You must be kidding!"

The next morning, the scene was repeated.

"Well, how about today? Can you assist me?"

"No. I'm still a technician."

"Why don't you go and ask the chief once again?"

"How many times am I supposed to plead my case?"

I wish Dr. Walter had left me alone, for the constant reminders hurt. It was clear that my boss could easily change my status if he wished. All my colleagues were certain of that. Other than the chief's total indifference, there could be no reason why I was kept in limbo. And that hurt the most, reminding me of the previous setbacks, such as the trick played on me by Dr. S. from the Bronx. However, I needed the salary, and so I still stood behind the surgeons' backs from 7:00 in the morning till 5:00 in the afternoon.

I decided to approach the chief of the general surgery department for a first-year position in his residency training program. I put together all the required documents and brought the package to his office. Two secretaries took their time, discussing over the telephone the goings-on at the parties the night before. Then one of them gave me a nod and proceeded to file her nails. While she was busy sculpting, I explained why I wanted to see her boss.

"He's very busy. Leave your papers and come by sometime later."

"When?"

"Let's say in a couple of weeks."

"It will be too late."

"That's the earliest he'll be able to see you."

The next time I brought them a box of chocolates. They magnanimously accepted the gift and suggested that I drop by in a couple of weeks, filing their nails all the while.

The fourth or fifth time, I told the secretary, "Do you know that I used to be a department chief myself?"

"Really? How interesting!" she exclaimed and slowed down the nail filing a little.

"But there was not a single time when I would not see anyone who wished to see me, much less a colleague," I went on.

"Really? How interesting!" she exclaimed, and her file resumed shuttling with blinding speed.

"Tomorrow," she said. "Come to my office tomorrow."

The next day, the nonmedical workers' union went on strike and the secretaries joined the job action.

Early in the morning, the police set up wooden barriers at the entrance to the hospital. Passing by, I saw both secretaries among the strikers. Together with the rest, they were fighting for a pay hike. Both were filing their nails, talking languidly. They waved at me, and I smiled back. I was glad that I had not joined the union and had no reason to stand by their side. Besides, I did not like the union leader, the fat woman who issued uniforms in the basement. Rumor had it that she was a superb organizer, but I could not imagine her in the role of a fiery leader. If she really was so terrific, why wasn't she anywhere to be seen among the strikers?

Even as that thought crossed my mind, an old Pontiac rolled up to the barriers, and the accursed female climbed out from behind the wheel, bullhorn in hand. She swaggered to the group of picketers, placed herself in front, put the loudspeaker to her mouth, and roared:

"What-do-we-want? A-con-tract! When-do-we-want-it? Right-now!"

Pigeons fluttered up, scared by the sudden outburst; the police officers came to life and stepped closer. She moved in a circle, leading the crowd in the chant. The entire group picked up the rhythm and began marching behind the leader.

"What-do-we-want? A-con-tract! When-do-we-want-it? Right-now!"

A few days later the management met all union demands.

As for me, I failed in my attempts either to see the bosses or to get my papers back. I came to see both secretaries a few more times. They were still occupied with nail filing and still gave me the same negative replies (for higher pay, though).

64

Irina and I strolled along Central Park West, discussing what to do. My three-month-long quest was a failure. I was still a technician. Meanwhile, all positions in the residency programs, particularly the ones in surgery, had been filled. There was a slightly better chance in rehabilitation and psychiatry.

"Don't you think it will be hard for you to endure five years of training in surgery?" Irina asked me.

"Of course, it will. No question about it."

"What's the duration of training in rehabilitation?"

"Three years."

"Maybe you should think of changing your specialty?"

I stopped in my tracks, astonished.

"Irina, it's out of the question," I said irritably.

"But why?"

"If a person has a special talent, it's his duty to put it to good use, not throw it away. All my life I've been an orthopedic surgeon. When I became a technician here, I watched my American colleagues at work. I thought that while I was first-rate in Russia, in America I wouldn't be anything but a clumsy oaf. I'm as good or better than most American doctors. If I abandon orthopedic surgery, it will be an injustice not only to me but also to my profession."

"I know, I know. But you should also think of your health," Irina said.

"Let's make one thing absolutely clear. I was born a surgeon and as a surgeon I'll go to my grave. And you're wrong if you think I'll be better off in a rehabilitation program. On the contrary, I'll die of boredom."

"I didn't want to wound your pride. I'm just trying to find a way out."

"There can only be one way out: to find a training program in surgery and start at the entry level."

"Have you finally gotten permission to assist at operations?" Dr. Walter asked the next morning.

"No."

"A good friend of mine works in another hospital. I'll talk to him, maybe he'll be able to offer you a job."

I made one last attempt to talk to the chief.

"Oh . . . yes," he said. "Yes, of course. . . . Maybe next year I'll be able to make you a house officer."

When I related our conversation to Dr. Walter, he flew into a rage. "He plans to give you dog work so you can slave for him without getting any credit. Tell him to go screw himself. I'll make it a point to talk to my friend about you."

"What hospital is it?"

"J. Hospital. It's small, but respectable."

"I know it," I said. "It's on the list of hospitals I applied to for the training program in surgery."

65

$\mathbb{A}$merica in the early 1970s was a promised land for foreign-trained physicians. Virtually any immigrant doctor could find a vacancy in a residency program, undergo full training, and stay in the country for good as a full-fledged doctor. In those years, America, like an international medical vacuum, sucked in doctors from all over the Third World. And Russian refugees were prominently represented in that influx of foreign physicians.

That period coincided with the peak of the Russian Jewish exodus. For Russian immigrants, who a few years before had not imagined such upheavals were possible, it was a golden age indeed. Not only did most of them contrive to reach America, but almost all managed to establish themselves in their new country. Even women physicians of advanced age, some in their late fifties, managed to gain access to training. Some of them were even so lucky as to get accepted in residency programs without passing the English-language qualifying exam, conditional on their eventual passing.

But the period did not last long—only till the early 1980s when it suddenly transpired that America had an excess of doctors and the ominous prospect of medical unemployment loomed ahead. Then the AMA cut back medical school enrollment, abolished residency programs, and turned down foreign applicants. Thousands of foreign-trained physicians rushed applications to scores of residency programs all over the country. The magnitude of the problem was highlighted by the fact that as many as 250 Russian doctors with all necessary qualifications failed to gain admission to any training program.

Reflections on the sad reality crowded into my mind one day in April 1982 as I was going by subway to an appointment with Dr. Reg, to whom Dr. Walter had referred me. I was anything but optimistic. It seemed to me a miracle was all I could rely on.

I emerged from the subway station and stopped in amazement. The panorama of a ruined city lay before my eyes. Elegant brownstones, big and small, stood without roofs, their walls crumbling, their empty windows gaping. Through breeches in the walls one could see all the way to the sky—inside there were neither partitions nor ceilings. The grim ruins seemed to leap straight out of World War II—vintage pictures of war-ravaged Stalingrad.

But the streets here teemed with life. The throng consisted almost entirely of blacks, mostly young men and teenagers, whose postures bespoke idleness. Some of them leaned, hands in pockets, against the walls; others shouted to each other across the street; still others listened to Latin music from powerful transistor radios. Although it was noon, there were quite a few drunks.

Tense with foreboding, I wended my way along the street, all the time expecting somebody to try to strip me of my attaché case or simply to approach. I tried to put on the nonchalant, indifferent air of an undercover cop. All my muscles were tense, posed to propel me instantly into running away or even fighting. In this way I reached the hospital. In its immediate vicinity the tension abated somewhat. Guards were posted at the entrance, an ambulance pulled up, and a guarded parking lot was nearby. I relaxed slightly and thought, Could providence lead me into such a depraved area for the sole purpose of exposing me to danger? Perhaps it is the last trial before I land a position in a residency program.

The first cursory glance inside, while I walked down the hospital corridor, showed a picture of desolation. The walls were dirty, a large Service Department sign hung on the third-floor landing. The pay phones were thronged by patients

sporting dressings and plaster casts, hobbling on crutches, rolling about in wheelchairs, hooked to IV pulls. They brought to
mind a wartime evacuation hospital teeming with wounded
servicemen. Cigarette smoke floated in the air; many of the
patients carried blaring radios; everybody tried to shout above
the din. My impression was that all the patients were recruited
from among the people I had just tried to dodge in the streets
outside.

Again a thought crossed my mind, Certainly if providence
has led me to this kind of hospital, it can't be merely as a
sightseeing tour. I have seen my share of hospitals for the poor
in Russia.

The surroundings changed drastically when I entered the
office of Dr. Reg, deputy chief of the department of surgery.
A lanky man with snow-white hair, he spoke in a gentle, soft
voice and immediately won me over with his elegant manner.

"Take a seat, Dr. Golyakhovsky," he said politely, man-
aging to pronounce my name correctly (a feat beyond the ability of most Americans).

"Thank you for coming. I looked through your credentials and was most impressed. Besides, my friend Dr. Walter
has pleaded very eloquently in your behalf. You're a perfect
candidate for our program; we need a man of experience. But
it's only fair to warn you that our hospital is in dire financial
straits, so as of today I can't promise you anything definite.
However, we're expecting to be merged with another hospital.
If the merger comes through, we'll get an infusion of money
that will enable us to take a few extra residents. I have your
name at the top of our respective lists."

"Thank you," I said. "When do you expect that merger?"

"Within a month. The municipal authorities have already
okayed it. As soon as the decision is finalized, we'll mail you a
notification and a contract for the first year of residency training."

I liked his calm and frank manner of talking. It was some
time since I had been treated with respect by anyone in a position of authority. When I walked back to the subway station,
the crowd of loafers in the street was even larger than before;

the noise, the music, and the number of winos increased pro-
portionately. I kept thinking that while the neighborhood was
awful, my co-workers-to-be might turn out to be better than
the denizens of more pacific places. After all, as the Russian
saying goes, it is the person who makes the place better, not
the other way around. The memory of Dr. Reg reconciled me
to any conditions. If only they would take me!

For more than four years now my family's motto was If
only they would take me (him, her, us)! Irina and I and our
son worked our tails off and paid an enormous price to achieve,
step-by-step, what is commonly defined as "good fortune."

When I told Irina about my visit to the hospital, hiding
nothing, she said with a sigh, "God, if only they would take
you!"

66

Junior was nearing the end of
his college studies. He was taking the last exams and spent
nights in his room studying. Although already accepted by a
medical school, he was not sure whether his college grades
would be good enough to graduate. Finally the last exam in
his major, physical chemistry, came. Junior repeatedly pro-
fessed his certainty that he would fail. His fears were conta-
gious. Poor Irina, also with a bad case of nerves, could speak
of nothing else.

"What happens if he fails?"

"He won't," I responded soothingly.

"Why do you think he won't?"

"Well, so far he's passed all his exams. Why on earth should he fail this one?"

"He says it's an extraordinarily difficult subject and curses himself for having chosen it as his major. If only he had majored in biology instead!"

"Don't worry, everything will be just fine."

But our worries about Junior's exam paled beside the anxiety with which we awaited the hospital's response. Irina constantly heckled me with questions.

"Did Walter call Dr. Reg?"

"Yes, he did. The decision's still pending."

"Didn't he say when it might be handed down?"

"He asked me to call in a week."

"God, I can't endure that torture any longer!"

"But what if this opportunity doesn't materialize? What will I do?" I asked anxiously.

We sighed—alternately and together. Our tired souls were again taut.

One day at my hospital I bumped into the chief of supplies, the lady for whom I had toiled in the basement my first few days on the job. She greeted me with a charming smile.

"How are you, Vladimir?"

"Fine, thank you. And how are you?"

"Awful. I have absolutely nobody to work for me. You should see the terrible mess in the basement. It's been terrible since the last strike."

"I am sorry," I mumbled.

"I've appealed to the management to let me have you again," she said brightly.

"What? But I'm going to enter residency training."

"While you're still here they promised to let me have you."

Horror-stricken by the news, I again asked Dr. Walter to call Dr. Reg.

Although in a hurry to get to the operating room, he took pity on me and stayed back to comply with my request. I personally dialed the number and passed the receiver to him. He had a brief exchange with Dr. Reg, then hung up.

"Great news, Vladimir!" he exclaimed. "The merger has

been approved at last, he said your contract would be in the mail. Congratulations!"

"Thank you! Thank you so much for what you've done for me!" I said again and again, overcome by emotion.

"Come on, what's so special about it?"

"Nobody else has lifted a finger to help me!"

"I know," he said. "All one can count on is connections."

It was true. That warning was the first thing I had heard from my wise old Aunt Lyuba the night I arrived in New York.

"Dr. Walter," I exclaimed, "I'd like to buy you a dinner at the Russian Tea Room! Let's celebrate!"

Tying up the gown at his back that day I thought, Praised be the Lord, the dreaded chore was at an end. Scrub nurse Ms. Fren dispatched me to haul heavy oxygen cylinders. I almost sang as I carried them. Now that at long last I had been accepted I did not have a care in the world. And I was not afraid of a little work!

All three of us waited with bated breath for the arrival of the coveted letter. My salary would be $25,000 per year, a net gain of $8,000. However, we had to pay $10,000 for our son's tuition and board. So the extra expenses would more than offset the anticipated increase. But I still had $3,000 left from the advance payment for the book.

"It's too dangerous to go to that hospital by subway," I told Irina. "Even in daylight it's a combat zone there. And I'll have to come to work at dawn and leave late at night as well as stay on call every third night. I'm afraid we'll have to buy a car. The down payment is not large, and the rest we'll be paying on an installment plan. What do you think?"

Psychologically I still felt ill at ease broaching the subject of such a huge purchase. I waited tensely for Irina's response.

"Of course, you must buy a car and drive to and from work," she replied resolutely. "I'd already thought of it." She paused. "After we make the first payment for Junior's tuition and the down payment for the car, will there be anything left for a vacation?"

I was aware of her fervent desire.

"I guess there will."

"Enough for us to go to Europe?"

A European trip was her cherished dream, and I had waited for her to voice it. I took her face between my palms and began kissing it.

"Of course, I'm going to take you to Europe! You thought of my need for a car; I thought of your need for a trip to Europe. Let's start planning right away."

"Where shall we go?"

"Take your pick. How about Paris?"

"Oh, wonderful!"

"And Amsterdam?"

"Yes, yes!"

I myself was dying to see Europe, but the desire to take Irina was even stronger. She had difficulty adapting to American life. She hated and feared New York City and never felt at home in it. Europe had a powerful attraction for her as an embodiment of all things intrinsically kindred, familiar, and beloved. We had been raised in the European spirit, and we felt more at home with European cultural heritage and traditions than in America. It seemed to Irina that a trip to Europe would let her inhale the air of her youth again.

67

Junior took his last exam and came home in a somewhat calmer mood. He did not know his score but felt that he had done well enough. Irina was relieved. She was all aflutter, looking forward to the forthcoming trip and conferring with the travel agent about the cheapest charter fare and reservations along the route we had worked out. For my part, I was trying to complete the alterations and additions to the first half of my manuscript. I wanted to have the translation on the publisher's desk before departure.

On May 1, I set out to buy a car, the seventh in my life. I felt I owed it to my new country to invest in a domestic one. I had owned the previous six cars in Russia where car buying, just as elections, was free of the bothersome problem of choice. All it took was putting one's name on a list and waiting for at least two or three years for the privilege to pay the entire purchase price in advance. There was no layaway plan and little choice, for the Russian automotive industry turned out just two models, although later the choice was expanded to three. Having put down his money, the lucky buyer had to wait another year or so and only then could he receive a car of a color available at the store. Such "simplicity" forced any prospective motorist to join the waiting list several times, so that when the first car wore out, he would already be signed up for another. I followed this rule and was able to buy six cars in the span of twenty-one years. Technologically, Russian cars were as far behind American automobiles as the Montgolfier brothers' hot-air balloon was behind a modern jet aircraft. Russian car buffs, myself included, in the streets of Moscow always ogled the rare American car, only in possession of foreign embassies. A parked American car invariably drew a crowd of admirers.

But now I was in for a different experience. I wandered around a cavernous showroom between scores of different cars, peering at the price stickers, sitting down behind the wheels, seeking a model and color most to my liking. Then I went to another showroom across the street. I planned to visit yet another but was too tired to follow through on my intention. Besides, what was the point of being choosy? I did not know one from another, only how much I wanted to spend. I returned to the first showroom and called Irina.

"Listen, there are so many cars and they all look so good that I've overstrained my powers of discrimination. But basically, I've made my choice. Can you come to have a look? If you approve, we'll buy it."

"But I don't know anything about cars," Irina protested. "It's up to you to decide."

"No. Please come if you can, I want you to have a look. Besides, it will be an interesting experience for you. It's high time we began adapting to American ways."

When she arrived, I escorted her to a 1982 Buick Skyhawk, opened the door, and told her to get behind the wheel.

"Try to feel like an American!"

Irina liked the car and opted for beige.

And so for the first time I drove in my own Buick through the familiar streets of mid-Manhattan. It was an eerie sensation. There was a time when I had walked the pavement here, rain or shine, to save the bus fare. Beautiful cars had passed by, blinding me with their headlights. They seemed to belong to a different life, far removed from my reality. But I had kept thinking, I'll do it! I'll be what I want to be! And here I was at last, driving my own car and blending with the traffic. Yes, I had merged into the mainstream of my new country. I had made it!

It remained for me to do a few things. I received the finalized half of the manuscript from my translator and took it to the literary agent. I filed an application for my new invention, Devices for Correct Application of Plaster Dressings, and took it to a patent lawyer.

Finally the contract for my first year of training in general surgery arrived in the mail. It qualified me as a Post-Graduate Year One (PGY-1). Signing it, I thought with a smile that by rights I ought to be a PGY-29 for I had completed my medical undergraduate studies as far back as 1953. Thus the contract made me twenty-nine years younger. Not bad!

68

I f I am asked what kind of entertainment is least entertaining, I answer without hesitation, American parties. Amazingly, in a society that has for centuries nurtured democratic principles, people have not learned to make merry at gatherings, whether at home or at the office. One almost never hears laughter; the sparkle of merriment that should enliven such social occasions is simply not there. Usually the revelers drink a little, eat a little, talk a little, keep silent a little, and get bored a lot.

Russian parties are generally far more lively. In spite of the generally bleak reality (or maybe because of it) people who get together try to have a good time. They tell jokes, laugh heartily, dance, drink a lot (even to excess!), and in general have fun. Perhaps the Russian party is an outlet for the Russians' gregarious nature.

I brought the wine and piroshki to the clinic, in effect throwing myself a farewell party. I made a mental vow to try to prod my guests into some merriment. The clinic nurses, a giggly Puerto Rican named Renée, and Marylin, a lithe and elegant black girl, helped me set up the spread. In the plaster cast room, they covered the orthopedic table with a white hospital-issue bedsheet and laid out the food. I delivered a lecture on the Russian piroshki and added that my mother had personally baked them. I tried to make my story funny and interspersed serious stuff with jokes to inject a dose of merriment and stir up the crowd.

"Ivan the Terrible and Peter the Great loved piroshki. Khrushchev, too, used to eat them. But my mother's piroshki are even better than those the Russian tyrants gorged themselves on. So you are exposed to the cream of the Russian cuisine."

My guests smiled, gingerly bit off tiny pieces of dough at the edge and peered inside at the stuffing.

"What's in there?" they asked.

"The stuffing is made of Russian missiles and tanks."

"Seriously, Vladimir! Really, what is it?"

I explained as best I could how piroshki were made and what they were made of. Gradually, the party was coming to life. Marylin and Renée presented me with a joint gift—a pen and a funny greeting card with the signatures of the entire surgical staff. The two girls embraced and kissed me from both sides, saying that they had never had and never would have such a wonderful technician. Moved, I made a brief speech.

The piroshki were a hit. Many were hungry at the end of the workday, particularly young residents who never had enough time to eat. They quickly figured out which contained what and began grabbing fistfuls.

Having had their fill, my guests became more talkative. As usual, they discussed their work. Once on the track of shop talk, the guests forgot about their host. I surreptitiously left the room and went to the subway station to go home. Thus I said good-bye to my first job.

At home, I found a guest, Junior's fellow student and friend Bob Gavallo, a pleasant lanky lad. They were drinking beer in the kitchen to celebrate graduation. Irina was not home yet and I sat down with the boys.

"Have you told your dad how you graduated?" Bob asked Junior.

"No."

"Why don't you?"

Junior kept mum, so I took the initiative. "Anything wrong? What are your grades?"

"Okay," he replied impassively.

"Come on, tell him," Bob insisted.

Junior again shrugged.

"He graduated magna cum laude," Bob told me. "The best in our class."

I glanced at my son, who was smiling shyly, as if embarrassed by his success. In a flash, I recalled the trials Junior had endured. If anyone had told me when we were leaving Russia or even when he was just starting in college that he would be graduated with honors, I would have laughed in the face of the prophet. Now I was smiling inwardly. Our son was the chief beneficiary of our travails. But hadn't it been our dearest dream from the very start, the ultimate goal of the family? He was the one who faced a long life in America; he was the one to start the American branch of our family.

The boys went to the movies while I sat alone and reflected, the smile never leaving my lips. When Irina came home she asked me right off, "What are you so happy about?"

"Junior was graduated from college magna cum laude!"

She looked at me perplexed, as if refusing to believe.

"Yes, yes," I repeated. "It's true. Our son has finished college near the top of his class."

On August 31, 1982, on the eve of the start of training, all new residents were summoned for orientation. Our hospital had training programs in all basic branches of medicine: internal medicine, general surgery, obstetrics and gynecology, pediatrics, pathology, and general urology. All in all, there were about one hundred first-year residents.

The freshman residents represented, on a miniature scale, what I had already seen at the board exam: Indians were in a clear majority, many Orientals, quite a few Caribbean blacks, a few Puerto Ricans and Cuban refugees, and a handful of native Americans—graduates of medical schools in Spain, Mexico, the Philippines, and the Dominican Republic. Finally there were six Europeans: four Russian Jews, a Pole, and a Portuguese. But there was not a single graduate of an American medical school; Americans had stayed away from that hospital. Naturally most residents were in their twenties, but there were a few Indians pushing forty. In the Russian group, not one was younger than thirty, and I was the patriarch of the group.

I had mixed emotions. While happy to have attained doctor's rank again, I was embarrassed in the midst of that youthful crowd, feeling much like an old rooster among young chicks. I realized that although I was able to crow like an adult, I would have to chirp like a chick; full-fledged doctor that I was, I would have to undergo training from the very beginning.

The first order of business was learning to scrub for surgery. The matron of the operating room demonstrated to us, in minute detail, all the stages of the double scrubbing procedure: this first scrubbing was supposed to go to the level of the wrists only; and how to dry the hands on a sterile towel. Listening to her talk, I recalled my scrubbing debut more than three decades ago. But what could I do? I had no control over my training program. So long as I bore the title of a PGY-1, I was required to behave like one. Therefore I did not let on that the matron's lecture covered familiar material and I listened to her with the eager attentiveness of a genuine freshman.

Our immediate teachers and guides were second-year residents. Most of them enjoyed their new positions of authority. For example, they meticulously checked whether we stuck to the rule prescribing exactly ten minutes of scrubbing, finding fault with our performance if they could. It was exactly like a second-year soldier hazing a fresh recruit in boot camp. And the victim must bear his suffering without a murmur—or else he is in for a lot of additional trouble.

PGY-2 Dr. Les, a Jamaican, took personal charge of me though nobody entrusted him with that responsibility, nor did I request his undivided attention.

"What country are you from? Russia? Have you ever scrubbed for an operation?" he asked me.

"A little."

"Let's see how you do it. Follow me. No, no! You handle the brush incorrectly! Once again, from the very beginning. No! I can see you're still a beginner."

I had a powerful urge to tell him to go to hell. However, conscious of being a freshman, I was reluctant to start my training by arguing with a superior.

The compensation came in the operating room when I was the one whose gown was tied up behind his back, not the other way around. When I approached the operating table for the first time as a physician in America, neither the surgeon, nor Dr. Les his assistant, paid the least attention. The procedure was a routine herniotomy and I was to perform the job of second assistant. The surgeons were bent over the wound, while I stood aside, holding my gloved hands at the ready and waiting for an invitation to take part in the proceedings. At last the surgeon turned his head.

"Are you a new resident?" he asked. "What's your name? Stand here and pull the retractors. Have you ever assisted at operations?"

"A little."

"Splendid. Now, since you've had some experience, take the scissors and snip off the loose ends in the knots I'm going to tie."

I tried to comply.

"For all your experience, you haven't learned to handle the scissors right." He turned my scissors in such a way that I could hardly use them at all. But rather than protest, I bent my body at an impossible angle to be able to manipulate the instrument, and we got through the operation.

The second day I drew my first night duty. My immediate superior was Dr. Yo, a lanky thirty-year-old Japanese. Making the rounds of all surgical patients on the nine floors, he explained and described my duties to me on the go, never breaking his stride. I was to examine newly admitted patients, take blood samples, and carry test tubes with color-coded stoppers to the many different labs. Then I was to collect the analyses at the labs, take them to the respective rooms, and enter the results in the patients' charts. Also, I was to be the first to respond to the summons of a nurse if anything had to be done for a patient: a new prescription, intravenous injection, blood transfusion, or change of dressing.

The Japanese scurried down the corridors at such a clip that I had difficulty keeping pace with him. I raced at his side, filling my notepad with whatever I managed to understand from his instructions; his accent was not easy to grasp.

Our chief was Dr. Saly, an Indian of about forty. He was in the fourth year of residency, that is, a PGY-4, and moved as slowly as an Australian koala climbing a tree. He spoke equally slowly and with a thick accent that was even more difficult to understand than Dr. Yo's. Dr. Saly showed me how best to write down analyses in a notebook for subsequent transfer of the notes to the charts of newly admitted patients, and then proceeded to lecture me on the political aspects of our job.

"Remember, the more important the attending physician, the more updated the analyses of his patients should be. For instance, here are two new patients. One of them is a private patient of chief attending physician Dr. R.; the other is a service patient looked after by junior attending physician Dr. P. You ought to take up Dr. R.'s patient right away, examine him thoroughly, enter your observations, in minute detail, in his chart. Only then should you handle Dr. P.'s patient. If you have any questions to your superiors, ask Dr. Yo, who will consult me. Yourself, you are not to bother either myself or the chief resident. Understood?"

"Understood. But what if the junior physician's patient is

in graver condition than the one of the senior doctor? What should I do in such a case?"

"It's not your job to decide which of the patients is sicker. You're not qualified yet to make independent decisions. Just call Dr. Yo, who will consult me. Understood?"

I understood that he was a horse's ass. Had he found himself under my control he would have been dismissed in an instant. Besides, he had somehow made it as far as the fourth year in this program, so apparently he knew what he was talking about.

At 9:00 P.M., a seven-year-old black girl with all the symptoms of appendicitis was admitted to the emergency room. I took her blood sample for analysis and watched Dr. Saly examine her. He seemed to vacillate between urgent surgical intervention and deferring the operation till next morning. I was surprised, for the faster the operation, the better the prognosis, but I refrained from questions or comments. The girl writhed in pain.

It was past midnight when Dr. Saly finally mustered up the courage to dial the number of the attending physician on call. But he was so coy and mumbled so incoherently that even sitting next to him I could not figure out the patient's condition. Not surprisingly, the sleepy surgeon had to ask repeated questions.

He hung up and proceeded to check my entry in the girl's chart.

"Why haven't you written anything about the patient's sex life?" he asked me.

"Sex life at seven! What kind of sex life can one have at such an age?"

"Everything's possible. You should make it a point to conduct a gynecological examination and record the results in the chart, whatever the patient's age. Remember, though, in case of a minor, the examination should be performed in the presence of witnesses and with her mother's consent."

"I would never have gotten up the nerve. But I guess I'll have to, if you say so."

The operation did not start until 2:30 in the morning. Dr. Saly was the operating surgeon, the attending physician his first assistant, and I the retractor puller. Although a PGY-4, Dr. Saly had no surgical skills. He poked the scalpel at the skin, unsure of where and how to make an incision. The attending physician had to guide him, trying to keep his temper in check. When he finally managed to expose the appendix, it became immediately clear that surgery was indeed urgently needed. Thank God, help arrived in time—just barely.

70

One of the first patients I saw was a seventy-year-old white woman suffering from hallux valgus—bent and distorted toes. She had come to the hospital on her own, complaining of pain. I was firmly convinced that the old lady needed no surgery, particularly insofar as she had a severe case of diabetes. All she needed was a pair of orthopedic shoes or even a set of supinators for her regular shoes. However, the young attending physician, Dr. Gav, an Indian fresh out of training at our hospital, talked the patient into an operation.

"Your pain will be gone and you'll be able to walk like a young girl," he promised. She obediently signed the consent papers. Dr. Gav performed the operation, resection of bone's exostosis on the right foot. He promised to operate on the other foot after the first one healed. But it would not; as is often the case with old people afflicted with chronic diabetes, she showed a flaccid healing pattern.

I did not like the way Dr. Gav treated his patient. Once, when I found myself alone with another resident, an Israeli PGY-3, I asked him, "Do you think that patient was in need of an operation?"

"Of course not," he replied.

"Why then did Dr. Gav subject her to it?"

My colleague eyed me ironically. "She didn't need an operation, but he sure did."

It was my first encounter with unnecessary surgery. In Russia, such a notion does not exist. On the contrary, the problem there is lack of surgery when indicated, the reason being that Russian surgeons have no income from their patients—unless, of course, they treat them privately on the sly.

My experience told me that the poor old woman had serious problems. Dressing her wound, I could see that she got weaker by the day. Drastic countermeasures were in order. But Dr. Gav was cramming for the national board exam and only rarely appeared for even a cursory examination of his patient. Considering my junior status, I was not supposed to intervene. My immediate superiors, PGY-2, PGY-3, and PGY-4 residents, also watched the patient's condition deteriorate but made no attempt to bother the busy physician.

The only person I outranked was M., an American-born medical student who studied in Mexico and was serving in our hospital for clinical experience. Senior residents almost completely ignored him and the poor fellow was cast adrift. So he hooked up with me, and I took pleasure in sharing my experience with the youngster.

The old woman exhibited symptoms of incipient gangrene of the foot. Dressing her wound with M.'s help, I expounded on what I thought needed to be done. He listened with obvious skepticism. Then the patient's general condition deteriorated still further and she developed diarrhea.

"Do you think it is common diarrhea?" I asked him.

"I guess so. Maybe food poisoning?"

"No way. It is incipient protein deficiency due to poisoning with the products of gangrene-related protein degradation."

"Really?" M. asked in surprise. "What's to be done?"

"Her foot must be amputated and she should be put on intravenous protein feeding without delay."

"Amputation? You must be kidding! Is it that serious?"

"Everything is serious in surgery. Any complication is a potential killer."

Several days later, M. was shocked to find out that the old woman had had her foot amputated because of gangrene that had set in after the first operation. Now we dressed her stump and fed her proteins intravenously—parenteral nutrition, although it was much too late.

He kept asking me, "What do you think, Dr. Vladimir, will she ever get well?"

"No. There's no way her life can be saved."

"I can't believe it! There are so many lifesaving drugs for critical patients."

"True, but they're only effective up to a point."

Distraught, he exclaimed, "But why, why did it have to happen to this wonderful old lady?"

It was the first tragic case in his medical experience. I knew only too well why it had happened and tried to explain it to him. The poor boy was torn between belief and doubt—it sounded too wild.

71

We residents were required to be on call one in every three nights—from 5:00 P.M. to 7:00 A.M., 14 hours on top of a 10-hour-long regular weekday. There was no break after a night on call; we went on our regular shift till 5:00 in the afternoon, officially, but actually till 7:00 or 8:00 P.M. because there was always too much to be done. Thus, coming to work at 6:00 A.M. on the day preceding night duty, we stayed on the job for 36 to 38 hours at a stretch. Once every three weeks we stayed on call the whole weekend, Saturday and Sunday, working till Monday night—a 60-hour stint. All in all, we worked anywhere between 110 and 116 hours a week, regularly spending two to three nights without sleep.

Young kids, my son's age, never missed an opportunity to complain to me, "Ah, Vladimir, if only you knew how tired I am!"

Lucky devils, at least they enjoyed the luxury of bitching. For fear of drawing attention to my age, I could not afford complaints.

Given their permanent state of fatigue, the residents nodded off at any conference, particularly when the lights were turned off to show slides or films. No sooner had a resident slumped in the chair than his head started to droop. From time to time, he would open his eyes in alarm and raise his head like a goose guarding his flock, but the next instant his head would loll to the other side. All residents suffered from a common postconference affliction: pain in the neck.

Surgical residents had to carry an even bigger load. We had to do everything all other categories of residents did plus spend from four to six hours a day assisting at operations and an equal amount of time at nighttime emergency surgical procedures. Also, senior residents rode over the greenhorns, forcing us to perform many of their own chores. Our beepers rarely stayed silent for any length of time; our superiors never stopped calling us to dictate new assignments.

In the dead of night, I received a call from Dr. Fon, a fourth-year Filipino resident.

"Bring me the X rays of such-and-such a patient, on the double! I'll be waiting for you in the third-floor operating theater."

His call found me in the midst of dressing a newborn infant two buildings away from the X-ray room and operating theater. I hastily applied the last few layers of gauze and sped off to fetch the X rays, without bothering to write anything in the chart because the resident had said "on the double." I was sure he was extremely busy if he could not find the time to climb to the next floor where the X rays were kept. When, panting, I brought the X rays to the doctor, I found him lounging in the operating theater anteroom, perusing *Playboy* magazine. He took his time admiring the centerfold, then cast a perfunctory glance at the X rays. "Take them back," he told me, and immersed himself in the magazine again.

Again I ran to write down the dressing procedure in the patient's chart.

As I ran past the emergency room, Dr. Gup, a PGY-2 Indian of twenty-eight, intercepted me:

"Where are you going?"

"To the Pediatric Building."

"What for?"

"To record the dressing procedures in the patient's chart."

"No hurry; you'll have time enough to do it later. Come help me suture a wound. Have you ever sutured wounds?"

"You might say so."

"Good. Now show me how you can do it. Don't be afraid, I'll help you if needed."

The wound was small and shallow, and I easily coped with the task.

"Hey, you can really do it," Dr. Gup said. "An excellent job, well done."

"Thanks," I said and ran back to write down my unrecorded dressing procedure—at long last. I did not tell him that I had learned to suture wounds when he was still in swaddling clothes.

Obviously I did myself a disservice by revealing my ability to Dr. Gup, because over the next night and half the next day he summoned me on several occasions to suture wounds for him. As a result, I piled up a huge backlog of unaccomplished tasks, uncollected analyses, and unrecorded procedures. It was already 3:00 in the morning and I still had not completed preparing the patients scheduled for next-day operations.

I knew my immediate night-duty supervisor, Dr. Yo, would be angry at me. He was very nervous and incessantly prodded me, checking everything I did. Given his propensity for walking fast, he rushed around the hospital at twice my speed, so whenever he appeared I was always behind. He would reprimand me, I would promise to complete the assignment, but just at the moment I was about to keep my word, Dr. Gup would summon me for the umpteenth time, and I would fail my superior's trust again. Dr. Yo was furious. Finally we came face to face at the hall of the biochemistry lab, where we both arrived to record the results of analyses.

"Why haven't you done it?" he shouted at me. "You promised you would!"

When he raised his voice, my jagged nerves gave out and I also began to shout, "Why are you yelling at me?"

"Because you're a liar!"

"I'm not. I just have not had time to fulfill all your assignments."

"A liar!" he screamed.

That did it. I assumed a fighting stance. He read in my face what was coming and crouched, preparing for action. I was bigger than my adversary and figured to knock him down with a single punch. But he was much younger, and it was too early to predict who would win.

Thus we faced each other, like two fighting cocks bracing for a scuffle! Then it suddenly occurred to me that the department chief and the hospital managers would certainly find out about the fight; that both of us would be sporting bruises and black eyes; that I was a freshman and nobody knew me; and that for all these reasons a fight would be an inauspicious start to my career. I paused . . . and restrained myself. A pity, though. I was dying to give him a thrashing.

72

Our 650-bed hospital was unprofitable. It had been built six decades previously in a neighborhood populated by prosperous white families, mostly Jewish. Initially the hospital had been staffed by fine doctors and had enjoyed an excellent reputation. But times had changed with the demographics. One after another, the big-name physicians had left, followed by other, less famous, doctors. Finally the composition of the staff had changed dramatically. Now it consisted primarily of foreign medical graduates. Native-born Americans were few; almost all of them had been graduated from foreign medical schools. By the time I started, only a handful of the oldest staff members remembered the good days.

The overriding concern of the management was to prolong the existence of the hospital, for it teetered on the edge of bankruptcy. Next to it stood the once splendid buildings of a school and a synagogue, now closed down and falling to pieces. If the hospital could not muddle through, its buildings were slated for the same refuse heap. The destructive force of the ever-growing local community held sway in that part of the city.

The locals, many of them beset by illnesses, suffered primarily from drug addiction and alcoholism. But they cared little about their own health. Many, if not most, were victimized by diseases and injuries directly related to their way of life: an assortment of infections and inflammations from self-administered drugs; pancreatitis and cirrhosis of the liver stemming from alcoholism; knife and gunshot wounds.

In medicine, just as in any other field, supply is shaped by demand. Those patients were satisfied with any kind of treatment, having no ability to discriminate between good and bad. Most of the poor were treated by inexperienced residents who did their best, but their best was not good enough.

Another large group of patients consisted of senior citizens, mostly women in their late eighties, inmates of nursing homes. They were covered by Medicare and were thus private patients of our attending physicians. They were put up in smaller rooms, given more attention, and in general taken good care of. Unfortunately, however, because of age and chronic ailments, they were generally in poor health, and treating them was not easy.

Middle-aged private patients constituted the smallest category. Attending physicians paid the most attention to this elite group and residents were allowed near them only under supervision. They received the best treatment available in our hospital.

It was not difficult for me to see the stark difference in the standards of two medical institutions—my previous hospital in Manhattan where most patients were private, and this one dominated by charity patients. I wouldn't want to be a patient at our hospital.

However, even our ill-equipped and poor hospital in a New York slum area was a palace compared to any Russian public health-care institution. Our patients never suffered from lack of basic equipment or medicines. We did not possess state-of-the-art equipment, but we did have everything we needed. The results of treatment were, on the average, adequate. Through the combined efforts of physicians and nurses, most of our patients recovered.

I liked the way our nurses worked—diligently, thoughtfully, and calmly—not easy considering that many patients brought their street manners to the hospital along with their wounds. When I came for the first time into Room 306 housing sixteen patients, all of them drug addicts or alcoholics, the nurse who was dispensing medicines asked me, "Please, Doctor, guard the medicine table while I give a shot to a patient in the next room."

Somewhat surprised by the request, I stayed at the cart with heaped-on medicines. No sooner had I turned aside than a patient slid off his bed and materialized at the cart. In a flash, with simian agility, he grabbed a fistful of drugs on the near side. I barely managed to catch him by the hand.

"Let go, Doc," he hissed.

"Put the medicines back or I'll kick you out of the hospital!" I said.

The other patients watched our confrontation with keen interest, but made no attempt to intervene. The patient whose hand I was clutching was a black fellow of about twenty-five, far sturdier than I was. I was not sure he would restrain himself from hitting me with the other hand. But at that moment the nurse returned. The scene she found was obviously familiar to her. She accosted my adversary so furiously that he obediently returned to his bed.

The nurse was a very small woman, like a sparrow. Dispensing the medicines, she stood over each patient while he swallowed the pill.

"Otherwise, they would spit them out and collect them," she explained.

"What for?"

"They either sell them to other junkies or dilute them in water and shoot themselves up."

All our nurses were black and hailed from the same places as the rest of the population. But their looks, intellect, professionalism, and good manners made them stand out in contrast to their patients.

Many of them were pretty, with lively expressions on lovely faces. Many had gorgeous figures, making it a real pleasure just to watch them. And all of them were affable and eager to help budding doctors. Not surprisingly, our young men fell for them, and they in turn flirted with residents.

For me the nurses were my best friends and allies in those

initial hard days. I did not know the layout of the hospital, nor where and how equipment was procured, nor the names of the commonly used medicines and devices. So I had to ask nurses for the most elementary information.

They never snubbed me and invariably treated me with patience and courtesy.

I don't know how young residents expressed their gratitude to the nurses, but I always had the pockets of my hospital jacket full of candies. I started my day on each floor by distributing them among the nurses, always accompanying the sweets with jokes and compliments. They liked the attention. Soon I had a nickname among the nursing staff: Candyman.

Gradually I made friends with some of the nurses. They asked me about Russia, about my plans—whether or not I was going to return to my homeland after training. I told them about that faraway, mysterious country. One of the nurses, a Costa Rican, even studied Russian—just for the fun of it. With great difficulty, she could manage to say a few Russian words. And I made it a point to say hello and good-bye to her in Russian.

To have friends among nurses was not only fun, but, much more important, useful. They never bothered a person considered a friend with trifling matters. A system of mutual trust was in operation. I was rarely off work earlier than 3:00 or 4:00 in the morning. Then I could finally go to my room to try to grab some sleep. But it was a rare night that the telephone would not ring or the beeper chirp the minute I closed my eyes. It took well-honed reflexes not only to hear the ring or the beep, but to sweep the cobwebs from one's brain in an instant and understand which nurse was on the phone, from which floor, and which patient she was calling about. It was far from easy, the more so since many of the nurses spoke a heavily accented English.

If the matter were serious, I was supposed to rush to the scene. But if the call was merely about which medicine to administer to a given patient, the nurse would usually say, "I am sorry, Dr. Vladimir. I realize you're tired. I've administered the medicine to the patient myself so you don't have to come and record the prescription. But please don't forget to do it in the morning."

"Thanks a lot," I would say. "I won't forget."

I would jot down a note in my pad and fall asleep again before you could say "soporific."

No matter how busy I was, how tired and sleepy, I still persevered in writing my book. I had to do it in snatches, one or two nights a week at best. It was difficult to work in such a way, but it never left my mind, even during night shifts. Sometimes I had an impulse to write down an observation literally on the run, while delivering blood samples to the lab or rushing back to record the analyses in the charts. Then I would stop, jot down a couple of words on my pad, and be on my way again. As a result, a typical page of notes looked something like this:

Patient S., Room 306, Bilirubin 10, Amylase 1080 . . .
Write a chapter about how I smuggled the originals of my
    documents out of Russia . . .
On the sixth floor, replace dressing for patient M . . .
Check x-rays of patient K., Room 510 . . .
Write: had to pay 500 rubles ($750) for the right to be
    stripped of my Russian citizenship . . .
Patient T., Room 606, Hemoglobin 14.0, Hematocrit
    42 . . .

Conversation with my son; I break my glasses in impotent
rage. . . .

Sometimes the notes were so cryptic that I myself had
difficulty deciphering them. I more than ever yearned to see
my book published. When I became a resident and had to do
work that I had done earlier in my career, my yearning became even more feverish. Running errands, swallowing insults,
restraining myself every step of the way, I dreamed that someday my colleagues would find out who I actually was. The only
means to that end was to have a book published.

But the progress was not as fast as I had hoped. The editor had to read the first half of the manuscript. It was important for me to hear his opinion so I could incorporate his
suggestions into the rest of the book. But he was busy. Time
dragged slowly by and I was constantly on edge. Finally he
called and invited me to the Library restaurant at Broadway
and Ninety-second Street.

I arrived at the restaurant straight from the hospital after
a night on call, sporting my white uniform jacket and ID card.
The Library turned out to be a small, simple restaurant. I
thought that a prosperous editor should meet with his newly
acquired author in a more appropriate setting. But I was not
surprised, knowing as I did that Americans did not care for
ceremony; European manners were alien to business-minded
Yankees.

I anxiously waited for his assessment of my manuscript. I
realized that in America it was silly to fear censorship, but the
old complexes would not go away. The loathsome feelings born
of encounters with Russian editors were still alive. How many
times had I had to endure their dictatorial admonitions: Forget
about this piece—the censor would never let it slip past him;
that part should be shortened—in its original form it sounds
politically dubious; here you should enlarge on the great
achievements of Communism. A writer's lack of freedom in
Russia is worse than anyone's bad dream. It is not an easy task
to shed Communist complexes, and it takes a lot of time.

But of course, with my American editor I discussed the

details of only what I myself wanted to write. He liked what he had read, but advanced a suggestion.

"You should prolong your story to its logical conclusion, to the point when you settled down in this country. American readers like a story to run from the beginning to the end. Your book should tell how you and your family began life anew in New York City."

"No, I can't do it," I replied. "These are two different stories."

"Why?"

"My life in Russia and my life in America are too dissimilar to be able to coexist under the same cover."

"Why not?" he asked in surprise. "You used to be a doctor there; you've become a doctor here. You used to be a writer there; you've become a writer here."

"There and here are entirely different things. Myself there and myself here are different persons. I'm trying to make the American reader see Russia through the prism of my perception, my experience. If I'm going to write about my life in this country, the sequel, if it materialized, should depict how dearly I had to pay for freedom acquired so belatedly and how wonderful it was to become free—even if belatedly!"

"Maybe you're right," he said.

74

Dr. Les became my new chief during night duty. I was glad to be rid of Dr. Yo, with his incessant carping, but Dr. Les pushed me around, if anything, even more zestfully!

"Hey, Russian, there's a ninety-two-year-old woman patient on the tenth floor. Tomorrow she's scheduled for an operation for hemorrhoids. Get her to sign a consent form."

I filled out a special form that was to be cosigned by a physician and a witness. I put my signature as the "physician" and went to see the patient.

"Good evening, how are you?" I began. She did not reply. I checked her pulse and breathing. She was in a chronically grave condition; hemorrhoids could not be the primary illness. I made another attempt to attract her attention by shouting into her ear: "Can you sign a consent form for tomorrow's operation?"

The patient did not react in any way.

"You're wasting your time," the nurse told me. "She doesn't respond to any stimuli. Her papers from the nursing home indicate she's in an advanced state of senility."

"Then how can we obtain her consent for the operation?"

"Any close relative will do, but the trouble is she has none; nobody ever visits her."

"What should we do?"

"There's a way out. It's called administrative consent. For this you'll need a representative from the hospital administration."

I explained the situation to Dr. Les. He called the attending physician at home. The old woman was his private patient.

"Okay . . . Fine . . . Will do . . . Don't worry, everything will be just fine," Dr. Les was saying into the receiver. He hung up and told me, "He said he doesn't care how we get her signature," he said, "but tomorrow morning everything should be in order so he can operate."

"What shall we do?" I asked.

"Let's go to the patient. We'll think of something."

When we approached the patient's bed, Dr. Les told me, "Keep the form in front of her. That's right!"

He grabbed the patient's hand, inserted a pen in it, and proceeded to move it across the paper, imitating the patient's signature. Then he put his own signature as the witness.

"Everything's okay now," he told me triumphantly.

Making the rounds of the hospital, floor after floor, and preparing newly admitted patients for next-day operations, I came across a young Hasidic Jew in a small private room. He sat on his bed, swaying in prayer. He had a yarmulke on his head and a prayer book in his hands. When I entered, he gestured for me not to interrupt and went on with his prayer. I stood at the door, looking through my notes—what else was I to do? I was about to turn and go away to drop by later, when he ended his prayer, covered the distance to the door in a single jump, and grabbed me by the flap of my gown. He stared at the ID card on my chest, read my name, and yelped in Russian, "A Jew from Russia?"

"Yes!"

"So am I," he shouted in wild joy and began jumping around me, firing questions. "When did you come to this country?"

"Four years ago."

"Where did you live before?"

"In Moscow."

"Aha! I placed you at a glance."

"And when did you come to this country?" I asked in turn.

"About two decades ago, when I was still a kid."

His motion was so intense it made me a little dizzy. "I must examine you in preparation for surgery," I said. "What's your complaint?"

"Hernia, but it makes no difference. First we must pray together."

Amazed at the turn of events, I tried to talk my way out. "I don't know how to pray."

"It makes no difference!" he shouted, jumping up and down. "I have everything for a prayer with me."

264

He pulled me up by force and began winding a tefillin on my left arm and draping a tallith around my shoulders.

"Please . . . maybe some other time."

"No, no, there can be no other time," he yelled. "Now, right now! Turn this way and repeat after me."

He put on another tallith and we both faced the wall. In reality I only prayed that a nurse would not barge in and find me in such embarrassing circumstances.

He recited a short prayer; I repeated it word for word.

"And now we must dance!" he announced.

"Dance?! Oh no, for dancing I certainly have no time."

"It's a special dance, one that symbolizes friendship. Do you want my operation to come off well?"

"Yes, of course, but . . ."

"No 'buts.' Let's dance to it! Put your arm around my shoulder—this way, and I am putting my arm around yours—there. Now let's go in a circle."

He jumped around, turning me as he moved.

"All right, that's enough," I said. "There can be no doubt your operation will be a success."

"No, it's not enough!" he yelled. "Do you want the Israelis to win in Lebanon?"

"Of course. But what does our dance have to do with their victory?"

"If you want them to win, pray with me."

Still dancing and dragging me in tow, he muttered a prayer. I repeated the last syllables. "What a sight we must be," I thought. "Some doctor on duty! If only Irina could see me now."

Finally, I prevailed upon him to lie down and let me examine his hernia. While I went about my business, he told me he lived in a neighborhood where the Lubavicher Rebbe's word was law, where all Jews had to obey a very strict code of rules and pray many times a day.

"Come and pray with me once more before bedtime," he concluded.

"I'll try," I promised. I did not keep my word. It was past

3:00 A.M. when I was finally finished and returned to my room. But I could hardly stretch out on the couch and close my eyes, when the telephone rang (it always did at inopportune times!).

"Dr. Vladimir, please come to Room three-oh-six. It's urgent!" the nurse said.

"What's the matter?"

"Please hurry and you'll see for yourself. Two patients—a male and a female—they are making love."

"What? Where?"

"Right here in the room."

On the run I thought furiously, trying to chart the proper course of action. I took a guard along.

When we arrived on the scene, the nurse led us to a bed.

"That's him," she said. "The woman jumped off and went to her room. I recorded everything in his chart."

The bed was occupied by a young man with a gunshot wound in his chest. A chest tube to vent the air from his pleural cavity sprouted from his middle, so he could only lie on his back. It was difficult to believe that he could physically manage to do what the nurse said he had done.

I asked him, "Hey, what is it you've been doing just now?"

But he pretended to be asleep and refused to answer. The guard shook him by the shoulder, but the patient only shut his eyes more tightly.

I told the nurse, "Let's have a look at her."

In the women's room, the nurse took us to a bed containing a young woman with a leg encased from top to bottom in a plaster cast. I felt totally lost. How in God's name could she make love with such an impediment?

The woman also pretended to be asleep.

The nurse said, "All right, let them feign sleep. I've described the incident in detail in his chart and will enter the story in hers as well. They are animals, worse than animals!"

I read the entry:

At 3:25 A.M., a woman, Mrs. X, from Room 307, bed 3, was found in the patient's bed. She was naked and sat atop the man, both of them making rhythmic movements

266

backwards and forwards. I told them to stop the obnoxious activity, but they did not heed my order and continued moving backwards and forwards. At 3:33 A.M. I notified by phone Dr. Vladimir, physician on call.

I could vividly picture the scene from this rather clear description.

75

$\mathcal{S}$oon we were to part with our son; Junior was leaving for Syracuse. It is said that we don't get our children from God forever, only borrow them for a time. This time he was leaving us for good.

I recalled how in 1975, when Junior had enrolled in the Moscow School of Medicine and Dentistry where I was a chairman and a professor, I had been looking forward to the joy of being my son's teacher. Now, by the time he graduated from medical school, I would have just completed my residency training. What if he enrolled in a training program in orthopedic surgery where I would be chief resident? Wouldn't it be marvelous—father and son residents in the same program?

As for Irina, her daily worries, concerns, alarms, and joys about him were about to dissolve. All she was left with were me and her work at the lab. Her worries about me diminished now that my professional career was finally started, and for all her distaste for many facets of American life, she was happy to be working at an American university, side by side with other Americans. She could not imagine or wish a better professional lot for herself. After two raises her salary had reached $20,000 per year—a not insignificant sum. Now that Junior was about to leave us, Irina would be able to concentrate more on her job. And my claim on her attentions would be better satisfied, too. But it also meant that she was about to cease being a mother on a daily basis, and what woman likes aging? Pondering all this, Irina was sad.

"Will you be able to take me to Syracuse in your car?" Junior asked me.

I remembered the day I rode home through snowbound Moscow streets from the hospital where he was born, holding him in my arms.

"Sure I will."

"Fine. Only remember, we'll have to start very early to get to Syracuse not later than eleven in the morning."

"Don't worry, I'll get you there on time."

Nowadays, my life revolved around night duty; I was forever either on call, or emerging from night work, or about to go on call. True to form, the day before Junior's departure I had had almost no sleep at all. So the night before I tumbled into bed exhausted. But already at 3:30 the next morning, we were hauling Junior's belongings downstairs to the car.

Driving in darkness, we crossed the George Washington Bridge and headed north on Route 17. Irina dozed off in the rear seat, sandwiched on both sides by our son's baggage, while Junior and I chatted in the front. When we approached the Catskill Mountains, dawn started to break. The sun edged upward from beyond the horizon; the road was eerily beautiful in the morning light.

As we neared Syracuse, Junior's excitement grew, and he impatiently counted off the remaining miles. At 10:30 I pulled up at the red brick building of the dormitory. A multitude of freshmen and older students who turned up to meet the newcomers milled around the entrance. As soon as we stopped, several students ran up to the car, asked Junior's name, grabbed his possessions, and led him to his room. He came to life, joined the general babble of conversation, and all but forgot about our existence.

His room was huge, comfortable, well lit and well furnished. What a far cry from the dismal students' hostels in Russia! There a typical tiny room would contain four or more cots, a plain table, a rickety wardrobe—and that was all. But even such miserable accommodations were scarce.

"It's really one of the happiest days of my life!" Junior told us.

And walking us to the car, he embraced us and said, "Well, thanks for everything." This "everything" was our life with him and for him.

On the way home we kept silent, listening to the sad music by Tchaikovsky and Chopin on a cassette Junior had given us for the return journey. Now the sun was setting. The receding daylight lit up the hills and wooded mountainsides, and the sunset was as sad as the music.

When we entered our apartment, Irina slowly went into our son's room and walked around it. I watched her from a distance. There was a feeling of desolation, the empty-nest syndrome.

76

I was gradually getting accustomed to my work and the people around me. I no longer depended on others to tell me where things were; I ran even faster around the labs; learned what to expect from each of my colleagues. But my status as the juniormost doctor, an errand boy as it were, was still the dominant factor in my life.

And often the mistakes of my superiors galled me.

The old woman whose signature on the consent form Dr. Les had obtained in such a curious fashion, died only five days after being operated on for hemorrhoids. She should not have been subjected to surgery, considering her condition and age.

The patient whose leg had been amputated below the knee continued to fade. Her condition was getting progressively worse, and Dr. Gav performed another amputation, cutting off her leg above the knee. She died three days later. The medical student was disconsolate.

"How could it happen?" he asked me.

Again I explained that in medicine, particularly in surgery, one had to contend with a great variety of complications.

Myself, I had seen so many complications and errors throughout my career that those cases did not surprise me. What did was the very fact that such egregious errors could happen here, in New York City, in a major health-care center, against the background of America's stupendous medical knowledge. The high standard of the health-care system was supported by billion-dollar outlays for research, equipment, and medicines. But my observations suggested that the standard dropped noticeably in hospitals such as ours, with a high concentration of foreign-educated physicians.

Our training was focused on a single goal: high scores on in-training exams. To this end we spent two or three hours every day doing question-and-answer exercises and cramming with textbooks like medical freshmen, not qualified physicians. Usually one of the chief residents would read a question and the multiple-choice answers to it, while we would take turns guessing which of the answers was correct.

I had great difficulty understanding the Indian accent of my colleagues, made particularly unintelligible by their rapid-fire manner of speaking. So when my turn came, I was unable to grasp either the questions or the answers.

"For shame, Vladimir, it's unconscionable not to know the

answer to such a simple question," Dr. Saly would reprove me. "It's *B,* not *C.* Clear as day! You should read more."

After the seminar I looked up the question to read what I had been unable to grasp in his rendition. I saw with annoyance what the right answer was and felt humiliated to have erred so flagrantly.

Soon after that incident a four-year-old boy was admitted to the emergency room. I diagnosed his condition as an inflammatory infiltrate in his abdomen due to untreated appendicitis. I had seen a lot of similar cases during my career. Dr. Saly decided to operate for appendicitis.

I told him, "The boy does not need an operation. He has an infiltrate and must be treated with antibiotics."

He ridiculed me, "Vladimir, are you crazy? What infiltrate? You should read more, Vladimir, you really should!"

He operated on the boy. After it was over, he said reluctantly, "You were right, it was an infiltrate. The operation was unnecessary. But how could you diagnose it?"

"Oh, it was really very simple, thanks to experience."

Chief residents realized that I could be entrusted with serious assignments, and, with increasing frequency, left me alone in the emergency room. I often was the first to examine surgical patients, diagnose their ailments, make on-the-spot decisions, and commence treatment. In all difficult cases I was required to call my superiors. In itself that kind of work was quite familiar to me—years ago I had performed emergency duties in Russian hospitals. But the working conditions here were different.

The emergency room of our hospital was hectic around the clock, but from 9:00 or 10:00 at night till 3:00 or 4:00 in the morning it was madness. Late at night the ambulance service as a rule brought the most critical patients: those with gunshot and knife wounds, victims of beatings and drug and alcohol poisoning. Patients and their kin thronged the cramped quarters; doctors, nurses, nurse's aides with stretchers, guards, policemen, ambulance paramedics, and personnel from the

D.A.'s staff maneuvered their way through the crowd.

I had never seen patients of this kind in such numbers in Russia. There, the category of emergency patients was dominated by alcoholics exhibiting the many consequences of their baneful addiction: injuries, diseases, poisonings. But there were no gunshot wounds because nobody had firearms. Nor were there as many junkies because narcotics were far less accessible. Muggings, rapes, and even murders did occur in Russia, but not as frequently as here.

Typical was the following dialogue I had with a twenty-seven-year-old nonworking man who patronized our hospital at three- to four-month intervals—now with an injury, now with poisoning, now with inflammation. All emergency room personnel greeted him as an old acquaintance.

I questioned him while filling out his chart, "Do you use drugs?"

"Sure do, Doc."

"What kinds of drugs?"

"Ain't nothin' I ain't tried, Doc. Since I was seventeen."

"Do you smoke marijuana?"

"Once did, Doc. Smoked it ten years. Quit—got no high from it."

"Do you sniff cocaine?"

"Sniff anythin'."

"Do you shoot heroin?"

"Shoot anythin', Doc. Three times a day."

"Now tell me, what do you need all those stimulants for? Just be honest, why do you do it?"

"You wouldn't believe the kind of pressure on me!"

"What pressure are you talking about?"

"Money, I need a hundred and fifty, even two hundred."

"Per week?"

"A day."

"Every day?"

"Know how much that stuff costs, Doc? Shoot up three times a day, fifty bucks a shot."

"Who gives you the shots? Yourself?"

"No, Doc, can't do it myself no more. Used to be I could shoot it up myself. See the tracks? That's all my work."

The patient's skin was covered with scores of scars from shots and inflammations—scars on his arms, legs, even neck where the veins came up to the surface.

"Ain't got no veins left, Doc. The last one I found on my cock, Doc! Honest! Messed that one up, too."

As proof he displayed his penis, bearing syringe marks. My eyes widened.

"But who gives you the shots now? And where?"

"A wizard, Doc. Charges fifteen bucks a shot."

Wizard was the nickname for experts who earned their living by giving drug injections to junkies with seemingly no unscarred veins left. They were capable of real miracles, unfailingly finding veins so small that not even nurses or physicians could locate them.

"Where does he shoot you?" I asked.

"He knows, Doc! Shoots me between the fingers."

It was the ultimate of skill to hit the tiny vein between the fingers with a hypodermic syringe!

I refrained from asking where the patient managed to get his daily $150 to $200. It was pretty clear he did not support his habit by withdrawing money from his checking account.

Persons with a normal family life were rare among our patients, but there were many mothers in their early teens.

Russian teenagers usually attain puberty by the age of fifteen or sixteen, and begin their sex life at sixteen or seventeen or even later. Schoolgirl pregnancy is extremely rare.

Needless to say, family and school upbringing in Russia is far more stringent than in America, let alone in the community that supplied most of our patients. But the way I see it, the root cause of the difference is Russia's incomparably harsher life. There, children draw no benefits, and to raise them even in a normal family with more than one breadwinner is a major undertaking. Single young women cannot afford the luxury of having a child. They have abortions—by the thousands.

Every day and especially every night in the emergency room, I saw dozens of crime victims—shot, knifed, beaten black and blue. There was no time to be astonished, the patients had to be treated without delay. Besides, I had seen a lot of similar things, except for gunshot wounds, in Russia.

But when criminals were brought to us handcuffed and under police escort, I could see that in one significant respect they differed from their Russian counterparts: Here, they were much younger—mostly teenagers or young men in their early twenties. When I had to suture their wounds, the policemen handcuffed the patients to the operating table.

"Why do you handcuff them?" I asked. "You're standing right next to me."

"You don't know their kind. They're quite capable of snatching the scalpel out of your hands during surgery, cutting you up, and attacking us."

Drunk, dirty, drugged, and blood-stained, our patients were the misfits of society. A normal human face was a rarity in the emergency room.

Resident Dr. Gup kept saying with disgust, "They're not human, Vladimir, they're animals!"

It was apparently for that reason that he increasingly kept a safe distance from those patients. To work with them was hellishly difficult. They were rude, negative, uncommunicative, and disobedient. It took patience to talk them into the simplest injection.

They had shot themselves up for years, but the sight of a hypodermic syringe in my hands drove them to panic.

"Easy, Doc, easy!" they'd yell. "I'm human, Doc! I'm human!"

They writhed and jumped on the stretcher so violently when I administered injections that sometimes the needle slipped out of the vein, forcing me to do the procedure anew. And to find their veins was a feat befitting a real wizard.

One patient behaved so violently, that he wrested the syringe from my hand and wounded me with the needle that had already been dipped in his bloodstream. Aware that I was likely to contract just about any disease from him, I recorded the incident on the chart that was made for me. The next day he died. I sent a sample of his blood to the laboratory for a check— to be on the safe side.

To tell the truth, Irina and I enjoyed living alone, without our son. What other reward can parents who have raised a child expect if not emancipation? The newly acquired freedom was wonderful. In spite of my workload we still spent much time together, more than ever, because now we were on our own. We were more attentive and tender to each other; we had no need to divert our attention to our son. Everything became as it had been once upon a distant and almost forgotten time.

To cheer up Irina when I was on call, I bought her a good radio so she could listen to classical music. I also made it a point to call her several times during the night. And when I came home, Irina always tried to cook something special, to make me relax and recuperate. Nowadays, Irina's best morsels and warmest feelings came my way, not our son's.

Enjoying our life together, we continued our joint effort to improve it. Now I had a new concern: to get into a training program in orthopedic surgery the next year. Irina proofread and typed the letters I dictated to her.

It was far from easy to land a position in an orthopedic program. However, I had amassed a few credits I believed would facilitate my task: I had completed one year of training in general surgery, thus meeting the most important requirement of the Orthopedic Board. Besides, I was a doctor already on his way, an entirely different proposition from being one about to start.

I requested applications from forty hospitals that had training programs in orthopedic surgery and again began putting together a package of credentials: diplomas, patents, lists of publications. The resultant package constituted a forty-page folder. I added new references from my job and mailed the applications out.

The project took two months. Helping me, Irina again began thinking of the forthcoming challenges and changes. We even discussed moving, although neither of us was eager to leave New York since she had a job.

"Imagine that the Mayo Clinic offers me a position," I would tell her. "It would be a unique opportunity, a dream come true to work at the Olympus of my profession. But if such an eventuality comes about, what are we going to do about your job?"

"Let's wait and see the offers you'll get. We'll have plenty of time to decide," Irina would reply prudently.

Beautiful fall came to New York, the best season of the year. The trees stood in golden attire, the air was fresh and crisp. We took every opportunity to go to the country in our Buick to marvel at the autumnal landscape.

I hoped for three to five interviews from the applications I sent out, interviews which would give me, I believed, at least a solid chance to gain admission to an orthopedic training program.

The first response came from the Mayo Clinic. When I returned home after a regular night on call, Irina handed me an open envelope with an expression on her face that left little room for doubt.

They did not want to interview me.

Well, so the Mayo Clinic was beyond my reach. I had dreams of being accepted by that clinic, but never counted seriously on such a stroke of luck.

I told Irina, "Relocation to Minnesota is hereby canceled. Unpack!"

She gave me a sad smile; the very first letter put her on her guard. Naturally, I was also upset.

A few other replies followed—all of them rejections. But they were from mediocre hospitals, none of which was in New York City. As the rejections piled up, Irina grew increasingly somber, while I bravely smiled (although each new smile required a progressively greater effort) and repeated, "Let's wait some more, it's not over yet."

Then came a letter from the Hospital for Special Surgery, which had one of the best training programs in the city. They, too, said no.

I sighed and found nothing to say to Irina. But deep inside I still thought: Let's wait, let's wait some more. Something will happen.

But rejections then came from St. Lukes-Roosevelt and the Hospital for Joint Diseases. Yale never even answered. Indeed, only one program director, from the Maryland State Hospital, invited me for an interview. I called him and made arrangements. So the haul was just one-fifth of what I had hoped for. I realized that my chances of making any training program were slim to none.

Whether because of a permanent depression because of the avalanche of rejections or because I worked too much and too hard, for several weeks I had felt enormous fatigue—so great that I constantly perspired. Trying to hide my condition from Irina, I wondered if I had contracted a disease. I checked the lab analysis of the blood sample obtained from the patient who had pricked me with the hypodermic syringe and died the next day from inflammation of the lungs. The analysis was negative, so apparently it was not an infection. But what could it be?

To be able to go to Baltimore for the interview, I had to swap a night shift with someone. All my colleagues had equally busy schedules, but finally I managed to talk Dr. Gad, an Indian, into an exchange. We swapped weekend shifts, so I was to work overnight on Friday and then the next Monday while he was to take over from me on Saturday and Sunday. The next weekend we would change places.

Irina and I set out for Baltimore in our car on a dismal, rainy day. Our spirits were in tune with the weather. I had little hope and only decided to go to the interview so I wouldn't reproach myself later for having missed a chance, however slight. Irina went along because she was concerned about my health and did not want to let me go alone.

There were eight candidates for three positions: seven medical students and myself. By that time I had grown accustomed to being around youngsters, what with my junior status, but to compete against students was a novelty. We spent the whole day being interviewed by attending physicians, all of them younger than me. Each interviewer began his talk with me by saying how impressed he was by my extraordinary credentials and my resolve to make a fresh start from scratch. Then followed a barrage of questions. But it was up to the director to make the decision.

He told me, "Your application with all those patents and diplomas made such an impression that we held a special meeting to discuss you. Let me tell you frankly, we would love to have a man of your experience in our program, but your age is a big handicap. You have no idea how hard you'd have to work!"

"I think I do. I'm already in residency training."

"Here it will be even worse. But if you still want to join us, we'll leave your candidacy open—in case one of these young men has a change of heart and leaves a vacancy. Agreed?"

I agreed, if only because I had no idea what to do next. All my expectations had been frustrated, all my plans foiled.

Almost the entire time we drove home Irina and I kept silent, thinking the same sad thoughts. Besides, I had to concentrate on my driving. It was dark and rainy and I was tired after a whole day of talking.

I was exhausted and felt ill. And the next day I faced the prospect of overnight work.

78

D̲r. Gad, with whom I had arranged to swap night shifts, called me on the phone in the early afternoon: "Listen, Vladimir, I looked through the weekend log and saw too many new patients. So I am calling off our exchange."

I was stupefied. We had arranged everything in advance! And he knew that if he backed out of our deal I would have to be on call four days in a row. Things are not done that way. Usually doctors never let one another down at a moment's notice. Besides, how could he be sure that his shift would be easier than mine? But I realized that no amount of persuasion would make him change his mind. I called home. Irina was glad to hear my voice. "I am waiting for you. How are you feeling?"

I did not want to scare her and said, "Everything is fine. Except that you needn't wait for me."

"Why? What happened?"

"That other doctor has changed his mind and backed out. So I'll have to stay on call three more nights."

What Irina said about that doctor propriety forbids me to quote.

Dr. Naz, an Iranian Jew and chief resident of the team on call, was astonished to see me on duty the next morning.

"Vladimir, you've swapped shifts, haven't you?"

I explained my arrangement with Dr. Gad.

Then Naz took me aside and whispered in my ear, "Vladimir, never trust Indians. They are a very cunning, perfidious, and self-seeking lot. Look at the powerful Indian mafia they've set up in our hospital: Indian attending physicians maneuver to accept only Indians in residency programs; everything they do is only for the benefit of their compatriots. Yech!" he finished with acute hostility.

That same day, Dr. Saly, an Indian, softly muttered to me when we found ourselves alone, "Iranian Jews think they're the salt of the earth. Just look, Vladimir, how many of them occupy key positions in this hospital. It's a veritable Iranian Jewish mafia! In fact they are nothing, just nothing. You shouldn't trust them, Vladimir."

A Russian resident in pediatrics took me aside and gave me an indignant earful, "Listen, it's a veritable loony bin, don't you think so? Just look at what they are doing! We've got a real Haitian mafia. Once a Haitian doctor gets his hooks into a patient, he passes him around to his compatriots like a football. And all for the purpose of squeezing the patient dry, but only within their Haitian circle. You can't imagine what's going on here! They actually steal patients from other, non-Haitian doctors. Boy, what a crazy place!"

The hospital was awash in barely concealed ethnic strife, each ethnic group trying to keep to itself and stay away from the others. We did not have a tradition of getting together to party, drink beer, discuss work and family matters. Each group socialized within itself and took no others into its confidence.

That night, I saw a patient pass a few bills to his visitor, receive a dirty hypodermic syringe containing some solution, and instantly inject its contents into the sterile catheter through which antibiotics were administered to him intravenously. The culprit was the young junkie who had complained to me of the woes stemming from his daily need for $150. We pumped him full of antibiotics, yet his temperature regularly shot up, bewildering me. Now the cause of his recurring fever was clear; by shooting up, he continuously reinfected himself.

"Hey, why have you done that?" I asked him.

"I ain't done nothin', Doc, nothin'," he replied indifferently.

"But I saw it with my own eyes."

"I ain't done nothin', Doc, nothin'!" A wild flame leapt into his eyes.

It was useless to insist—and not too safe. The other inmates pricked their ears, while the visitor, who had brought the syringe, eyed me malevolently. If I accused him of pushing drugs, he was likely to turn nasty. I cut the conversation short and left the room.

I related the incident to the nurse on duty.

"Why, everybody knows that he shoots up heroin through the intravenous catheter," she said. "That's why his temperature is so irregular. But let me give you a piece of advice, Dr. Vladimir: Leave him alone. So far as I'm concerned let them do all the drugs they like. I'm not going to be the one to stop them, it's too risky."

A few hours later, the nurse called me on the phone, "Dr. Vladimir, that patient wants an immediate discharge right now, in the middle of the night. He is running a fever again, but he insists on a discharge right away. Could you come and talk to him?"

When I stepped into the room, the restless patient rattled in a choking voice, "Doc, I wanna get discharged, Doc! Lemme go, Doc!"

"It's too early for you to go home, you have a fever."

"Doc, I wanna get discharged, Doc! Lemme go, Doc!"

"Please try to understand. You shouldn't leave the hospital."

"Doc, I wanna get discharged, Doc! Lemme go, Doc!"

Under the law I had no right to keep him in the hospital against his own will, but he was required to sign a statement that he was leaving of his own free will. When he wrote his signature, I tried to remove the catheter from his vein, but he shoved me aside and ran out of the room.

"Hey, wait a minute! Where do you think you are going?" I yelled. "I must remove your catheter. . . ."

But he had already disappeared. I looked at the nurse helplessly. She shrugged.

"Don't you see, Dr. Vladimir, that he needs the catheter to shoot up? When you caught him red-handed he got cold feet that you would remove his catheter. That's why he decided to leave. But don't worry, he'll be back in a couple of days, when the catheter gets clogged up. It's not the first time. Besides, he needs the money for the drugs."

"I wish I knew how he gets it," I said, recording the incident in the fugitive's chart.

"We'll be better off staying ignorant," the nurse observed. "Maybe he steals and mugs, or even kills. That's the kind of people they are—ready for anything to support their habit."

I felt rotten and asked her for a thermometer to take my own temperature. It was 102°F.

"Please give me a couple of Tylenol pills."

Looking over her shoulder, she furtively took a key out of her pocket, unlocked the medicine cabinet, gave me the pills, shut the door, locked it, and put the key back with the same precautions.

"If they notice where I keep the key, they'll steal it for sure," she said by way of explanation.

I swallowed the pills and went to my room barely able to move my feet. Something was happening to me, but what, I could not understand.

I felt awful, but the next day, I was constantly on my feet and could not relax. I was to examine patients scheduled for surgery on Monday; record all the procedures in their charts; treat patients in the emergency room; and assist at urgent operations. I raced around the hospital like a rabbit chased by hounds. The beeper on my belt chirped so frequently that often I had to respond to two or three calls at the same time.

I noticed that my urine was unusually dark. At first I thought that fatigue had obscured my vision, but no—there was no mistaking it. Could it be something was wrong with my liver? Hepatitis? I could not ponder the question too long. The beeper came to life and I was urgently summoned to the emergency room. The patient had a cranial fracture and needed a CAT scan. Our hospital did not possess the scanner, it was too expensive for our meager resources. The patient had to be taken to a large hospital nearby. It took me over an hour to make all the arrangements over the phone. Finally an ambulance arrived. The rules prescribed that the patient should be accompanied by a physician, and the chief resident dispatched me as the juniormost member of his team. It was already 3:00 in the morning when we finally started. The procedure revealed a brain hemorrhage and the patient stayed on in that hospital.

I grabbed a ride back in an ambulance. The streets were dark and deserted. At a corner, we came across a brand-new Mercedes-300 that swerved from the roadway and stopped at the closed gate of one of the many body shops that dotted the street. "I wonder who had the bright idea of bringing in such a car for repairs at almost five in the morning, particularly since it shows no damage?" I thought. Then the gate opened, the driver climbed out of the car, and I saw with a start that he was none other than my patient, the junkie who had himself discharged the day before. He exchanged a few words with someone whom I could not see, and drove the Mercedes inside. The gate closed and my amublance rounded the corner. "What could it be?" I thought. "Clearly, it's not his car. Whose then? And at such a time. He had stolen it! Of course! And now he wants to sell it. So that's why he was so adamant about a discharge!"

I had barely returned to the hospital when a summons came for me to go to the third floor. Two patients picked a fight and one of them yanked from his opponent's arm an intravenous catheter through which medication was administered. There was pandemonium in the room. Hospital security guards had already tied up several combatants and were in the process of imposing peace on the others. Amid the tumult I had to insert a new catheter in the victim's arm.

The female nurse's aide who was dozing off on a chair looked at me with interest and asked, "What country are you from, Doctor?"

"Russia. And you?"

"I'm from Jamaica. Do you miss your homeland?"

"No. I like it here in America."

She sighed, "And I hate this country, hate living here!"

"Why don't you go back then?"

"Doctor, are you crazy?" she exclaimed. "Do you know the kind of apartment I have here? I live in a house left behind by a Jewish family. I have a real nice eight-room Jewish apartment. I own two cars, a refrigerator, a washing machine. And I am also planning to buy a dishwasher. I would be crazy to part with all that!"

It was 6:00 in the morning. I was exhausted and felt rotten. With only an hour left to have a nap, I refused to debate the nurse's aide on her hatred for America and went to my room. My urine was even darker than before and I made a mental note to go to the hospital's health station the next day.

Falling asleep, I recalled the words of the nurse's aide. And I saw in my mind the flocks of ducks that spent the winter on the reservoir in Central Park. Defying the laws of nature, those migratory birds refused to fly away for the winter. There was plenty of food in New York and apparently they saw no point in leaving for the south. Although, if asked, they would probably also aver their distaste for New York and their preference for southern countries.

79

In the hospital's health station, a Haitian physician was perusing an old newspaper. Yet I had to wait while his secretary talked on the phone, describing how she had spent the previous night. Finally, she put down the receiver, turned her attention to me, and let me through to see the doctor. The latter glanced at me over the rim of his newspaper.

"Hi there. Take a seat. Anything new?" Again he immersed himself in yesterday's news.

"Something's wrong with me: weakness, perspiration, dizziness."

"Go to see the nurse and have your temperature taken."

But the nurse had stepped out and did not reappear until half an hour later. Then she took my temperature: 101°F.

The thermometer reading was all the doctor required to arrive at a confident diagnosis: "Common cold. Take a few aspirins."

"Yesterday, I had a higher fever," I protested. "And my urine's turned dark."

"Let's wait a couple of days. If your condition doesn't improve, come see me again."

His nonchalance stunned me. If he was so indifferent toward his own colleague, what could common patients expect?

"I think I have some kind of liver condition."

"Okay. Go to the nurse and tell her to take a blood sample."

Late at night, I heard my name on the PA: "Dr. Vladimir, you're urgently needed at the E.R.!"

Another emergency! I ran into the emergency room to find one of our residents on a stretcher. Pale as snow, he was clutching his blood-splattered arm with his right hand.

"What happened? What's the matter with your arm?"

"I was shot by a mugger. He took my wallet and ran away."

"Where?"

He told me that the mugging took place in the guarded lot across the street from the hospital when he parked his car. He was lucky to get away with a mere perforation wound and a broken arm. Had he not ducked, he would have been dead by then.

Other residents arrived and we began working on our

comrade, dressing his wound and calling the police. Everybody was shaken and agitated. Even my fatigue was gone.

In our dangerous neighborhood, doctors and nurses from the hospital had been assaulted before, but so far there had been nothing more serious than plain mugging. It was the first instance of a direct threat to life. Any one of us could be the next victim.

The next day, the entire hospital discussed the assault on the doctor. Everybody was worried, feeling impotent and defenseless in the face of the underworld. Thuggery was so widespread in that area that there was no avoiding the danger.

Native New Yorkers shrugged their shoulders. "Well, such is life in this city. We have to pay a price for our American freedom."

Immigrants and native-born Americans debated the issue hotly. The former insisted that there was too much freedom for all.

Yes, of course, there is much more freedom in America than in the rest of the world. But is there such a thing as excessive freedom? The way I see it freedom cannot be excessive any more than there can be too much air to breathe. Lack of law and order is not evidence of too much freedom, but rather an indication of people's inability to use the advantages of freedom.

For instance, in Bolivia there is far less freedom than in the United States but crime is even more rampant. Crime, whether individual or collective, is a matter of individual and national morality. Israel is almost as free a country as America. And the people there own weapons in far greater numbers (and of a far deadlier variety—assault rifles!), yet crime is all but nonexistent. No one in Israel uses submachine guns designed as a means of protection against an external enemy to shoot up their compatriots, because in Israel the level of public morality is very high.

Throughout my surgical career in Russia I had treated thousands of crime victims and knew the magnitude of crime there as well as anybody. And yet I could not help being amazed by the scale of crime in America. Who are American criminals by and large? Those whom I saw were incredibly backward individuals, most of them immigrants, many of them illegal aliens. They never went to school and never worked. They were ignorant of the basic law of life: *Work is the only way of achieving anything.* Finding themselves in the midst of a highly productive society, they wanted only to consume. To achieve their goals, they hunted human beings much like our savage ancestors had hunted animals.

Rich, democratic America pulled them in like a gigantic vacuum cleaner. But America's freedom and abundance only let their worst instincts loose. They were not sufficiently developed to appreciate freedom or to understand the proper uses of democracy. So far as I am concerned, the only way to keep these people in check is to educate them, and work is the best educator.

80

After four days of continual work I was delirious with weakness. The next day my vacation was to begin, and I dreamed of getting home to get a good night's sleep and then start looking for a dependable private doctor.

Again I thought bitterly about the failure of all my attempts to regain my lost professional standing. No matter how feverishly I sorted out all available options, I could see no glimmer of hope. I really had no idea of what was in store for me, even in the near future. Besides, something untoward was going on in my body. I had never felt so bad in my life.

I was summoned by phone to the health station.

"Listen, you have a very high level of liver transaminases," the doctor said.

I looked at the figures and realized immediately that I must have contracted hepatitis.

Still, the doctor made no attempt to examine me.

"What do you think it is?" I asked him.

"Hepatitis."

He had diagnosed my condition on the basis of analytical data alone.

"But what form of hepatitis—A or B?"

"What difference does it make?" he replied indifferently.

The difference was crucial, of course. Hepatitis B, caused by an Australian antigen, is far more treacherous and fraught with many more complications, including, prominently, liver cancer. It is transmitted with patients' blood. I counted the days and figured out that I had been infected by the hypodermic syringe dipped in the blood of the emergency room patient who had died the next day.

Driving home along the West Side Highway, I tried to keep in the right lane in case I fell asleep from fatigue or succumbed to a bout of the disease. My head was swimming and I could think of one thing only: Get home, get home as fast as possible. . . .

Terrified by my condition, Irina asked the chief of her lab to refer me to a private physician. The very next day I sat in an East Side office in Manhattan. The doctor examined me the proper way: he asked relevant questions, palpated and inspected what he was supposed to palpate and inspect, and took all the required tests. It was a pleasure to watch the crisp professional way he worked. He was a genial man roughly my age, a genuine American.

"There's little doubt that you have hepatitis," he said. "But which form we'll only know from the analyses. Besides, you're suffering from general inflammation with cardiac complications. Stay in bed and wait for my call with the lab results. Then we'll see what to do next. But it's very likely you'll need hospitalization."

The bad news about the heart complication and the prospect of spending my vacation in a hospital hit us hard. Irina was even more distraught that I was. I could see she was in a state of panic. I spent the next days on my back, totally drained, while she came home from work, bringing delicacies, sat down at my side, felt my forehead, took my temperature, tucked in my blanket, spoon-fed me—all the time looking worried and heaving sighs. At night, she again rose a dozen times to feel my forehead, bring fresh pajamas, and change my underwear because I perspired constantly.

During the day, after she left for her lab, I worked on my manuscript, incorporating the editor's suggestions—mainly by making deletions. I mercilessly cut out all irrelevant material much as a sculptor chops off excess pieces of marble to create a finished work of art. It was a pity to delete whole stories, interesting in themselves, and to abridge the remaining text, but I worked with gusto.

A book is a symphony in words. It must clearly present the main idea and the principal themes—"melodies." If there are too many of them, the main thrust of the symphony will be lost and it will turn into a cacophony. And so I tried to leave only the most important and interesting material in my book.

But my capacity for work was largely undermined. Every half hour I had to lie back on the pillow and close my eyes to fight fatigue and dizziness.

Returning home from work, Irina asked me reprovingly, "You've worked on the manuscript again, haven't you? Why are you indulging in masochism?"

"Well, maybe a little. . . ."

"Please stop it. You'll have plenty of time to finish your book afterwards."

"Who knows what will happen afterwards? I want to go to the hospital knowing that the publisher had the finished product. This book is my gift to America for having given us refuge. I know it's a good book."

My condition deteriorated day by day. I perspired at night more than ever, the fever never abated, I was constantly dizzy, and I was getting weaker. Meanwhile the laboratory procrastinated. Irina called my doctor with please to speed up the proceedings only to hear that he needed just one more analysis to be absolutely positive about the diagnosis.

Late at night, I was awakened by Irina's muffled sobs. "My God, I had a premonition that it would end up just like this! One cannot suffer so much and swallow so much humiliation without paying a price in health. I'm mad at America. I think you love America more than it loves you. All these years you have been pressing your considerable talents on her, trying to be useful, but all you've seen in response has been outright rejection. Not a single person has expressed the least bit of desire to help you. If I were in your shoes, I would be filled with hatred for everything and everybody here. Yet, you are still in love with America."

"Of course, I am; it's my country. Just as you are my wife."

"Ah, it's unimportant now. It's even unimportant whether or not you'll reach your goals. Only one thing matters now—your health."

"I'll get well, don't worry. Everything will be just fine, everything will come together. I'll make it. I'm sure. . . ."

But to tell the truth, I was no longer sure of anything.

Finally, the doctor called, "Vladimir, bad news: hepatitis B. And unfortunately that's not all: You also have subacute bacterial endocarditis. Your blood culture shows streptococcal infection. You must be hospitalized immediately."

I took the blow hard. "Endocarditis? Are you sure?"

"There can be no doubt. You'll have to stay in the hospital for at least four weeks."

"Four weeks!"

So that was why I felt so weak: endocarditis, inflammation of the inner heart envelope, a serious disease. The price of untreated endocarditis is sure death; that of a treated one, an average of five years off one's life.

The doctor told me he had already reserved a bed in a Bronx hospital where he had privileges and that the hospital staff had been informed of my impending arrival so that intravenous antibiotic treatment could begin the moment I checked in. The last thing I managed to get done before going to the hospital was to mail the finished manuscript to my editor. Irina and Mother escorted me to the cab, supporting me on both sides. I was so weak I could hardly move my feet. The last thing I saw as the cab was pulling out was my mother's tear-streaked face.

I did not see a doctor until after I had been in the hospital for seven hours. Finally, a doctor appeared—a young female first-year resident. She made an awkward attempt to stick a syringe in my vein, pricked both my arms all over, but failed. Mortified, she apologized. I have large veins and an experienced person would have had no trouble at all with them. But I was patient and joked with the poor girl. Finally she appealed for help to a second-year resident, another young woman with very long, straight hair. When she bent over me, her hair smothered me—a pleasant sensation to be sure, but not what I needed most. Somehow she managed to insert a catheter into my vein and the treatment began.

I had never been a patient at an American hospital, so it was interesting to get a patient's-eye view of hospital life, particularly since the medication had a fast and dramatic effect: my fever abated and I ceased to perspire and began regaining my strength. I was put up in a four-bed room in the company of three old men suffering from grave chronic illnesses, all three terminally ill. Such an environment did nothing to cheer me up. Had I not been a physician myself, I would have been scared and hardly able to stand such company.

The nurses took excellent care of us. Everything was done on time, amiably, with sensitive hands. The nurses were all young women, black and white, and very friendly. I gave them candies, joked with them, and soon we became friends.

Resident physicians were rare visitors in our room. They came randomly for brief visits and always ran in and out. They were forever behind schedule, spent much time in discussing things among themselves, and by and large, ignored the patients. I was the ward of three lady doctors.

One of them usually appeared around noon and said while still in the doorway, "Hi there! How are you doing?"

"Thank you, better I think."

"Good. I'll drop by later. See you!"

Another one never came earlier than 2:00 or 3:00 in the afternoon. "How are you feeling?" she would ask.

"Thanks. Better, I think."

"Has my colleague been here?"

"Yes."

"Good. I'll drop by some time later." She would disappear.

The third one came after dinner, pulled a chair up to my bed, and plopped down. "You can't imagine how tired I am," she said.

"Yes, I know. It's time for you to go home."

"Are you kidding? I never go home before ten."

"Why do you have to stay so late?"

"Work. So much work!"

"Yes, I know."

"Yeah. And how are you feeling today?"

"Thanks, a little better, I think."

"Have my colleagues been here?"

"Yes, they dropped by."

"Good. All right, let's listen to your heart."

She bent over me, covering me for a minute with an avalanche of hair so that I had to hold my breath lest I draw some of it into my lungs.

"Okay," she would say. "See you tomorrow."

Soon afterward, the other two would arrive.

"Has our colleague been here? Did she listen to your heart? Good!" Then they would vanish.

On the fifth day of continuous intravenous infusion of liquid medication, I felt a stab of pain at the point near my elbow where the catheter protruded from my vein; the skin reddened and a little swelling appeared—telltale signs of thrombophlebitis caused by the catheter that overstayed its welcome. The rules stipulated that a catheter could be kept in one place two or three days at most. I complained sequentially to all three of my lady doctors. Each one of them cast a cursory glance at the inflamed vein and promised to replace the catheter. Yet none kept her word that day. Late at night, the nurse applied an alcohol compress to the inflamed area.

The next morning, I asked the nurse to summon any one of them; the vein had swollen so much that the infusion was blocked. My doctors called back on the phone and ordered the nurse to withdraw the catheter. They also promised that one of them would be along to insert a new one. I waited for twelve hours without antibiotics. My condition took a turn for the worse and I began to run a fever again.

Irina came to visit me after work. "Why aren't you getting antibiotics intravenously?" she asked.

"I'm waiting for a new catheter to be installed."

"How long have you been waiting?"

She was terrified to find out. "I am going to get the doctor myself," she said menacingly.

I don't know what she told them, but very soon one of my ladies came on the run.

My private physician visited me daily, keeping an eye on my chart. I did not report the young residents to him. What was the point of complaining? If that was the way things were, there was no reason to believe that a rapid change was possible. Once I had been a beginner myself and realized that it took a lot of time not only to master the medical skills, but also to learn to be a doctor, to learn to commiserate with the patient and master the proper bedside manner. But I told my physician there was no way I would remain in the hospital for four weeks. I was fed up with staying in bed.

Vladimir Junior came to visit his infirm father. I had not seen him since the day we had taken him to Syracuse. He entered the room and bent over my bed. "Hi, how are you feeling?"

"Now I am all right."

"How did you manage to get sick?"

"I shared the lot of many surgeons: got infected by a patient's blood."

"Let me listen to your heart."

Although merely a freshman, he tried hard to show off his medical competence. He inspected the room intently, commenting on every detail. I watched him closely; he had clearly changed within that short time. He looked much more self-assured and positive than before—the picture of a true-blue American!

Gradually I recovered and began taking walks along the corridor, looking impatiently out the window—when will they let me go? But the better I felt the darker were my thoughts of the immediate future: What awaited me? Again I had to look for a job, any job, to seek a transfer. A transfer where? I realized that my prospects had deteriorated still further. And I no longer counted on preferential treatment. Bitter experience had taught me that to expect understanding, sympathy, or just plain kindness was an exercise in futility.

continued antibiotic treatment long after being discharged from the hospital, Irina giving me the shots. With my rear end thickly covered with syringe marks, I began taking short strolls in Central Park, pondering the same old problem: how to find a job and what kind of job?

My editor praised my manuscript and predicted success. I mulled over plans for other books and set about drawing up a new proposal. Perhaps I would be able to earn a living by writing? I liked the idea as a way out of my predicament.

No creative work should be done listlessly. I had always been an enthusiast of surgery and regarded it as a form of creative endeavor. But now circumstances conspired to deprive me of any chance of returning to orthopedic surgery. And I had to admit, painfully, that my enthusiasm for surgery was gone. Walking through the park, I vowed never to try to return to the operating table.

But a person given to intellectual pursuits must be a productive worker. My productivity as a doctor had dropped to the vanishing point for the simple reason that I could do nothing else than secondary, auxiliary work. Of course, even a great actor can sometimes agree to a minor part but would not be content to play nothing but minor parts. And my present duties were akin to episodic parts whose performers got no billing at all so small were their roles. It was not productive work, definitely not my line. Pondering my situation, I came to realize with increasing clarity that as a man of letters I could be far more productive than as a second-string doctor.

My editor tried to persuade me that it was well-nigh impossible to earn a living by literary work. I was aware that winning literary recognition of sufficient degree to earn a decent living would take a lot of time. For a Russian writer to win over American readers is a tall order; one must develop unmistakable instincts for the subject matter and form that would appeal to the readership. Yet I did not have enough time. I pondered the problem at great length from all angles, but invariably came up against insuperable barriers.

Poor health and incessant brooding drove me into a depression. And to top off my misery, my lawyer received a letter from the journalist Stanley demanding compensation and threatening to sue me if I did not oblige. It was the last straw, Stanley wrote that he had spent over a year of his time working with me and in the process sacrificed several book projects of significant income potential. He had been driven to such heights of selflessness by sheer fondness for me, Stanley explained. He insisted that he had incurred expense in his search for a publisher, and in entertaining me at his home. He had counted his expenses down to the last cent, including the number of cups of coffee I had drunk while enjoying his hospitality. His losses amounted to $10,000, he claimed, and he demanded to be reimbursed in full.

I knew that Americans loved to litigate and that some lawsuits took years to be brought to conclusion. But I certainly saw nothing appealing in such a prospect. Furious, I wrote a reply to Stanley worded so strongly that even Irina judged it to be excessive. My lawyer had to rewrite the response, draining it of venom to the extent it was possible.

I was not so angry with Stanley as stunned by my misfortune. I even began to think that Irina was right and I lavished too much love on undeserving America. True, America had given us shelter, but she had consistently turned down all the gifts I offered her—my knowledge, my skills, my love.

I decided it was time to leave America for a while to put things in perspective. Where to go? To Israel, of course, only to Israel! I still had some sick days, and I yearned to see with my own eyes the Promised Land, the country to which my coreligionists had always aspired. I needed positive emotions for medication.

I had not notified my Israeli friends of my coming, because I wanted some time alone, face to face with the country. I needed to walk in the streets, to drink in the faces of passersby, to try to grasp the individual character of the nation. How were Israelis different from other peoples? I walked along a quay in Tel Aviv, observing the kaleidoscopic diversity of facial features. It was a stupendous feeling to realize that everybody around me was Jewish. All my life I had known that Jews were a minority. We were a minority in Russia where Jews were mistreated so badly they had good reason to hide their ethnic identity. We were a minority in America where we were not hurt as often or as flagrantly as in Russia, but a minority nonetheless. But here everybody, without a single exception, was Jewish! And another striking fact: Israeli Jews were starkly different from their Diaspora brethren. I looked into the faces of tall and slim beautiful girls and young men (many of them in reservist uniforms and toting assault rifles) exuding power and manliness; I looked in the faces of old men and women whose age-dimmed eyes reflected quiet dignity. And I realized what distinguished the Israelis: proud and dignified bearing, the bearing of masters of their own land.

I recalled how upon my arrival in New York I had been upset by the appearance of Broadway crowds that clashed with my notion of what Americans were supposed to look like. Here the crowd surpassed my notion of what Jews should look like.

Watching the Israelis, most of whom were young men and women, I suddenly realized what it was that had struck me in my son when he came to visit me at the hospital: His behavior was akin to that of the Israelis; no longer an immigrant, he had begun feeling as much a master of his homeland as the Israelis felt in Israel.

Meetings with friends followed. Dr. Zanuk, a former Communist Zionist just recently emigrated, celebrated his sixtieth birthday, and I was a guest of honor at the festivities. He introduced me to his guests.

"This is my American friend. He has come all the way from America to see me."

The words *American* and *America* were pronounced with respect and a special meaning. The guests, all of them recent Russian immigrants, pelted me with questions.

"Are you really from America?" "How do you like it there?" "Must be good, eh?"

"Wonderful," I said. "A far cry from Russia."

"Oh sure, no question about it. America is such a rich country! We should certainly try to come to America and have a good look at it."

"Yes, you must come. You'll like what you see."

I met an old friend, a nice lady, Dr. Ida Uchitel.

"Let's have a look at our new American," she said, opening her arms to me. "Well, you've got some new silver in your head. Now take a seat and tell me all about your America, one thing at a time. Was it difficult to start everything from scratch there?"

"You bet it was!"

I rode to Jerusalem and went straight to the Old City. Four millennia of history opened up to my eyes as I wandered about the ancient streets holding my breath. I spent the whole evening at the Wailing Wall, sorting out my memories, dreaming and praying as best I could. I did not beseech God to ease my plight in America. I thanked him for granting me an opportunity to live in America.

Then I rented a car and drove all over the country. In Caesarea I sat on the ruins of a Roman stadium where two and a half thousand Jews had been sacrificed once in A.D. 70. Since then almost two thousand years had passed and during World War II, another six million Jews were sacrificed. Has the world changed? No! But the Jews have; they are now masters of their own country.

While I thus sat deep in thought, a squadron of fighter-bombers, American-made F-16s, streaked across the blue sky with a deep rumble. I watched them with satisfaction; it was a pleasure to know that my country, America, was helping the Israelis.

Close to the end of my brief sojourn, I went to Masada, an ancient fortress on a cliff where a handful of Zealots had held a powerful Roman army at bay for three years. A strong wind was blowing on the mountaintop. I turned to face it, trying to feel what the ancient patriots had felt. It was a wind of valor. It instilled the feeling of power and confidence in me.

I was returning home—to America.

There is a standard pattern to a love affair: A sudden conflagration followed by a gradual process of disillusionment. It takes a very strong love for familiarity not to douse the flames of affection. But even strong love is not immune to crises. I knew it from my own experience.

I loved America with all my heart. The crises had been fed by low morale born of illness. But I returned to New York from Israel in a state of inner peace, reconciled to reality: Come what may, I had been lucky to choose America as my new home.

Department chief Dr. Ler and his deputy Dr. Reg greeted me warmly.

They made me an offer: "Why don't you work for a year at the lab, conducting experiments and helping young residents master research techniques?"

"Sounds great! After all, I've been in research all my life."

"You'll be considered still in training, so you'll have to see patients at the outpatient department."

Thus I switched to easier and less hectic duties. I helped my young colleagues, examined patients, diagnosed their ailments and initiated treatment. But never again did I approach the operating table. My enthusiasm for surgery was gone.

It is a pleasure to enjoy a lull after a powerful tempest. I was content; my life became almost devoid of stresses. Occasionally gusts of the old winds touched me, but they no longer cut me to the bone.

Then one day, my book, *Russian Doctor,* came off the press.

To hold one's published book for the first time is the same as taking one's newborn baby in one's arms. When I brought home the first three copies of the book, I lay down in bed and put the books next to me—like my children. And just as parents admire their child, so I leafed through the books and delighted in them. I had spent almost five years to see the project to successful completion. But the period of struggle was finally over. I immediately signed a contract for a sequel— the one you are reading now. And plans for yet two more books were taking shape in my mind.

Some time later I received the U.S. patent for the devices and method that increase ease and accuracy when applying plaster casts to patients with fractures and dislocations. This way I utilized my experience and gave my young colleagues a helpful guide in their everyday work. And I was very pleased when in our hospital's newspaper the following was written about me: "The hospital is proud to have such a distinguished physician on its staff."

Curiously, I became so estranged from all things Russian that even speaking Russian on the job was harder for me than to speak English. At home Irina and I still spoke Russian, but outside I fell out of the habit of using the language. I was not losing my fluency, but uttering Russian words for the benefit of others I had a strange feeling of doing something alien to me. Besides, I could see that some immigrants began to forget the hardships of life spent in Russia. They even came to idealize their past, which sounded in their tales much brighter than it really had been. As a corollary, they criticized their present life in America. What they failed to understand they chalked up as bad.

It ran against my grain, but I was powerless to change them. Dissatisfaction is as human as forgetfulness.

Once at a clinic reception, I examined a Russian immigrant from Latvia, a very sick woman of sixty-five. Among her many, many ailments, she suffered from arthritis and deformation of the toes. While I examined her, she said, "You know, Doctor, I think all my diseases can be traced back to my Siberian exile."

"You did time in Siberia?"

"Yes, when the Soviets seized Riga in 1940, I was just twenty-three. Together with many other Jews, I was deported to a Siberian gulag and rotted there for twenty-eight years, doing hard labor in horrible conditions. Could it be that that's where my feet went out on me?"

"Judging by your story, it's quite possible."

"Yes, I am certain that's where I lost my health."

Then she started complaining that she had seen several American physicians, but none of them could help her or even talked to her.

"Believe me, Doctor," she exclaimed, "a human being is treated here even worse than in Russia! People there were warmer, they liked to talk."

And she went on venting her spleen.

"Those Americans all have their brains topsy-turvy."

Once Irina and I went to Hartsdale to visit American friends.

"Recently, a very rich Russian immigrant, a millionaire, has bought into this community," the host said. "He lives in a big house and drives luxury cars."

"A recent Russian immigrant a millionaire?" I asked in astonishment. "How has he made his fortune?"

"They say he's a watchmaker who has struck it rich by selling cheap Russian movements in the guise of Swiss watches."

"Show me his house," I asked my friend.

We drove up to a mansion with a Mercedes-500 and a Cadillac in the driveway. Nearby I saw their owner—that same former America-baiter. I decided not to bother him; my Buick Skyhawk was no match for his conveyances. But a thought crossed my mind: As it happens, the Russians are not altogether mistaken to think that each American is a millionaire. Potentially he is.

For over five years I had no contacts with Russia, but I felt no pangs of nostalgia. Even the pictures of that country, once so familiar, began fading in my memory: gray sky, bad climate; dreary expanses of fields interspersed with ravines; white birch and aspen trees at the edges of dismal woods; miserable villages with knee-deep mud puddles and gray peasant hovels. Even the sights of Moscow and the faces of old friends were no longer clear in my mind's eye.

Then all of a sudden, a telephone call and Russian speech: "Hi, old boy!"

I did not recognize the voice. "Hello! Who is it?"

"Don't you recognize me?"

"Sorry, but I don't . . ."

"It's Savva, Savely Ghusev. Do you recognize me now?"

I was stunned. "How on earth? Where are you?" He had been one of my oldest friends in Moscow.

"I've come on business for a short while and decided to find you. So I looked up your name in the telephone directory, and here I am."

"I'm sorry not to have recognized your voice, but I never expected to hear from you."

"I understand. Listen, I'm calling from a pay phone in the street, because I don't dare use the phone in the hotel room. I have a Russian roommate and besides, somebody is always likely to overhear. So let's make arrangements for a get-together."

"I'd be glad to see you any time and any place you find convenient."

"Here's what we'll do. In a few days, I'll try to call you again and then we'll see each other. But I don't know when I can find the time so nobody knows."

"I'll be waiting for your call."

I hung up and began reminiscing. Savva and I had gone to high school together, but later our paths diverged. Occasionally we met at parties, but we had nothing in common except for a lingering mutual attraction. He was a pure ethnic Russian of proletarian stock. And he also was a topnotch athlete who built a successful career in sports in the late 1950s when the Soviets were just edging into international competition. By the time I left Russia he had advanced to a top position in the Soviet sports establishment. And since he was allowed to come to the United States now, in the midst of the 1983 chill in Soviet-American relations, it could only mean that his position was unassailably high. On the other hand, his decision to seek me out implied that he was still an independently minded person. It would be a thrill to see him!

After he called the second time, I drove up to the Hilton on Sixth Avenue and waited in my car. There he was! Aha, he had expanded and aged, but overall looked to be in good shape. I came out of the car and waved to him. He saw me and made a barely noticeable sign indicating that I shouldn't approach him. Then he looked warily around, nodded to me, and turned the corner. I raced up to him, but he said without stopping, "Drive up in your car. I'll be walking along the street and you'll pick me up."

When he jumped into my car I did not stop until we drove for a couple of blocks. Only then did we embrace as old friends, pounding each other on the back.

"I am sorry I couldn't say hello right off," he said. "But you see I'm here with a delegation and I would hate anyone to see me with an American. You've probably forgotten about such things, but I must be constantly on my guard."

"I still remember," I said. "Now tell me, can we go to my place or have you no time for that?"

"Let's go to your place. Tonight is the only time when I have nothing to fear. I want to see Irina and spend an evening with you."

While we drove home he told me that the purpose of his visit was to make arrangements for the arrival of Soviet athletes to take part in the Los Angeles Summer Olympics.

"Between you and me, the Politburo has already decided to boycott the Games. Those doddering idiots, our leaders, are afraid that too many of our guys would defect. It's a pity to miss the opportunity to compete against American athletes on their own turf, but what can I do? Politics! But as long as the boycott decision hasn't been officially announced, we make believe that everything goes on as planned. And who am I to complain? Thanks to this mess I was able to come to America."

His story was evidence of his old, clear-thinking self.

"Listen, that's some car you have! And looks brand-new too. Boy, does it handle! Looks like you're okay. Are you a millionaire by any chance?"

"Not yet. As a matter of fact, it's a relatively cheap car. It's only that all cars look gorgeous and have powerful engines in this country. But then this is America."

While we were passing the doorman and waiting for the elevator in the mirrored lobby of my building, he looked around with undisguised admiration.

"Whatever you say to the contrary, you still live like a filthy capitalist," he joked. "In Moscow, only really big shots live in buildings with doormen and mirrored halls."

"Well, here this luxury is affordable to the middle class."

Irina came out on the landing to meet us. She had already set the table with American food so as to give our guest a glimpse of our life-style. Savva took a bottle of vodka out of his pocket.

"This is genuine Russian stuff. Bought it before departure. Drink it to remember your old friends who haven't forgotten you either."

"Thanks for the gift. But Russian vodka can wait. Tonight, we are going to drink American whiskey."

"To you!" He downed a tea glass filled to the rim, Russian style. I almost forgot that liquor could be consumed that way.

"Well," he said, "and now you should tell me everything step by step: How you have settled down; are you satisfied or not? Mind you, I have not the slightest idea of what it's like to be an immigrant."

And the evening of reminiscences was on.

From time to time our guest interjected, "It hasn't been a bed of roses, you bet!" He listened to me intently and sadly. Then he said, "Well, best of luck to you! You certainly deserve whatever you have achieved braving such terrible odds. But I have one more question to ask you, if I may."

"Shoot."

"Tell me, was it worth it?"

I weighed my answer carefully. We were old friends dispersed by fate to different corners of the earth. Perhaps I would never see him again. And he would probably convey my last word to some of my old friends in Moscow. The answer had to be so accurate and unambiguous as to defy misinterpretation by people on the other side.

"One has to pay a high price for freedom," I said.

84
_____

On August 18, 1983, our immigrant existence came to an end. We became citizens of the United States of America.

In the morning we took a cab to the U.S. courthouse in downtown Manhattan. As we rode, I remembered how five and a half years before I had been riding through Moscow streets to surrender my internal passport of citizen of the U.S.S.R. For the privilege of being stripped of citizenship and getting an exit visa each emigrant had to pay 500 rubles ($750). Paying 2,500 rubles ($3,750) for the five members of the family, I asked the glum teller with fake naïveté: "How much would it cost me to have my citizenship back?" She looked at me as if I was crazy. "Fifty kopecks [seventy-six cents]." A thousand times cheaper!

In the beginning I had not the remotest idea of how difficult immigration would be. I plunged into its rigors at the age of fifty. Irina was three years younger, but for a woman it is an age associated with tremendous physiological and psychological upheavals. For these reasons, a wholesale reevaluation of values was especially trying and painful for both of us. We had to be born anew to cope. A denizen of the ocean deep faced with the need to adapt to life on the mountaintop would find his task no more difficult.

I had chosen to strive for the real mountaintop—America. It is a country of boundless opportunities for immigrants. But it takes several generations to open all the doors. So what if I had failed to regain my status as an orthopedic surgeon? Maybe my son will.

About four hundred immigrants assembled in the cavernous building of the old courthouse. While we waited for the ceremony to commence, I looked at faces and clothes and listened intently to speech patterns, trying to place my new compatriots. The crowd was dominated by Hispanics and the babble of voices around me was mostly Spanish in a variety of accents. The second largest group was made up of Indians. There were also many Orientals, mostly Filipinos and Koreans. The few blacks spoke either Spanish or Creole. The smallest minority was represented by whites—all of four families.

We had nothing in common—except that all of us had come to America in search of a better life. Yet now we were to become members of a single community—the United States. It seemed strange. But I knew that the next generation, born on American soil, would have no problem viewing themselves as members of the same nation. That's what was really astonishing!

We were all summoned to a huge courtroom. We took our seats, acutely conscious of the solemnity of the occasion. The procedure was explained to us. Many immigrants did not understand English and others translated for them in whispers. I, too, translated for my mother. But we intoned the oath in a fairly cohesive chorus. And then, one by one, we received our certificates and returned to our seats. When my family's turn came, Mother whispered, "Thank you, God!" and burst into tears.

My eyes also filled with tears. So now I was a citizen of America, a wonderful country created by immigrants—both voluntary and brought by force. And I recalled the pioneers. One of them, William Bradford, the *Mayflower* chronicler, wrote: "Being thus passed the vast ocean, and a sea of troubles . . . they had now no friends to welcome them, nor inns to entertain or refresh their weather-beaten bodies."

In a brief period, crowds of immigrants had transformed savage America into the most advanced and highly developed country in the world. With their labor they had given preeminence; with their love for freedom they had kept her free.

A fearless lot, poor but burning with dreams of success, they have populated this land and built its glory. And I was proud to call myself one of them.

Music started playing and a clear voice sang, "God Bless America . . . " Everybody in the courtroom sang along, even those who did not know the lyrics. And together with everyone else, I sang.